1/14

MW01341968

JEFFERSON COUNTY LIBRARY
620 Cedar Avenue
Port Hadlock, WA 98339
360) 385-6544   www.jclibrary.info

DATE DUE

Nov. 8 2013	
Dec. 21 - '13	
3/5/14	
JUN 14 2014	
OCT 4	
3-15	
MAY 31, 2018	
DEC 1 1	
JUN 2 9	
11-6	

DEMCO, INC. 38-2971

A Sound Defense

Military Sites, Lighthouses, and Memorials of Puget Sound

Nancy L. McDaniel

A Sound Defense
Military Sites, Lighthouses, and Memorials of Puget Sound

Published by Nancy L. McDaniel

Copyright© Nancy L. McDaniel, 2013

Library of Congress
2013 908272

ISBN
978-0-9759044-2-8

All rights reserved. No part of this publication may be reproduced, distributed, or transmitted in any form or by any means, including photocopying, recording, or other electronic or mechanical methods, without the prior written permission of the publisher, except in the case of brief quotations embodied in critical reviews and certain other noncommercial uses permitted by copyright law. For permission requests, write to the publisher, addressed "Attention: Permissions Coordinator," at the address below.

Nancy McDaniel
PO Box 275
Chimacum, WA 98325

Please purchase only authorized electronic editions and do not participate in or encourage electronic privacy of copyrightable materials. Your support of the author's rights is appreciated.

Dedicated to my father and mother,
Leonard and Aileen McDaniel

Gone . . . but your memories and the gifts you gave me of travel, curiosity and the advice of "do it right the first time" live on.

Table of Contents

Chapter 1: Whatcom County   1

    -Fort Bellingham   2
    -Pickett House   5
    -Heritage Flight Museum   5
    -U.S. Coast Guard Station Bellingham   6
    -Semiahmoo Harbor Light   8
    -Birch Bay Air Force Station / Blaine Air Force
       Station   10
    -Whatcom County Map   14

Chapter 2: Skagit County   15

    -Burrows Island Lighthouse   15
    -Fort at Lone Tree Point   18
    -Skagit County Airport   19
    -Fort Whitman   20
    -Skagit County Map   22

Chapter 3: Snohomish County   23

    -Mukilteo Light Station   23
    -Mukilteo Explosive Loading Terminal /
       Mukilteo Tank Farm   25
    -Paine Field / Paine Air Force Base 26
    -Naval Station Everett   31
    -Arlington Airport   32
    -Flying Heritage Collection   35
    -Snohomish County Map   38

Chapter 4: San Juan County   39

    -"The Pig War" – English Camp & American Camp 39
    -Friday Harbor Radar Station   44
    -Patos Island Light   45
    -Turn Point Lighthouse   47
    -Lime Kiln Lighthouse   49
    -Cattle Point Lighthouse   51
    -San Juan County Map   55

Chapter 5: Island County 57

-Naval Air Station Whidbey Island   57
-Fort Casey and "The Triangle of Fire"   60
-Fort Ebey   67
-Red Bluff Lighthouse   70
-Admiralty Head Lighthouse   72
-Crockett, Davis, Ebey & Alexander Blockhouses   75
-Fort Nugent   78
-Deception Pass: West Beach, Reservation Bay, Reservation Head, Gun Point   78
-Brush Point Lighthouse   79
-Island County Map   80

Chapter 6: King County 81

-Fort Lawton   81
-West Point Lighthouse   89
-Alki Point Lighthouse   91
-Nike Missile Locations: Seattle Defense Area   93
- Cougar Mountain / Issaquah
- Bothell / Kenmore
- Redmond
- Lake Youngs / Renton
- Renton
- Kent / Midway
- Vashon Island

-"The Oozlefinch"   98
-Coast Guard in Seattle: Pier 36, Base Support Unit Seattle, Integrated Support Command Seattle   98
-Coast Guard Museum Northwest   101
-Sand Point Naval Air Station   102
-Museum of Flight   108
-Boeing Airplane Company, Seattle   109
-Battle of Seattle (1856)   111
-Sites of Blockhouses   113
- Fort Lander
- Black River Blockhouse
- Fort Dent

- Fort Henderson
- Fort Tilton
- Fort Alden (aka Fort Alder)
- Fort Thomas
- Fort Duwamish
- Fort Slaughter (Camp Muckleshoot Prairie)

-Lend-Lease Depot, Auburn   115
-Submarines & Naval Shipbuilding in Puget Sound   119
-Jefferson Park, Highland Park, Laurelhurst Playground, Froula Playground, Delridge Playground, Grand Army Of the Republic Cemetery near Volunteer Park, Sears Building in Downtown Seattle   124
-Barrage Balloon Causes Air Raid Scare   126
-Two Airports: King County and Seattle-Tacoma   127
-Naval Reserve Armory   129
-Seattle City Hall Park & the Seattle Air Defense Wing   131
-Naval Receiving Facility, Seattle, Pier 90 – 91   132
-Des Moines Memorial Way South   134
-Third Seattle Army Becomes Seattle Center House   135
-White River Massacre Site   137
-King County Memorials   138
-Naval Training Center, University of Washington 139
-Seattle Naval Hospital   139
-Point Robinson Lighthouse   140
-King County Map   144

Chapter 7: Pierce County   145

-Fort Lewis   145
-Units at Fort Lewis   150
-Fort Lewis Leaders and Legends   152
-Life at Fort Lewis in World War II   153
-Mount Rainier Ordnance Depot   156
-Prisoners of War, Fort Lewis   159
-Camp Harmony (Puyallup Assembly Center)   161

- Fort Steilacoom   162
- Browns Point Lighthouse   167
- Fort Nisqually, DuPont, and
  Point Defiance   169
- McChord Field / McChord Air Force Base   172
- Joint Base Lewis – McChord   179
- McChord Air Museum   180
- Camp Murray   180
- Tacoma Narrows Bridge   185
- Fort Hays and the Battle of Connell's Prairie 189
- Fort White   189
- Fort Hicks   190
- Fort Maloney   190
- Fort McAllister   190
- Camp Montgomery   191
- Pierce County Map   194

Chapter 8: Thurston County   195

- Puget Sound Mounted Volunteers,
- Blockhouses and Stockades   195
- Fort Henness   196
- Fort Chambers   197
- Fort Eaton   198
- Civil War Memorial, Masonic Cemetery,
  Olympia   198
- World War I Memorial   199
- World War II Memorial   200
- Korean War Memorial   201
- Vietnam Veterans Memorial   202
- Olympia Airport   203
- Thurston County Map   206

Chapter 9: Mason County   207

- Naval Air Auxiliary Station Shelton   207
- Vietnam Veterans Memorial,
  Mason County   210
- Mason County Map   212

Chapter 10: Kitsap County — 213

- Fort Ward   213
- Puget Sound Naval Shipyard   216
- Puget Sound Navy Museum   224
- Naval Undersea Warfare Engineering Station, Keyport   225
- Naval Undersea Museum   232
- Naval Submarine Base Bangor   234
- Nike Missile Sites   240
  - Poulsbo
  - Kingston
  - Winslow
  - Olalla
- Middle Point Military Reservation   240
- Manchester Navy Fuel Depot   243
- Point No Point Lighthouse   244
- Port Gamble   246
- Vietnam Memorials, Monuments, and Sites in Kitsap County   247
- U.S.S. *Turner Joy*, DD951, U.S. Navy Destroyer Museum Ship   249
- Kitsap County Map   252

Chapter 11: Jefferson County — 253

- Fort Townsend   253
- Fort Worden   258
- Puget Sound Coast Artillery Museum   269
- Point Wilson Lighthouse   270
- Fort Flagler   273
- Marrowstone Point Lighthouse   281
- Cape George Military Reservation   283
- Naval Magazine Indian Island   284
- Coast Guard in Jefferson County   289
- Jefferson County International Airport   293
- Memorial Sites   294
- Point Hudson   294
- Marvin G. Shields Memorial   297
- Destruction Island Lighthouse   298
- Jefferson County Map   300

Chapter 12: Clallam County   301

- Fort Núñez Gaona   301
- U.S. Coast Guard Station Neah Bay   303
- United States Life Saving Service
  Station #1, Station Waddah Island   304
- Camp Hayden and Striped Peak   305
- Cape Flattery Lighthouses   308
- U.S. Army Spruce Production Division
  Railroad   312
- Army Air Corps in Port Angeles   315
- Slip Point Lighthouse   316
- Lookout Stations, Aircraft
  Warning Service   318
- Ozette Lake Coast Guard Station   321
- LaPush and Kalaloch Beach
  Patrol Stations   322
- Quillayute Naval Auxiliary Field   324
- Ediz Hook Lighthouse   328
- U.S. Coast Guard Air Station,
  Port Angeles   330
- Motorboat Lifeboat Station,
  Quillayute River   332
- New Dungeness Lighthouse   333
- Cape Flattery Military Reservation,
  Makah Air Force Station   336
- Clallam County Map   340

Acknowledgements

Many thanks to my husband of nearly 34 years, Glenn Davis, for understanding when piles of books, papers, maps, and drafts loaded down the south end of the dining room table for nearly three years. When company would come I'd scoop them up and hide them in a back bedroom. Thankfully he said he understood. I'm not sure I would have persevered if not for him.

Many thanks to the members of the Coastal Defense Study Group who have done so much work in recording the details of history which should never be lost. Their publications and newsletters provided inspiration and information. Much gratitude goes to the many people who responded cheerfully and enthusiastically to requests to use photos and stories.

This book was written over a three year period of time. Sometimes I wrote when I couldn't sleep. Sometimes I wrote when I put pressure on myself to get it done. Sometimes the lack of quality and bad grammar showed up. Editing a collection of information requires patience, tact, expertise, and endless red pens. My unending gratitude goes to Lois Stanford, who took a rough manuscript and applied all of the above attributes and handed me a manuscript almost ready to go to the publisher. She insists that she enjoyed what she was reading. I hope so. It was her final touches that made this readable. I can't say enough about Lois and her unwavering optimism. I wanted to quit a couple of times, but her motivation kept me going.

Kroll Map Company of Seattle was extremely instrumental in developing the maps showing significant sites. Maria J. Brown of Kroll Maps patiently put up with my cryptic messages and my requests to add things that I had forgotten in my first submission. Their help and professionalism made the incorporation of maps much easier than I had anticipated. My never-ending thanks to this wonderful, professional, and knowledgeable company. Working with a company in Seattle where the staff knew and understood the challenges of this project made it all come together.

Thanks go to the Jefferson County Historical Society. I would have been inclined to quit a couple of times on the way to completion. The Trustees' encouragement and the advice and counsel of William Tennent were invaluable. Becky Schurmann and Marsha Moratti helped with supplying photos of Jefferson County's sites. Board members kept asking me how it was going. As a result, I felt I should actually finish this book. The Historical Society's support, comments, insightful questions and words of encouragement (and expectations) were worth more than I can say.

Greta Gohn is a brilliant artist. We chatted for a few minutes over tea about a cover for this book. My ideas were kind of bland. In reality, my ideas were lame at best. Her interpretation of my vision of "something with a map" and her talent developed into a cover design which surpassed my mundane ideas and dreams.

Kandace Nevin, a best friend (almost a sister) of many, many years was also a supporter and a provider of moral support. E-mails asking how the book was coming made me get back to the tasks at hand. Her support from hundreds of miles away created a sense of friendly motivation that made it a quest instead of a job.

Keppie Keplinger provided encouragement, photos, support, asked the right questions, and kept me going on this. She made the trip to Seattle with me to talk about maps. She listened as I rambled, and then put me back on track. Her insight into the details of getting a project like this done was essential. She kept telling me I could do it, and with her help and wise counsel, it eventually turned into a finished product.

Every individual I contacted for photos or for insight responded with enthusiasm.

Lighthouse supporters throughout Puget Sound provided inspiration to keep going on the project. I looked at the investments they made in these treasured lighthouses and realized I couldn't stop. Not a single organization had given up their dream to restore and preserve "their" lighthouses. As a result, I couldn't stop until I got this job done.

The job, however, isn't really done. As decreased public funding makes maintenance and restoration more difficult, some of these remaining treasures are at risk. Hopefully the communities, organizations and local governments will see fit to keep these pieces of our history alive for future generations.

Introduction

I grew up on the Olympic Peninsula in the State of Washington. For most of my childhood I was aware that there were forts and gun emplacements nearby. I only thought they were interesting because they were fun to climb on and they were near the beach.

When I went to college at the University of Puget Sound, there were constantly aircraft overhead — mostly C-141s and C-5s in those days. They were on their way to McChord Air Force Base. I used to drive by McChord and wonder what was behind those gates.

Then I was granted a commission in the Air Force. I had completed AFROTC and was commissioned a second lieutenant on the same day. I left Washington for 27 years as I built a career in the military. I would come back on various occasions and visit those old forts. Some had become state parks. Some were just stories in history books. I then started to take a little more interest in what was there and the people who had served at those installations.

The Puget Sound area has several military installations, both past and present. Some served our country from the days when settlers were concerned with encroaching Native Americans. (I smile at this point because I am descended from those natives who were displaced by encroaching white settlers). Other installations were established to protect the Pacific Northwest during World War I and World War II.

Lighthouses established long before Washington achieved statehood still guide ships through the fog and provide important reference points around the many navigation hazards of Puget Sound. These lighthouses often served as a first line of defense during times of national crises and were important links in the defense of our country.

There are installations which still are active, and there are many which have been transformed into recreational areas. Some sites do not exist at all anymore except in historical documents.

This book is written to recognize these installations, but also to recognize the people who served on their grounds. My hope is that perhaps this book may inspire you to visit some of them yourself so you can stand there and remember these people too. Another hope of mine is that you might be inspired to assist if possible in ensuring that these sites are preserved and restored so that their history is preserved. As years go by, the costs of maintaining these sites may be topics of discussion for local communities. Become involved and advocate that they remain as vital reminders of the historic contributions that these sites have made to the defense of the nation.

The book is organized by geographic area with the thought that you might take a drive to an area and have a reference for old and active sites there. Each chapter describes the military sites or attractions within that county. Maps are not designed to provide definitive directions to each site, but are included to show the relative locations of sites.

Keep in mind that active bases may have limited access to some or all areas. Call ahead to ascertain what credentials might be required to access the base. These entry requirements may change periodically when heightened national security levels change. Some sites are closed and now are private property and may not be accessible.

Western Washington's military sites have been national assets for decades. While shots may not have been fired in anger from many of these sites, please consider "what might have been" if these installations had not been built. Deterrence, readiness, and security have been bolstered by these assets.

Visit, enjoy, remember, and celebrate the long history of our nation's military personnel and enjoy the installations and assets which are part of a rich military history.

Chapter 1

Whatcom County

Whatcom County, established in 1854, had been part of the Spanish claim in 1775. It was later claimed by Russia, by England, and by the United States.

Bellingham Bay was named by Captain George Vancouver of the British Navy during his expedition into the waters of Puget Sound in 1792. Fur trappers and traders were the first non-Indian residents to settle in and Hudson's Bay Company set up shop from 1825 to 1846. Prior to the Europeans, however, Whatcom County was home to several Northwest tribes including the Lummi, Nooksack, Samish, and the Semiahmoo.

In the mid-1850s, settlers throughout Western Washington were feeling threatened by natives who were quickly being displaced by increasing numbers of farmers, loggers, and fishermen arriving in the Pacific Northwest.

Several treaties, including the Point No Point Treaty and the Treaty of Point Elliott, had been signed. These treaties established reservations which were designed to isolate and concentrate natives on grounds set aside for their use.

In only a few instances were these grounds near traditional hunting and fishing grounds. For most natives, the new reservations were located away from traditional lands, and were viewed as places to go to die. Forced to go to these reservations before the treaties were even ratified, many natives viewed these "agreements" as provocations for sporadic warfare throughout the territory between 1855 and 1858.

Native peoples from Canada were paddling southward. They came south in war canoes from the Queen Charlotte Islands, southern Alaska, and what is now the north coast of

British Columbia. The increased presence of the natives was starting to alarm the settlers on Whidbey Island, in Port Townsend, the San Juan Islands, and Bellingham Bay.

Fort Bellingham

By 1855, increased number of settlers and increased economic growth warranted a fort to protect the area. Federal units had already arrived at locations to the south near Fort Steilacoom. Troops had yet to answer the calls for support at new communities to the north. While waiting for federal help, the townspeople built a blockhouse west of Whatcom Creek on Bellingham Bay. They formed Whatcom Company, a citizen based unit, and banded together for their own protection.

Captain George Pickett was stationed at Fort Steilacoom. Receiving orders from Washington D.C., Pickett was dispatched by the Ninth Infantry Regiment to construct a fort on Bellingham Bay. The fort's establishment was designed to develop a U.S. military foothold and provide protection for settlers and U.S. resources. Sixty-eight men comprising Company D, accompanied Captain Pickett to what is now Whatcom County to build what would briefly be known as Fort Bellingham. First Lieutenant Robert H. Davis, nephew of Secretary of War Jefferson Davis, and Second Lieutenant J.W. Forsythe were part of the officer cadre. Forsythe would later die in infamy at Wounded Knee. Pickett would lead "Pickett's Charge" at the Battle of Gettysburg.

Real Photo Post Card Old Fort Bellingham. Author's collection

Located on a prairie at the edge of a bluff, the chosen site had access to a freshwater spring capable of providing water for the installation.

The only problem was that the site was a homestead and it was occupied. Mr. and Mrs. Roberts had claimed the land, filed homestead papers and had cleared trees and brush from the site. Mrs. Maria Roberts' husband was away. In his absence, Mrs. Roberts refused to give up her claim. The troops simply removed the roof of her house. Mrs. Roberts, in advanced pregnancy, walked three and a half miles into Whatcom for shelter. Negotiations continued however, and the couple was later allowed to build a cabin on the beach, where they remained for many years.

Construction on Fort Bellingham began in late summer of 1856. Pickett used his soldiers and hired civilians from Whatcom to dig latrines and garbage pits. Trenches for the palisades were excavated. Inspector General George Mansfield wrote in his report of 1858: "The barracks, and officers' quarters are within an enclosed square of about 80 yards the side." [The fort is] "made of palisades set in the ground, loopholed for musketry and flanked by two Blockhouses two stories high, pierced for mountain howitzers and loopholed; and is provided with 3 gates — All the buildings are one story." He added that the officers' quarters were roomy and that "The buildings are wood framed. Barracks had a mess hall & kitchen & bakery attached, and was ample." The blockhouse near the shore was "occupied by the guard."

Other buildings included a hospital, two wardrooms, a kitchen, laundress' houses, a carpenter shop, a smith shop, barns, an outhouse, and a store. The fort also had a large garden. Officially, Pickett lived at the fort, but most of his time was spent in a small house he had built in the village of Whatcom.

According to Mansfield, the soldiers were not well trained. When tasked with target shooting at a target 200 yards away, only one out of 40 men could hit the target. Mansfield commented that "this showed a want of instruction and practice."

On November 11, 1856, order and discipline was tested when two soldiers broke into the fort's store and stole more than $160 worth of clothing. The stolen goods included pants, socks, shirts, and three table covers. The thieves returned to the camp and had several other soldiers take the goods to a home located near the camp. Richard McCann and

Thomas Handley appeared before a jury in a trial conducted by the 3rd Judicial District. They were acquitted of burglary but found guilty of petty larceny after a short trial. They were the only soldiers brought before a full civilian court at Fort Bellingham.

General George Pickett. Photo courtesy National Archive

Many of the men "married" Indian women. Records indicate that Pickett required his men to go through a marriage ceremony indicating their commitment to their wives, and commitment to their offspring. Lieutenant Davis married a Swinomish woman, producing a son, Sam Davis.

Captain Pickett married a Haida woman by the name of Sakis Tiigang while at Fort Bellingham. Her name means "mist lying down" or "morning mist" in the Haida language. Pickett built a home on what is now Bancroft Street in Bellingham.

Morning Mist gave birth to a son, Jason Tilton Pickett, in 1857. She never fully recovered from the difficult delivery and died within weeks of his birth.

When Lyman Cutlar, an American settler on San Juan Island, shot a Hudson's Bay Company pig, unrest between England and the United States broke out. Pickett's company was sent to San Juan Island to protect American interests in the dispute. Several British warships were sent to protect British interests. Pickett's men began to dismantle one of the blockhouses and some other assets at Fort Bellingham and reassembled them on the south beach of San Juan Island. Following the British and American agreement to jointly occupy San Juan Island, what remained at Fort Bellingham was removed. In 1863, the fort was officially closed. In 1868, 320 acres were returned to Mrs. Roberts, who had since remarried and was known as Mrs. Tuck. She continued to live there and farm the land for many years. Today, rows of greenhouses cover the site.

When Fort Sumter fell and Pickett answered the call to return to fight in the Civil War, his son was placed in the hands of friends. Departing from Fort Bellingham in 1861, Pickett left without ever seeing his boy again. His son would later grow up to be a noted artist. Some of his paintings are on display at the Whatcom Museum of History and Art in Bellingham.

Pickett House

Pickett House, 910 Bancroft St., Bellingham, WA. Photo by Author

Pickett House was originally a simple two-story home of undressed planks. The main section only measured 15 feet by 25 feet. Two rooms comprised the home's first floor and two bedrooms comprised the second floor. A lean-to on the west side contained the dining room and the kitchen.

Many changes have occurred to the Pickett House over the years, however much of it remains in its original state. The Pickett House was designated as a museum in 1941 and in 1956 it became home to the Daughters of the Pioneers. The Pickett House is on the National Register of Historic Places.

Heritage Flight Museum

Founded in 1996 by Apollo 8 astronaut Major General William Anders, the Heritage Flight Museum is a non-profit, 501(c)(3) organization dedicated to the preservation and flying of historic military aircraft.

The Museum settled at Bellingham International Airport in 2001, and has been developing displays and community programs since then. Visitors are welcome to get an up-close look at the collection of memorabilia and artifacts, and a selection of flying World War II, Korean, and Vietnam era aircraft. The collection includes: a P-51, an A-1, a PT-19, a T-6 Texan, an L-13, an H-13 Sioux, O-1, and an F-89 Scorpion. The collection also includes engines, simulators, and military vehicles.

United States Coast Guard Station Bellingham

The Coast Guard has had a permanent presence in the Bellingham area since 1947. Fourteen personnel comprised the crew of an 83-foot Coastal Patrol Boat, and a crew of eight manned a 50-foot Harbor Patrol Boat. In 1966, patrol boats were replaced by the 65-foot Harbor Tug *BITT WYTL-65613*, which was later transferred to Valdez, Alaska. The first station was commissioned in 1977 with a crew of six.

As the mission definitions expanded, new facilities were added in 1986 and again in 1999. The present station, commissioned on July 19, 1999, can accommodate 48 people. The Coast Guard Investigative Service also has an office at Coast Guard Station Bellingham.

Station Bellingham is the northern-most station in Coast Guard District 13. Because of its proximity to Canada, the station works with a variety of other federal, state, local, and Canadian law enforcement agencies to provide a credible presence and deter threats. USCG Station Bellingham was an integral contributor to the safety of the 2010 Winter Olympics held in Vancouver, British Columbia.

The day-to-day responsibilities of the Station's staff and resources include the San Juan Islands and north to the Canadian border. Each year, resources are deployed on an average of 150 search and rescue cases and provide additional security by performing an average of 300 maritime law enforcement boardings each year.

USCGC Sea Lion. *Photo courtesy of U.S. Coast Guard*

USCGC Terrapin. *Photo courtesy of U.S. Coast Guard*

In 2004, USCG *Sea Lion*, an 87-foot Coast Patrol Boat, was placed into service with a crew of ten. It joined the USCG *Terrrapin* in providing Coast Guard service at Station Bellingham.

Additional missions include helping to maintain aids to navigation, providing marine environmental protection, enforcing fisheries conservation, and port safety and security. As part of the Integrated Border Enforcement Team (IBET), Station Bellingham has participated in numerous drug related arrests, and the seizures of thousands of pounds of drugs and nearly a million dollars in U.S. currency.

Semiahmoo Harbor Light

The Semiahmoo Harbor Light was first lit in 1905. Increasing numbers of ships passing through the area prompted residents to petition the Lighthouse Board in 1897 for a lighthouse and fog signal station.

The Board acknowledged the petition, but delayed any action until after the Spanish-American War was over. In 1900, the town postmaster, Orison P. Carver, tried again and the petition was approved. Congress funded the $25,000 for construction. Carver subsequently became the first lighthouse keeper.

Edward Durgan followed him in 1913, and he served until 1920 when he died while on duty. Accounts indicate that he suffered from a heart attack while raising the keepers' boat up via pulleys. His wife, Estelle, succeeded him briefly in the job. Several other keepers followed, but the position was eliminated in 1939 when an automatic light was installed.

Semiahmoo Harbor Light 1943. Photo dated 17 July 1943, courtesy of the website: uscg.mil/history/LHWA.asp

Little in the way of photographs or stories remains of early Semiahmoo operations. Organizations and historians including those from the *Lighthouse Digest* welcome any stories or photographs pertaining to the light or keepers and their stories of service with the light.

Located near Blaine, the lighthouse provided navigational aids into and out of the Port of Blaine. Constructed on pilings and made out of wood, it had an octagonal house capped by a cylindrical lamp cupola, a fourth-order lens and showed a fixed red light. Its fog signal was a trumpet. The light station was deactivated and dismantled in 1944. Replaced by an 18-foot pyramid house, this too was dismantled in 1971. Today a functional metal tower sits at the site in Semiahmoo Bay.

Courtesy of Lighthouse Digest Magazine, Amisa Pollard Collection

Birch Bay Air Force Station / Blaine Air Force Station

Blaine Air Force Station (AFS) was an integral part of the radar network of the Air Defense Command (ADC). As the Cold War became the focus for the U.S. military, it was imperative to gain control of the air space over the United States. As a result, the mission of the Air Defense Command, established in 1946, was to organize and administer the integrated air defense system of the Continental United States (CONUS), exercise direct control of all active measures, and coordinate all passive means of air defense.

At the beginning of the Korean War in 1950, the Secretary of the Air Force sought approval from the Secretary of Defense to speed up the construction of a permanent radar network which would ultimately provide security to the United States. Approval was granted on July 21, 1950, and the Army Corps of Engineers proceeded with construction. The entire station comprised approximately eighty acres of what was once was rolling farmland near the community of Birch Bay. The sea-level location allowed certain radars to provide long range scans.

The 757th Aircraft Control and Warning Squadron (AC&W) was activated at Paine Air Field near Everett in November 1950. The initial cadre of personnel arrived at the Birch Bay site on March 14th 1951, to operate a pair of AN/FPS-10

radars. In March 1952, a MARS (Military Amateur Radio Station) was initiated.

The base could house approximately 200 airmen in five barracks and 20 officers in the BOQ.

Initially the station functioned as a Ground Control Intercept (GCI) site. The job of a GCI site was to act as a guide for interceptor aircraft as they launched to intercept intruders on the unit's radar. GCI operators were tasked with monitoring thousands of square miles of watching the sky and waiting to identify an intruder into friendly airspace.

Birch Bay AFS was re-designated Blaine Air Force Station on December 1, 1953. Technology continued to progress and by 1959 the unit had switched to an AN/FPS-20 search radar and AN/FPS-6 and AN/FPS-6A height finder radar.

The Semi-Automatic Ground Environment (SAGE) system was coming on line and in 1960, Blaine AFS joined the SAGE system and provided data to McChord Air Force Base near Tacoma. The unit was then re-designated as the 757th Radar Squadron (SAGE) in April. By 1963, the conversion was complete to the AN/FPS-24 search radar, and the AN/FPS-26A height finder radar. As the years went by and radar technology advanced, the station was upgraded to improve both efficiency and accuracy.

The 1970s saw even more changes in the role of the unit. The station's mission focused on Long Range Radar. The growth of the base grew by leaps and bounds due to the staffing issues crucial to the mission of serving as a back-up station if the SAGE system went off line. The 1970s saw the assignment of women to the unit. Approximately a dozen women were stationed at the 757 during the 1970s.

By 1978, Air Defense Command was being inactivated and antiaircraft radar stations were being drawn down. Three radars (AN/FPS-24 long-range search radar, the AN/FPS-6A, and the AN/FPS-26A long range height finder radar) were being operated up until the site was closed. Personnel were gradually reassigned, and a skeleton crew was left to disassemble the radar units and to close up the buildings. Orders were given to keep the dining hall intact, so potential buyers could use it in some manner. The 757th Radar Squadron was deactivated on January 1, 1979.

Many of the station's buildings are still intact; however the properties are undergoing redevelopment into a conference and recreation center.

Blaine AFS. To the south, Radar and Operations buildings. Courtesy of Radomes, Inc., The Air Defense Radar Veterans Assn: http://www.radomes.org/museum

Blaine AFS. To the east, Barracks. Courtesy of Radomes, Inc., The Air Defense Radar Veterans Assn: http://www.radomes.org/museum

**WELCOME TO
BLAINE AIR FORCE STATION
WASHINGTON**

HOME OF THE 757TH RADAR SQUADRON
AEROSPACE DEFENSE COMMAND (ADCOM)

Welcome brochure. U.S. Air Force Publication

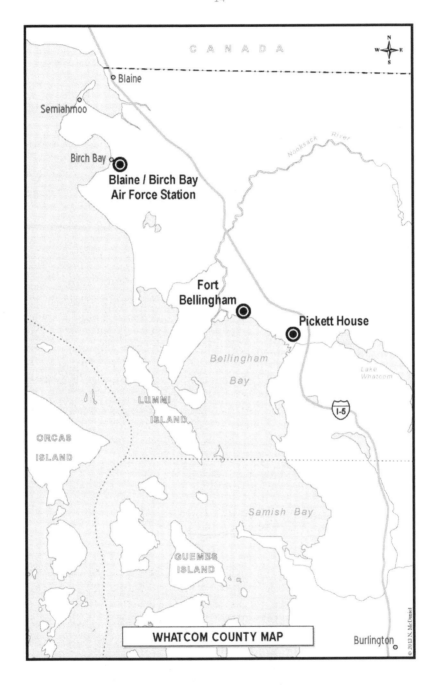

Chapter 2
Skagit County

The Washington Territory officially was formalized on March 2, 1853. At that time, Skagit County was part of Island County. The first Island County also included today's San Juan, Island, Whatcom, and Snohomish Counties.

In 1854, after lengthy discourse, a few settlers broke away from the original Island County and established Whatcom County. In November 1883, Skagit County separated itself from being governed by Bellingham, and established a separate county named after the Skagit Tribe.

In this diverse county with rich farmlands, islands, timber, and fishing, the first settlers quickly set about the business of building an infrastructure of roads, villages and towns, and lighthouses.

Burrows Island Lighthouse

The Burrows Island Lighthouse is located on the southwestern end of Burrows Island. Watercraft heading from Bellingham Bay south through Rosario Strait to the Strait of Juan de Fuca have to contend with strong eddy lines and tide rips. The Burrows Island light provided warning for the nearby Dennis Shoal and Lawson Reef.

The first mention of the light was in the 1901 Congressional Record (57th Congressional Report #419 dated December 16, 1901):

> *To establish a light house and fog signal at Burrows Island, Rosario Strait, State of Washington. There is much traffic through Rosario Strait, which will naturally increase in the future. During certain seasons of the year fog and smoke from forest fires prevail. Burrows Island is a point of departure for most vessels plying the strait. The tides and currents here are strong and variable, and there are several dangerous reefs in the immediate vicinity. A light and fog signal at the southwest point of Burrows Island would be of great use to commerce and navigation. It is estimated that they be established for not exceeding $15,000 and it is recommended that an appropriation of this amount be made therefore.*

Designed by C. W. Lieck, the light was first lit in 1906. Mr. Lieck also designed the Mukilteo Lighthouse around the same time. The Burrows Island Light is a wood structure with a 34-foot square tower. It is attached to a fog signal building which originally held a Daboll trumpet fog signal.

The fourth-order Fresnel lens, a white light with a red sector, was removed after the light was automated in 1972. The lens is now at the Coast Guard Station in Port Angeles.

Legends about the lighthouse include a short account of the fog horn utilization. It is said that the horn never blew during the first three months after it was installed. In the following year, the horn reputedly blew for 329 hours out of the year.

The Lighthouse Service operated the light until 1939 when it was taken over by the Coast Guard. The Coast Guard operated the lighthouse with personnel stationed on the island until 1972. After it was automated, the boathouse and keeper's house were closed. A modern optic lens replaced the Fresnel lens in the lantern room.

A helipad now occupies the ground where the keeper's house was located. The island's shoreline is comprised of sheer rock with sharp drop-offs. Steep hills covered with trees or grass, define most of the island. The light station was built on one of the few level spots on the island.

Originally, the station included the combination light tower and fog signal building, a keeper's house, a boathouse, and other outbuildings.

Burrows Island Lighthouse. Photos courtesy of the U.S. Coast Guard

A bungalow was built north of the original keeper's house to house an additional keeper. When electricity came, a power plant was added. Every eight months fuel was delivered by the buoy tender *Fir* to keep the generators going.

The forty acres comprising the grounds are owned by Washington State Parks. The lighthouse itself was made available to an eligible entity with the passage of the National Historic Lighthouse Preservation Act of 2000. In 2010, the transfer of the facilities to the Northwest Schooner Society was initiated. Plans include creating an interpretive center within the structures and lighthouse programs where participants can occupy the keepers' facilities

A two hour cruise, departing from Anacortes offers an opportunity to see the lighthouse from a water view as well as other attractions including orca whales and the vistas of the San Juan Islands. Kayak tours are also available.

Fort at Lone Tree Point

Lone Tree Point. Photo courtesy of Jerry Sorensen

Washington Territorial Volunteers constructed and manned a blockhouse at a site approximately three and a half miles northwest of LaConner in 1856. With the signing of the various treaties with Native Americans, the tensions that had been building between settlers and Natives began to lessen. As a result, the blockhouse was staffed for only a few months.

Nothing remains of the blockhouse; however the tree on Lone Tree Point is still evident and a prominent site. The site is currently part of the Thousand Trails Campgrounds on property leased from the Swinomish Tribe.

Skagit County Airport

Skagit County's first airport began as a single runway, built in 1933 in Bayview (approximately three miles west of Burlington) as a joint project of the Works Progress Administration and Public Works Administration.

As training missions increased at Whidbey Island Naval Air Station, alternate airfields were required to facilitate training and increase safety. During war years, military aircraft were a common sight as pilots prepared for overseas deployments and utilized the airfield as an alternate landing site for training and emergencies. The U.S. Navy took over the site about 1943 to serve as an alternate airfield for Whidbey Island Naval Air Station during World War II, and built a triangular runway-taxiway landing strip which looks much the same today.

After the war the airport was operated by the federal government until being transferred to Skagit County in 1958. The current terminal facilities were constructed in the late 1970s. Today, the airport serves general aviation needs, charter flights, the Civil Air Patrol, and military aircraft on occasion. Estimates indicate that the airport serves approximately 60,000 aircraft per year.

Airport ca. 1950s. Courtesy of Port of Skagit County

Fort Whitman

During the 1880s, Secretary of War William Endicott proposed an upgraded coastal defense installation and weapons system. He convened the "Endicott Board" which recommended a huge $127 million construction program including breech loading cannons, mortars, floating batteries, and new installations for approximately 29 locations on the United States coast line. As a result, coastal fortifications built between 1885 and 1905 are often referred to as Endicott Period forts.

Land purchased for $3,000 in 1903 became the site for Fort Whitman. Construction began in 1909 and was completed in 1911. Only one gun battery was built along with a separate mine field control and observation post southwest of the gun battery. Battery Harrison was a single story 6 inch disappearing gun battery with mounts for four guns with barrel lengths of 277 inches. (Model M1908 guns manufactured by Watervliet). Guns were mounted on raised platforms with two magazines between the guns.

The guns arrived by barge and were hauled up Goat Island's 80-foot bluff by a steam drive tramway. On February 21, 1911, Battery Harrison was transferred for service to the Coast Artillery.

The first garrison of the fort was a four-man caretaker detachment headed by Corporal Thad Eastwood who stayed as caretaker until the start of World War I in 1917. The fort was expanded during WWI but was once again reduced to caretaker status in 1919.

Battery Harrison. Photo courtesy of USforting.com

During December 1941, Battery C, 14th Coast Artillery Regiment was sent to garrison Fort Whitman. Two officers and 46 enlisted men comprised the unit. Temporary buildings and tents housed the troops. A 37mm AMTB battery, built in 1942 on the west side of island facing Saratoga Sound, remained active until 1944. The 14th Coast Artillery disbanded in October 1944 and the fort was once again returned to caretaker status. The temporary buildings were torn down in 1945.

Goat Island was deeded to the Washington State Game Department in 1947 and is now part of the Skagit Wildlife Area. The island is accessible by kayak or small boat. Exploring the fort requires a short, but steep hike up the 80-foot bluff. The only remaining structures are Battery Harrison, a latrine, and a mine control and observation post approximately 800 feet southwest of the battery.

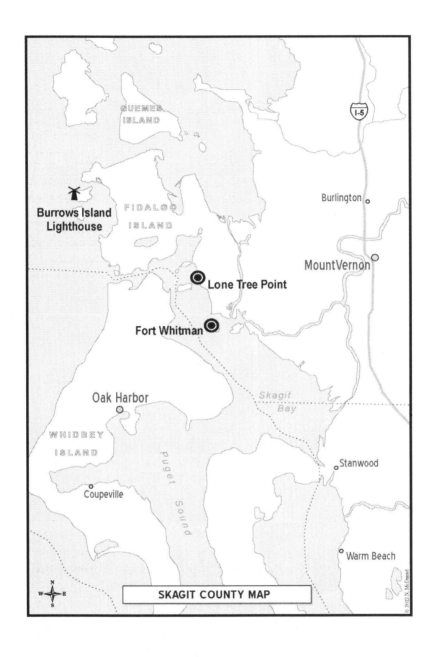

Chapter 3

Snohomish County

Snohomish County was and still is an important asset for the protection of Puget Sound and the nation. Ranging from light stations to major air fields, the installations found in Snohomish County are remarkable.

Mukilteo Light Station

Mukilteo Lighthouse, ca. 1960. Photo courtesy U.S. Coast

The Mukilteo Light Station is situated in historic downtown Mukilteo adjacent to the Washington State Ferry dock. Its light marks the turning point for ships entering into Possession Sound. It still provides an important navigational aid for Washington State Ferries operating between Mukilteo and Clinton.

The light was built in 1905 on the site

where the Point Elliott Treaty was signed on January 22, 1855. A monument in Mukilteo at Third Street and Lincoln Avenue commemorates the signing of the treaty.

Captain George Vancouver named the point where the light station was built "Rose Point" for the wild pink roses which covered the land.

In 1901, the U.S. Lighthouse Board recommended that a light and fog signal be built on the point to help guide vessels. Construction began in 1905 and it took eight months to complete the station. Consisting of the light and fog-signal building, two large two-story houses, an oil house, and a windmill, the entire station cost $27,000 to build.

The light was lit for the first time in March 1906. The thirty- foot tower, designed by Carl Leick, Lighthouse Service architect, was made of wood. The kerosene lantern was magnified by a fourth-order Fresnel lens. The fog signal included a Daboll trumpet signal which had been invented by Celadon Daboll of New London, Connecticut.

The first keeper assigned to manage the light was Peter Christiansen. His wife and four children occupied the station until 1925 when he died of an apparent heart attack after helping unload a shipment of coal for the light station. Christiansen was a Norwegian immigrant and had served as a member of the Lighthouse Service for 31 years. Christiansen was followed by Edward Brooks, who came from the New Dungeness Light Station near Sequim. In 1927, electricity was installed at the Station. An attempt made to change the lamp from kerosene to an electric bulb was unsuccessful. As a result, the lens was exchanged with the New Dungeness station. This lens, still in the lighthouse, was made in 1852 by L. Sautter & Cie, Paris, France. In 1939, the

Mukilteo Lighthouse. Photo by Author

Lighthouse Service was merged with the U.S. Coast Guard which took up the mission of aids to navigation throughout the country. In the 1960s, the Coast Guard planned to replace the Fresnel lens with a modern rotating aero-beacon, but the Mukilteo community protested this upgrade. Officially designated as a Historic Place by the Washington State Advisory Council on Historic Preservation, the lighthouse was placed on the National Register of Historic Places in 1977. In 1979, the Coast Guard automated the lighthouse and fog signal. The beacon's characteristic is a two-second white flash every five seconds and is visible for 14 miles. An electric fog horn is activated by an automatic sensor which detects moisture in the air, sounding one three-second blast every 30 seconds.

The exterior of the Mukilteo Light Station is almost the same as it was in 1905. Painted the traditional white with green trim and red roofs, it continues to provide a visual landmark. Today, the grounds are property of the City of Mukilteo and the area has been named "Mukilteo Lighthouse Park." The park provides great subjects for photography of both the lighthouse, and Washington State Ferry vessels.

Open to the public, the old fog signal building contains a fascinating display about the lighthouse, and has historic photos of the first lighthouse keepers and their families who occupied the facilities. Accounts of the historical events of the area are also on display. A copy of the Point Elliott Treaty between the various tribes of the area and the government is available for view at the visitor's center. It was signed in 1855 near the location of the lighthouse. The exact location is not known.

The gift shop and visitor's center are open to the public on weekends from April through September.

Mukilteo Explosive Loading Terminal / Mukilteo Tank Farm

During World War II, a mill located on the waterfront in Mukilteo provided a dock facility which was perfect for loading military ships. The mill property was sold to the Army and the Mukilteo Explosive Loading Terminal was established. The Terminal provided facilities for loading ammunition onboard ships bound for the Pacific theater. The Mukilteo location provided easy access for rail, barge, and road transportation.

The harbor was relatively protected and in close proximity to nearby military installations.

Original structures built by the Army included administration buildings, auto maintenance shops, an ammunition repair shop, and several rail spurs which ran through the property to bring in the ammunition.

In 1951, the Air Force purchased the property and constructed ten bulk fuel above-ground storage tanks for use as a fuel storage and transfer facility. It was called the Mukilteo Tank Farm and was also known as the Mukilteo Defense Fuel Support Point. The piers were reinforced, and fuel pipelines were extended to the end of the pier.

By 1953, the facility was operated under the auspices of McChord Air Force Base. The facility supplied JP-4 (jet propellant number 4) and other aviation gasoline fuels to military installations throughout the Pacific Northwest. In 1973, the Air Force transferred the facility to the Defense Logistics Agency which continued to operate the fuels distribution facility as a government-owned contractor-operated storage and transfer terminal.

Fuel came in by barge and then was sent to the military installations by barge, train, and tanker trucks. In 1955, the Air Force Fuels Laboratory began operating on the site. The fuels laboratory remained in operation until 2003.

By the late 1970s, the pier at the Tank Farm was in disrepair and was no longer available for loading fuel onto railcars. In 1987 the Mukilteo Tank Farm was closed and the mission was consolidated to the Navy facility in Manchester. In 1989 fuel storage and transfer operations were finished.

The only tenant on the site now is the National Oceanic Atmospheric Administration, through a permit to continue operation of the Mukilteo Biological Field Facility by the National Marine Fisheries Service.

Plans and activities are underway to transfer the property to the Port of Everett.

Paine Field

During the Great Depression, one of the largest relief projects in the country was the building of Paine Field. The project was designed to create a first-class airport and bring jobs and economic growth to the Pacific Northwest. On a direct route from Portland to Vancouver, British Coumbia and then on to Alaska, the site just southwest of Everett seemed to be ideal. Consisting of 640 acres, the property was purchased from Merrill Ring Logging and the Pope and Talbot Company. Snohomish County matched the dollars and initial work began by the Works Progress Administration (WPA) on September 10, 1936. When completed it was to have four runways.

The large commercial airport that was originally planned for Everett in the 1930s never came to fruition. National priorities dictated that the newly constructed air field should become an important asset for the military.

Originally built to be the County's commercial airport, World War II changed its use to a military airfield, operated by the Army Air Corps from 1941 to 1946. When the U.S entered World War II, there was a need to protect the Bremerton Shipyards and the Boeing plant in Seattle which was producing B-17 and B-29 bombers.

Paine Army Airfield 25 February 1942. U.S. Air Corps Photo

It was once again used as a military field in 1951 to support the Korean Conflict. It continued to see mixed military and commercial use until the mid-1960s when Snohomish County took over full management of the site.

The field was named Paine Field to honor a World War I Snohomish County resident and Army Air Corps Pilot, Second Lieutenant Topliff Olin Paine. His boyhood residence was a two story house located at 2020 Wetmore Avenue in Everett. He attended the University of Washington, majoring in Civil Engineering. When the United States entered World War I, he enlisted with the 12th Company of the Army Infantry in Everett. He attended ground schools and subsequently entered flying training at March Field in California. With his pilot training he also received a commission into the Army as a second lieutenant in 1918. After his discharge from the Army at the conclusion of World War I, he flew as a commercial pilot in California and was subsequently appointed as a pilot with the Air Mail Service. His experiences flying the route from Rock Springs, Wyoming to Salt Lake City, Utah are legendary. Flying in near blizzard conditions, he is reported to have landed several times in nearly impossible conditions.

His feats are commemorated at the National Postal Museum in Washington D.C., for his early contributions to establishing the Air Mail Service. Paine died of an accidental gunshot wound in 1922. In 1941, the Earl Faulkner Post of the American Legion suggested that the new field be named in honor of Lieutenant Paine.

When the Korean War broke out in the 1950s, the Puget Sound's war supporting assets once again needed protection. In 1951, a United States Air Force Aerospace Defense Command unit was stationed at Paine Field. The field's name was officially changed to Paine Air Force Base.

Paine Air Force Base main gate. U.S. Air Force Photo made available by Matt Cawby

The 4753rd Air Base Squadron was designated as the official organization. In January 1952, rosters indicated that there were four officers and thirty-three airmen stationed at Paine Air Force Base. Their prime job was to rebuild the base into a tactical air defense installation. During this period, the control of the base was shared between Snohomish County and the military. The Air Force, however, had priority over the use of the airport. The 4753rd was re-designated as the 86th Air Base Squadron, which later changed to the 529th Air Defense Group. In 1955, the 529th Air Defense Group gave way to the 326th Fighter Group (Air Defense). In 1961, the 326th Fighter Group was discontinued and was replaced by the 57th Fighter Group.

In the 1960s, the field was designated as part of the 25th NORAD (North American Air Defense) region and supported the 25th ADC (Air Defense Command) station at McChord Air Force Base in Tacoma. It was part of a coastal horizon radar system that linked all ADC bases.

Aircraft stationed at Paine Air Force Base over the years included the: P-38, P-39, P-40, B-25, B-26, F-84, F-86, F-89, F-102, and F-106.

321st Fighter Interceptor Squadron F-89 Scorpions on the ramp at Paine Air Force Base, 1956. U.S. Air Force photo

Paine Field. USGS photo, 1990

In 1966, the Air Force began the process to close the base. In the same year, Boeing bought adjacent property for the fabrication of the 747. Since then, the former Paine Air Force Base has continued to develop as a major center for several aviation, engineering, maintenance, flight schools, and service companies including Alaska Airlines, Willard Flying School, Curtiss-Wright Flight Systems, Crown Aviation, Honeywell, and Goodrich Aviation Technical Services.

Over the years, Paine Field has hosted many small businesses by becoming a small business incubator. The combined Boeing – Paine Field aviation oriented business community is the Snohomish county's largest employer and has become one of the county's most important economic generators.

Paine Field is a destination for aircraft enthusiasts. It is the site where the Boeing Company manufactures the 747, 767, 777, and the Dream Liner 787.

Paine Field is also home to the Future of Flight Aviation Center and Boeing Tour, the Flying Heritage Collection, Historic Flight Foundation, Legend Flyers, and the Museum of Flight Restoration Center. The center and tour are made possible through the collaboration of the Boeing Company, Future of Flight Foundation, Snohomish County Public Facilities District and the Snohomish County Airport/Paine Field.

Naval Station Everett

Naval Station Everett's history began in 1983 along with the Navy's Strategic Homeport concept. Everett was selected in 1984 from 13 other eligible ports. Construction funds were approved in 1986, followed by an official ground breaking ceremony in November 1987.

Construction contracts to build the $56 million carrier pier were awarded in 1988. Less than four years later, three Navy ships participated in the formal opening of the new pier.

The Navy Support Complex at Smokey Point saw its own groundbreaking ceremony in 1993. The commissary, exchange, family support service center, thrift shop, education offices, bachelor and visitor quarters, chapel, and various recreation facilities were soon built at Smokey Point. Naval Station Everett officially began operation on January 4, 1994

Naval ships which have been assigned to Naval Station Everett include:

- USS *Ingraham* (FFG 61)
- USS *Ford* (FFG54)
- USS *Paul F. Foster* (DD 964)
- USS *Callaghan* (DDG 994)
- USS *Chandler* (DDG 996)
- USS *David R. Ray* (DD 971)
- USS *Fife* (DD 991)
- USS *Rodney M. Davis* (FFG 60)
- USS *Momsen* (DDG 92)
- USS *Shoup* (DDG 86)
- USS *Abraham Lincoln* (CVN 72)

Aerial view Naval Station Everett. Courtesy U.S. Navy

Arlington Airport

In 1934, President Roosevelt made the announcement that the Works Progress Administration was to receive several million dollars to work on airstrips which could be used for defense of the nation. Residents of Arlington petitioned city officials to apply and make property available for such a project in Arlington.

The original strip of land measuring 400 feet by 4,000 feet was leased from Mr. Mirckenmeir for $100 per year for a term of five years. The logged land was cleared, graded and a light asphalt strip was laid at the total cost of $760. Later on in the fall of 1935, additional funding was procured for a 2,000 foot by 400 foot crosswind runway, which became the northeastern runway.

The airport was used by local fliers and also by the Forest Service for transporting supplies to firefighters in the Cascades. When the lease expired in 1939, economic conditions prevented the Town of Arlington from purchasing the land. City fathers asked the War Department for financial assistance.

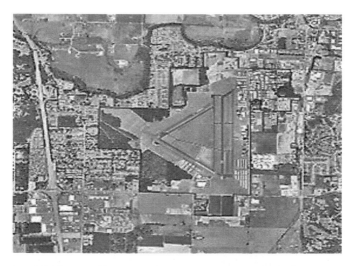

Aerial view Arlington Airport, Courtesy City of Arlington, http://www.arlingtonwa.gov

By 1940, the airport was known as U.S Naval Auxiliary Air Station, Arlington. The airstrip was initially utilized to support naval air training facilities in Seattle.

In 1942, preparing for war became more important for the country. The Navy authorized the Army to develop a strategic base for medium bombers which could meet and counter the growing threat of an invasion of the Aleutians by Japanese forces. Additional land was purchased and additional runways were constructed. Two 5,000- by 150-foot, asphalt surfaced runways with connecting taxiways, a control tower, barracks and living quarters, and a dining hall were constructed.

By 1943, the threat from Japan began to diminish. At the same time aircraft carrier operations were increasing and additional training facilities were required. The Navy took control of the properties once again and continued to build more barracks, a dispensary, theater, and hangars. The Army retained the right to use the facilities if national military strategy required them.

By June of 1943, the station was commissioned as a Navy facility once again. As the field was being used, the need for several major improvements was noted. The frequent northwesterly winds blowing across the north-south and northeast-southwest runways presented hazards for many of the aircraft in use at the time. The narrow landing gear of aircraft such as the F-4F made landing in these crosswinds difficult and dangerous. Authorization to build a third runway was received in early 1945 and it was completed in August 1945. At the same time flush lighting was installed along all three runways and taxiways.

Roadways around the installation were also subject to dust in the summer and potholes when it rained. By September 1945, contracts and construction were completed on roadways throughout the installation. Hangars for aircraft maintenance were also completed. Link trainers, communication facilities and training facilities were completed in the years 1944—1945.

Squadrons trained at Arlington include:

- VB-139, July 1943
- VC-55, August 1943
- VC-3, September-November 1943
- VC-4, September-November 1944
- VC-77, January-February 1944
- VC-78, January-February 1944
- VC 87, February-June 1944
- VC 90, February-August 1944
- VF 38, June-August 1944
- VT 38, June-August 1944
- VF 49, August 1944

By August 1945, Arlington was a complete station. Just a few weeks later as war efforts were nearing completion, reduced funding and operations dictated that the installation would be closed. The Chief of Naval Operations directed that the air station be reduced to caretaker status on December 1, 1945. At this point, it was used primarily for an emergency landing field for Naval Air Station Whidbey. Military personnel were reduced from approximately 600 to 200. By December 1946, the Town of Arlington received a permit to operate the station for commercial and civilian flying. The town leased the flying facilities to Wesley Loback, then the manager of Snohomish Airport, who operated an accredited flying school-Arlington Aeronautical School of Flight and Engineering.

In 1959, the United States General Services Administration declared the property as surplus and gave the airport to the City of Arlington through a quitclaim deed.

Alternate uses for the runway emerged during the 1950s. Drag racing became a focus for the runways and taxiways. By 1964 the FAA prohibited racing along the north-south runway. The venue changed but was not curtailed and racing continued along the northeast-southwest runway until 1969.

Today, the facilities of the Arlington Airport provide a venue for one of the biggest fly-ins in the nation. The Northwest chapter of the Experimental Aircraft Association (EAA) hosts the fly-in in July of each year. Aircraft from around the country come to AWO for this continually growing event.

On a daily basis, Arlington Airport is the home to a vibrant aviation industry base including maintenance and flying schools. The airport also serves as the home base for a wide variety of restored aircraft, helicopters, ultra-lights, upholstery, aircraft cover manufacturing, vintage military aircraft, and a host of other aviation related business.

Flying Heritage Collection

The Flying Heritage Collection at Paine Field is not technically a military site; however the planes within it are definitely part of military history.

The main part of the collection is aircraft from the 1930s

and 1940s with the main emphasis on combat aircraft from World War II. British, United States, German, Russian, and Japanese aircraft are part of the collection.

The aircraft have been completely researched and reassembled to achieve the highest authenticity in restoration. The collection began in 1998 when Paul Allen began the acquisition and preservation of wartime aircraft. Many of these aircraft are the last of the production line for their kind. Allen recognized that if these aircraft were not restored, they would likely disappear. Aircraft within the Flying Heritage Collection are meant to fly and have been restored to be capable of flying again.

Restoration at the Flying Heritage collection is painstaking and complete. The restoration team researches the original vendors of parts and components to be able to construct the aircraft as closely as possible. If vendors are no longer available the team is able to reconstruct the components, using authentic materials, to achieve the highest possible level of authenticity. Everything from cotton-coated wiring to paint is authentic. Original radios are procured and repaired to outfit the cockpit to perfect or near perfect original state.

Factory drawings and specifications have been studied to ensure the aircraft are returned to "showroom" condition. Each aircraft's individual history including its manufacturing location, its deployments, its combat record, post-war roles, and its repairs are all carefully documented. As a result, the aircraft's own history is discovered as well as the contributions it made to history.

The Curtiss JN-4D "Jenny" is one of the more well-known aircraft in the Flying Heritage Collection. The Russian Polikarpov U-2/PO2 is also a popular part of the collection.

The Curtiss P-40C Tomahawk on display is purported to be the only remaining P-40C in flying condition in the world. This particular aircraft never flew for the United States but was instead purchased by Great Britain in 1941 and then subsequently sold to Russia under the Lend-Lease program. According to Soviet research this particular aircraft arrived in Murmansk via a convoy in early 1942. It flew combat missions for Russia against the Germans in World War II. The P-40C was forced to make a belly-landing in a field near Murmansk on September 27, 1942, after enemy fire pierced the oil tank. This damage was sufficient to render it "grounded". The plane was abandoned. Soviet records indicate that the battle lasted approximately 25 minutes.

References to the aircraft were non-existent until January 5, 1944 when it was removed from the inventory of the 1st Combined Air Division. It was a common practice to retain irreparable aircraft on the inventory for a period of time. The aircraft was discovered by satellite photography in 1993.

The Collection provides visitors the opportunities to see the aircraft, but it also provides an insight into how the aircraft of today evolved. The Flying Heritage Collection is open seven days a week from Memorial Day to Labor Day. Outside of that period the facility is closed on Mondays.

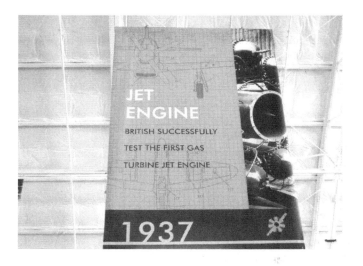

Educational display, Flying Heritage Collection. Photo by Author

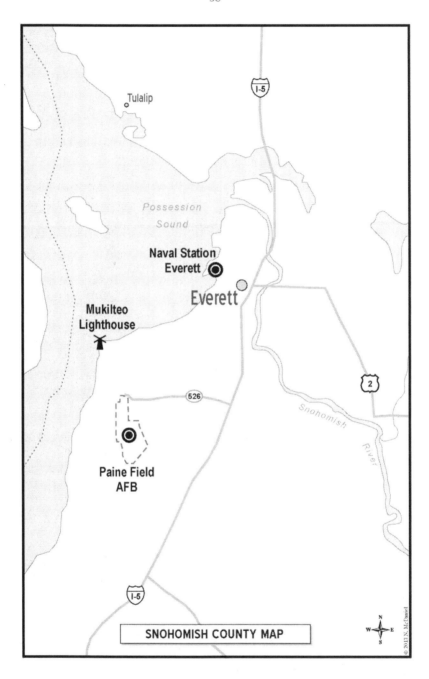

Chapter 4

San Juan County

"The Pig War"

The San Juan Islands have always been regarded as primer real estate. Plentiful timber, good soil, an important strategic location, and a temperate climate made the islands desirable to Spain, Great Britain, and the United States. All three countries staked claims, but by 1818 Spain had abandoned its claim and an Anglo-American agreement had provided for joint occupation of the area.

Trade agreements and capital investments by both countries were soon overtaken by the tensions resulting from American impatience with the British residents. Presence of the British seemed to fly in the face of the "manifest destiny" philosophy which was prevalent in the United States at the time. The British regarded the treaties, explorations, and activities of the Hudson's Bay Company in the area as the basis for her claim.

In 1846, the Oregon Treaty was signed in London. This treaty between Britain and the United States established the 49th parallel as the permanent boundary between United States and Canada. In most places it resolved the questions over competing claims to the Oregon Territory, and did a credible job of establishing the boundary until it got to the west coast. There the status of several of the largest of the San Juan Islands in the United States and the Canadian Gulf Islands remained in dispute.

The intention of the treaty was to designate all of Vancouver Island as British territory, but it defined the boundary at this point as the middle of the channel separating the continent from Vancouver Island. The definition of what was the "main channel" was unclear. The British felt it was Haro Strait, east of San Juan Island. The Americans believed it to be Rosario Strait, on the west side. As a result, whether Great Britain or the United States was the owner of these islands was in question.

The Hudson's Bay Company claimed ownership of the island in 1845. The company built a salmon-curing station there in 1845 and in 1853 began to develop a sheep ranch called Belle Vue Farm. Washington Territory was created in 1853 and Whatcom County claimed San Juan Island. The British regarded the claims as illegal but by 1859, approximately twenty-five to thirty Americans were living on the island.

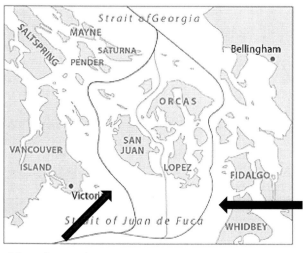

Line favored by the U.S.

Line favored by Britain

On June 15, 1859, Lyman Cutlar, an American settler noticed a rather large black pig belonging to the Hudson's Bay Company rooting in his garden. He shot and killed the pig. When he refused to pay for the pig, the Company's farm manager demanded payment. The British regarded Cutlar's refusal as illegal and demanded he be arrested. The other American settlers sent a petition to Brigadier General Harney, the very "anti-British" commander of the Department of Oregon. He quickly responded by sending troops from the

Ninth Infantry under the command of Captain George Pickett (then stationed at Fort Bellingham) to the island. Pickett arrived on the island on July 27, 1859. Captain Pickett, was a West Point graduate and a Mexican War veteran. He was the first U.S. commander on San Juan Island.

At the same time, James Douglas, Governor of the Crown Colony of British Columbia, dispatched a naval force to protect Britain's interests. He had advised the commander of the British unit, Captain Geoffrey Hornby, to try and avoid conflict if possible, but when Hornby's superior, Rear Admiral Robert Baynes arrived on the island, he was surprised to find that the United States and Great Britain were very close to going to war over the demise of the pig.

Both countries were moving more forces into the area. By mid-August, 461 Americans were supported by 14 cannon dug into earthen redoubts. Eight 32-pounder naval guns had been removed from the USS *Massachusetts* and placed in a redoubt excavated under the direction of Second Lieutenant Henry M. Robert (who would be the future author of *Robert's Rules of Order)*. Five British ships carrying 167 cannon and nearly two thousand troops were squaring off against the Americans.

English Camp as it appeared in late spring of 1860. Photo courtesy National Park Service

President Buchanan was shocked by the news from the far northwest region. He immediately sent General Winfield Scott to try and defuse the situation. Scott and Douglas began to correspond over the dilemma and both countries agreed to withdraw most of their respective forces. By mid-September, officials in London and Washington D.C. agreed to a joint military occupation of San Juan Island until the matter could be further settled through more discussions. Captain Pickett resigned his commission on San Juan and went on to lead his Confederate division in the charge that bears his name at the Battle of Gettysburg.

The Royal Marine Garrison on San Juan Island, pre-1867. Photographer unknown, photo courtesy National Park Service.

The joint occupation continued for the next twelve years with both countries maintaining garrisons at opposite ends of the island. American Camp remained as an active Army post throughout the Civil War with soldiers regularly rotating between the Northwest and battles in the East.

In 1871, the United States and Great Britain submitted the boundary matter to Kaiser Wilhelm I of Germany to make a binding, arbitrated decision. On October 21, 1872, the decision was made in favor of the Americans. British troops withdrew from the island in November of that year. Several years after the war, American troops left San Juan Island in 1874.

No shots were fired in the "Pig War" and no casualties resulted with the exception of the pig.

American Camp had several names during its existence as a military facility. It was once named Camp Pickett, then Post of San Juan in 1863. It was renamed as Camp Fred

Steele in 1867 and then Camp San Juan Island in 1868. When Lieutenant Colonel Silas Casey arrived to reinforce Pickett's troops, he established a separate camp which became known as Casey's Camp. Another name found in the records for American Camp was Camp Reynolds.

Casey's Camp (American Camp), ca. 1860s. Photo Courtesy National Park Service

Today, the sites of the Americans and the British garrisons are distinct parts of the San Juan Island National Historic Park. The San Juan Island National Historic Park commemorates the resolution of this boundary dispute. The Park is divided into the American Camp and the British Camp. The grounds are open all year from dawn through 11:00 p.m.

The site is an important part of United States history, even though many high school history books no longer even address the incident. Visitor centers provide interpretive displays of the camps.

American Camp. Photo courtesy National Park Service

British Camp. Photo courtesy National Park Service

Friday Harbor Radar Station

A World War II radar station was located at Friday Harbor on San Juan Island from 1942 -1944 providing early warning coastal defense during the war years. The site was disbanded in 1944.

Patos Island Light

Patos Island Fog Signal building with large trumpet, ca. 1900. Photo courtesy U.S. Coast Guard

Patos Island is the northernmost island of the San Juan Islands lying just northwest of Orcas Island. Spanish explorers named the island in 1792, Isla de Patos.

The English translation of the name is the Island of Ducks. The lighthouse is at Alden Point on the western end of the island.

It is located in a critical maritime area where passing steamships traveling from Nanaimo, British Columbia, to Alaska could be in danger of running onto the rocky islands. The station was first established in 1893 with a post light and a fog signal. Two dwellings, which were torn down in 1958, were part of the original facility.

The most notable keeper, Edward Durgan came to the island with his thirteen children in 1905 following his assignment to the Turn Point Light. It was a 26-mile trip into Bellingham for supplies. Isolated, especially in bad weather, the conditions proved to be tragic when seven of the Durgan children contracted smallpox. Trying to attract the attention of passing ships, the lightkeeper flew the American flag upside down as a symbol of distress.

Accounts of life on the island were recorded by one of the Durgan children, Helen Glidden, in her book *The Light on the Island*. While a fictionalized account, her descriptions help understand the difficulties of growing up in such a remote location. The book chronicles life on the island from 1905-1913. It also described the fun and positive challenges of growing up in such a place. The stories recall a time and place where smugglers, nature, religion, and family were part of the fabric of life. The book also provides a classic recipe for

Puget Sound Clam Chowder. The facility was always considered a good post, but families of light keepers were challenged by its isolation.

The facility underwent improvements in 1908 when a new fog signal and a 38-foot tower equipped with a fourth-order Fresnel lens was added. The light was automated in 1974.

Today it flashes a white light once every six seconds, with two red sectors marking dangerous rocks. The original Fresnel lens is on display at Admiralty Head Lighthouse. The lighthouse is now part of Patos Island State Park

A non-profit organization, Keepers of the Patos Light, was formed in 2007 with the goal of renovating the lighthouse and preserving the pristine environment of the island. Working with the Bureau of Land Management and the Orcas Island Fire Department, the preservation efforts continue. New doors, roof, windows, downspouts and paint have been part of this preservation effort. Repairs have also been made to the foundation, tower, and chimney.

Admission to the grounds is free.

Patos Island Lighthouse, ca. 1900. Photo courtesy U.S. Coast Guard

Patos Island Lighthouse after 2008 remodel, Photo by Linda Hudson, Keepers of the Patos Light

Turn Point Lighthouse

Turn Point Lighthouse. Photo courtesy of the U.S. Coast Guard

The Turn Point Lighthouse is located on the west side of Stuart Island, approximately eight miles east of Sidney, British Columbia. Turn Point is opposite the only place where a change of course is necessary to pass through San Juan Channel.

After the Pig War was settled, Stuart Island was surveyed in 1874 with the primary purpose of defining lots for homesteading. Two parcels were not made available for settlement but were retained as possible locations for a lighthouse. By 1888, Canada had a light on Discovery Island and there was a proposed light at the north entrance to the Canal de Haro. Having a light at Turn Point would make the channel well marked and provide safer passage. By 1888, the Lighthouse Board recommended that a light and a fog signal be established. The estimated cost was $15,000.

In 1891, Congress appropriated the funds and the final site was selected. In December 1892, a construction contract was awarded to build a duplex dwelling, a fog-signal building, barn, water tanks, and other minor outbuildings. The light was placed on a post located near the point. By fall of 1893, the facility was ready for operation.

Lightkeeper Edward Durgan and his assistant Peter Nicholai "PN" Christiansen occupied either side of the duplex. On February 16, 1897, a ship's whistle sounded near the facility. The two keepers found that the tug *Enterprise* had run aground on nearby rocks. Using pike poles, the tug was pushed off the rocks and moved to secure moorage. The captain was not alone on board, but had several drunk sailors below deck. In addition, he had put other crew members on board a barge which he had cut loose.

The barge was located and all crew members were brought ashore. The story continues, however, with an account of one of the drunk sailors pulling out a butcher knife and threatening his fellow sailors. The captain, with help from some of his men, overpowered his crew member and put him in a straight-jacket. The story goes on to indicate that the sailor was locked into the ship's hen house. Both Durgan and Christiansen received a citation for their efforts during the rescue.

In 1936, the station was updated with the addition of a concrete tower, a 300-millimeter light, and a foghorn. During World War II, additional Coast Guard personnel were stationed at Turn Point to staff a watch tower looking for ships entering Puget Sound and the Strait of Juan de Fuca area.

*World War II era photo of Turn Point Lighthouse.
Photo courtesy of U.S. Coast Guard*

The light was automated in 1974 and the station still provides critical services for the San Juan Islands. Researchers from the University of Washington utilize the quarters for a whale migration study base.

Restoration efforts in 2005 included replacement of windows using "wavy glass" to more closely replicate glass used in the original buildings. Work has also been done on the roofs and on installation of a power station, which includes an array of solar panels adjacent to the station.

The Turn Point Lighthouse Preservation Society provides education for the public. The Bureau of Land Management and the Coast Guard have worked together on restoration. Plans are to fully restore the buildings.

Lime Kiln Lighthouse

In 1860, a lime producing operation began to operate in what is now part of the State Park where the Lime Kiln Lighthouse is located. For 60 years, the area adjacent to the park was quarried for limestone. Kilns were built to fire the limestone to produce lime. Buildings were built, roads were cut and much of the island was logged to feed the fires of the kilns.

Located west of Friday Harbor, the lighthouse, established in 1906, still operates today and provides mariners important navigational aids. The U.S. Coast Guard operates the area adjacent to the lime operation as a lighthouse preserve.

In 1919, the Lime Kiln Lighthouse and two adjacent lighthouse keepers' quarters were built. The fourth-order Fresnel lens, installed in a 38-foot octagonal concrete and masonry tower with an attached fog-signal building, began operation on June 30, 1919.

Lime Kiln Lighthouse, ca. 1950. U.S. Coast Guard Photo

Two lighthouse keepers were required to keep constant vigils in alternate 12-hour shifts, seven days a week. Their salary was $800 per year plus housing. Lime Kiln was the last major lighthouse established in Washington. It was also the last major Washington lighthouse to receive electricity in the early 1950s. Until the early 1950s, an incandescent oil-vapor lamp was used as the light source in the lens. In 1984, the Coast Guard turned the property over to Washington State Parks and the park was created. The Fresnel lens was replaced with a non-rotating, 375-mm drum lens that utilized an electric lightbulb. Two electric foghorns were installed in the fog-signal building.

At a height of 55 feet, the beacon is visible for 17 miles. When visibility drops below three miles, photoelectric cells activate the electric foghorns powered by a battery system, emitting one three-second blast every 30 seconds

The Coast Guard still maintains the lighthouse as an active aid to navigation, but the building is used for orca whale research, interpretation, and lighthouse tours. The exterior of the building is almost exactly as it appeared in 1919. One of the lime kilns was acquired by State Parks in 1996 and has been renovated and interpreted for the public.

The site is one of the best whale watching locations in the State. Orcas, minke whales, porpoises and seals are often seen near the lighthouse.

The Lime Kiln Lighthouse was officially listed on the State Historic Register and the National Register as an Historic Site in 1978.

Cattle Point Lighthouse

*Cattle Point Lighthouse.
Courtesy U.S. Coast Guard*

There are at least two versions of the story as to how Cattle Point got its name. One version is that a ship loaded with cattle was stranded off the point and that the cattle were forced to swim to shore. The other version is that the Hudson's Bay Company unloaded cattle at a dock there prior to the "Pig War" dispute. Perhaps both stories are true.

Cattle Point was first noted on British maritime charts in 1858. As part of the American

Camp during and following the Pig War, the current site has become part of history.

The first light on the site was established in 1888. The light was maintained by a soldier who had been stationed at American Camp. After his Army days were over, he stayed on the island and raised sheep. George Jakle received provisions by a lighthouse tender which dropped off supplies and kerosene every couple of months throughout the year. Jakle would fill the lantern's oil reservoir once a week from the five-gallon kerosene barrels which were offloaded at Griffin Bay by the tender.

In 1921, the Navy built a compass radio station near the light. This aid to navigation used similar radio signals from Smith Island and from New Dungeness to help maintain safe navigation through rough weather using the principle of triangulation. The Navy built a radio tower, a transmitting station, a concrete powerhouse, and living quarters for sailors who were assigned there to operate the radio compass. The Navy also took over the responsibility to maintain the light.

In 1935, the Lighthouse Service replaced the kerosene powered lens lantern with a 34-foot octagonal, concrete tower and a fog signal building. The tower, on top of a 94 foot bluff, used a non-rotating 375 mm drum lens inside the lantern. It used an electric lightbulb that could produce a 1,500 candlepower light that could be seen for seven miles. The foghorn was powered by an electric air compressor and was mounted outside the fog signal building.

Automated in the late 1950s, Cattle Point Lighthouse was one of the first to be upgraded in the State of Washington. The tower had its lantern removed and it was replaced with a small 250-mm drum lens displayed on a short mast on top of the tower. The optic flashes white every four seconds. The electric foghorn automatically senses moisture in the air and sounds one two-second blast every 15 seconds.

Cattle Point Lighthouse received a temporary makeover in 1984 when it was used as a backdrop for an Exxon Oil commercial. In the video, it had a false hip roof and a lantern room. Both of the additions were removed after the filming of the commercial. Despite its fame as a wedding site and the backdrop for the Exxon commercial, it is endangered. Erosion is currently taking its toll. Due to its surrounding sensitive environment, a construction project will require careful and lengthy precautions, but is needed to prevent the lighthouse from toppling off its foundation.

The lighthouse and the restored Navy radio compass

station are owned by the Coast Guard. Located next to American Camp, a section of San Juan Island National Historic Park, the facilities at Cattle Point help round out the historical aspects of the area. Although the lighthouse itself is closed to the public, the grounds can be visited by taking a short walk up a trail from the parking area near the end of Cattle Point Road.

Cattle Point Lighthouse with lantern, ca. 1950. Courtesy of the U.S. States Coast Guard

Cattle Point Lighthouse. Courtesy U.S. States Coast Guard

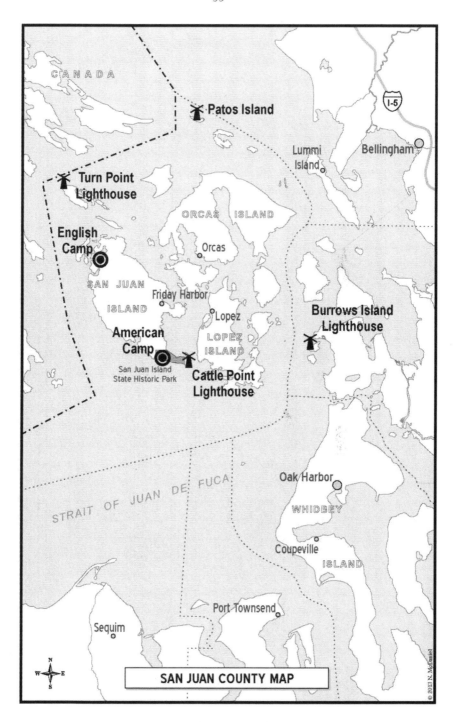

Chapter 5

Island County

**Naval Air Station
Whidbey Island**

Approximately eleven months before the bombing at Pearl Harbor pulled the United States into World War II, the Chief of Naval Operations asked the Commandant, 13th Naval District, to find a location for arming and refueling Navy patrol planes. Defense of Puget Sound was becoming of more critical concern as the potential for war grew.

Within ten days, several locations were examined including Lake Ozette on the west side of the Olympic Peninsula, Indian Island near Port Townsend, and Keystone Harbor, Penn Cove, and Oak Harbor on Whidbey Island. Terrain, long supply lines, and bluff shorelines resulted in the rejection of all these locations except for Oak Harbor, where an area adjacent to Crescent Harbor and Forbes Point appeared to be suitable for a seaplane base. Seaplane landings and takeoffs under instrument conditions could be accomplished more effectively there than at any of the other proposed locations. Dredging, filling, installation of water and power lines began at the new base.

By November of 1941, the search was also begun for a land- plane site. Approximately four miles to the north of the seaplane base, in an area known as Clover Valley, surveys were being carried out at what would soon become Ault Field. Owners of approximately 20 farms comprising 4,325 acres began to turn over the titles to their land for what would become runways and hangars. Many of the families moved to the Skagit Valley and began to farm once again.

Seaplane base under construction, 1942. Courtesy of the National Archives

Seaplane base ca. 1950s. Courtesy of the U.S. Navy

The location of the new base provided a strategic component for the defense of Puget Sound. The field was well-drained and was accessible from all directions. It was far enough away from populated areas so that live loads and operational training could be carried out without the restrictions imposed at many other stations. There was enough acreage available so that there was room to grow.

Construction began on March 1, 1942. On August 5, 1942, the first plane landed. Pilot Lieutenant Newton Wakefield landed his SNUJ single-engine trainer at the new, still-incomplete field. Six weeks later on September 21, 1942, Commanding Officer Cyril Thomas Simard read the orders and the new U.S. Naval Air Station Whidbey Island was commissioned.

The missions of the new base included seaplane patrol operations, rocket-firing training, torpedo overhaul, and training for both new recruits and petty officers. The name Ault Field was bestowed on the land-plane base in memory of Commander William Ault, who went missing in action in the Battle of the Coral Sea. The first planes to arrive included the F-4F Wildcat which was replaced by the F-6F Hellcat. They were followed by PV-1 Venturas, SBD Dauntless divebombers and many others.

In the 1970s, the Grumman EA-6B Prowler became a focal point for aviation on the base. Units and aircraft from NAS Whidbey played prominent roles in the Korean Conflict, the Vietnam War, Desert Storm, and in continuing efforts in Iraq. With the arrival of the Prowler, the base has had a primary mission of attack/electronic warfare. The base is the home of Patrol Squadron (VP) 46, which has the distinction of being the oldest American maritime patrol squadron, and the second oldest squadron, in the U.S. Navy.

Ault Field is the central operational facility and the location where most military and support functions are performed. With the phase-out of the seaplanes, the pier at the seaplane base is used primarily as a mooring facility for visiting Coast Guard vessels. In 2008, the EA-18G Growler arrived at Whidbey to continue the tradition of training and operations. Training is supported by an outlying field south of Coupeville where touch-and-go landings and takeoff from aircraft carriers can be practiced.

A prominent memorial to the PBY has become reality after many years of planning and dedication. The PBY Memorial Foundation has an office and static display at Building 12, located on 315 Pioneer Way on base. A PBY originally stationed at Whidbey was returned and restored by the Foundation. It provides a unique insight into aircraft once stationed at the facility and a photo opportunity for visiting veterans. The aircraft provides an important focus for the seaplane base as well as for all of NAS Whidbey Island. The foundation's museum is generally open on Thursdays through Saturdays.

PBY-5A of VP 62 on the ramp at Oak Harbor Seaplane Base, NAS Whidbey Island, WA, 1944. Photo courtesy of the National Archives

Fort Casey and "The Triangle of Fire"

The history of Fort Casey cannot be told without an explanation of the critical relationships between three forts which were constructed to defend Puget Sound. Fort Casey, Fort Worden and Fort Flagler share a similar history and a similar mission. They provided what has come to be known as the "Triangle of Fire" in providing harbor defense of Puget Sound. As a result, it is important to regard all three forts as a coordinated defense system.

In 1860, the War Department recommended that a single line of fortifications stretching from Foulweather Bluff on the

Kitsap Peninsula to Double Bluff on Whidbey Island be built. The recommendation also included construction of a fortified island built in the middle of Admiralty Inlet. The Civil War, 1860 - 1865, intervened and no immediate action was taken. Following the war, however, President Andrew Johnson issued an executive order which would set aside military reservations along Puget Sound.

In 1872, Army engineers were sent to the Pacific Northwest to scout out sites which would be suitable for permanent fortifications. Due to excessive costs, the engineers decided that building a fortified island in the middle of Admiralty Inlet would be too expensive, but they did agree that forts near Foulweather Bluff and Double Bluff would be advantageous.

The report was shelved. In 1891, the Puget Sound Naval Station was established in Bremerton. This was the first military facility of value that needed protection. In 1896, the Army engineers came back to assess the risks and develop a plan for defense of Puget Sound from maritime attack. Three sites along Puget Sound were selected: Admiralty Head on the west side of Whidbey Island, Point Wilson across the bay near Port Townsend, and Marrowstone Island between Port Townsend and Whidbey Island in Admiralty Inlet. The cost of these fortifications was estimated at $7 million.

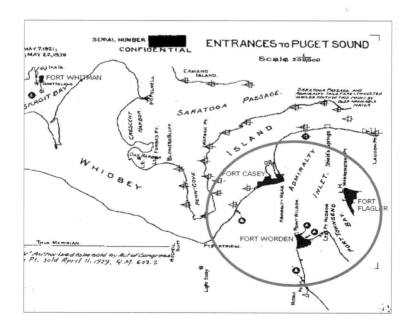

Work did not begin until after the USS *Maine* was blown up and sunk in the Spanish-American War on February 16, 1898. The protection of the Puget Sound Naval Station from the Spanish fleet became more of an imperative.

Construction materials were purchased from lumber mills in Port Townsend, Port Hadlock and Port Gamble. Sand and gravel was sourced from local pits. Cement was imported from Antwerp, Belgium, in barrels weighing approximately 400 pounds each. Guns, carriages, and other armaments were sent from Tacoma by rail and then barged to the respective sites. Tramways to haul equipment from the barges to the tops of the bluffs at each of the sites were constructed.

Fort Casey, built on Whidbey Island, was on the ground originally set aside as a military reservation. (In 1897, Dr. John C. Kellogg sold the government 23 acres for $7,200 to build gun emplacements.) The lighthouse at Admiralty Head was already sited exactly where the Army wanted to build a 10-inch gun battery so the lighthouse was moved several hundred feet north of its original location. When it was rebuilt, it was fortified to withstand the concussion from the firing of the nearby big guns. The new fortification was named Fort Casey in honor of Brigadier General Thomas Lincoln Casey, who had been a former commander of the Army Corps of Engineers.

The fort was activated in 1901 with a small, temporary garrison. The permanent garrison arrived in 1902 and was composed of men from two Coast Artillery companies coming from Fort Flagler and from Alcatraz Island. Later, an additional Coast Artillery company came from Hawaii to complete the force stationed at the fort.

Forces lived in tents while barracks were constructed. The first set of facilities built consisted of three enlisted barracks, six officers' quarters, a hospital, administration buildings, an exchange, commissary, bakery, stables, and central power house.

The first armaments consisted of six gun emplacements: Batteries Worth, Moore, Kingsbury, Seymour, Schenck, and Turman. Between 1904 and 1907, four additional gun emplacements were added: Batteries: Moore, Trevor, Van Horn and Valleau. When it was completed, Fort Casey had 34 pieces of artillery sitting 100 feet above Admiralty Inlet. These pieces included: six 10-inch disappearing guns, six 6-inch disappearing guns, two 5-inch pedestal guns, four 3-inch pedestal guns and sixteen 12-inch mortars.

Visiting Fort Casey today, you can see that Battery Worth has two 10-inch guns with disappearing carriages on display. These guns were obtained in the 1960s from Battery Warwick, Fort Wint, Subic Bay, Philippines. Battery Trevor also has two 3-inch rapid fire pedestal guns on display.

Fort Casey Batteries			
Battery	No.	Caliber	Type Mount
Schenck	8	12"	Mortar
Seymour	8	12"	Mortar
Worth	2	10"	Disappearing Carriage
Kingsbury	2	10"	Disappearing Carriage
Moore	2	10"	Disappearing Carriage
	1	10"	Disappearing Carriage
Parker	2	6"	Disappearing Carriage
Valleau	4	6"	Disappearing Carriage
Turman	2	5"	Balanced Pillar
Trevor	2	3"	Pedestal Mount
Van Horne	2	3"	Pedestal Mount

Four hundred troops eventually manned the fort after its opening in 1901. The guns, which could lob shells more than 10 miles, were never fired in anger.

Prior to and during the time the guns were being constructed and installed, shore-based armaments had greater accuracy and range than the guns aboard ships.

However, technology was rapidly changing and developments in armaments resulted in obsolescence. By the time WWI was looming on the horizon, improvements in shipboard armament made the shore-based armaments much less effective than they had once been. As a result, the forts could have become the target for shipboard guns rather than the ships being targets for shore-based guns.

71st Coast Artillery Corps making camp at Fort Casey, 1912. Real Photo Post Card, Author's collection

Fort Casey Battery Worth. Ten-inch gun on a disappearing carriage. Photo by Author

The mission of the forts began to change and instead of being the tactical bases which could stop ships with guns, the facilities' function changed into valuable sites for training. Fort Casey was used for this purpose during World War I with a mission of training soldiers for European duty. Thirteen of the 35 artillery batteries were dismantled and shipped to Europe.

After World War I was over, the remaining artillery batteries were dismantled and the fort was put into caretaker status. The grounds and facilities were used for Army Reserve Officer Training Corps summer training and Washington National Guard training. The post deteriorated under caretaker status and by the mid-1930s it was necessary to repair those structures that could be saved and tear down the rest. The WPA established a work camp on the post and worked through 1940. All three of the barracks were sold by 1939 and three of the six officers' quarters were salvaged by the WPA along with numerous other buildings.

In 1941 a massive building program took over and Fort Casey was transformed into a World War II post even before the war started. By June 1941 the post had added nine new 63-man barracks and three new mess halls. Officers' quarters were added and the existing quarters upgraded. Once again, Fort Casey became a prominent Army induction, training and mission support facility. The fort's guns were rearmed with anti-aircraft guns. The Harbor Defense Command also built Fort Ebey on Whidbey Island at Pigeon Point, north of Coupeville.

Following World War II, Fort Casey was vacant and became a site for vandalism. The fort was officially deactivated in June of 1953 and the grounds were declared as government surplus. In 1955, the Washington State Parks and Recreation Commission acquired 100 acres of Fort Casey for use as a state park and a national monument. Seattle Pacific University purchased 87 acres to be used as a conference center.

The present Fort Casey State Park includes the Keystone Spit area.

The National Park Service included Fort Ebey, Admiralty Head Lighthouse, and Fort Casey State Park in the Ebey's Landing National Historic Reserve. This National Historic Reserve extends approximately six miles on either side of Coupeville and is one of the largest historic districts in the country. It has nearly 100 structures listed on the National Register of Historic Places.

Battery Trevor at Fort Casey. Photo by Author

Fort Casey looking toward Fort Worden. Photo by Author

Fort Ebey

Plans to defend Puget Sound were already effectively being developed when Japanese forces attacked Pearl Harbor on December 7, 1941. Puget Sound Naval Shipyard assets in Bremerton, Boeing's aircraft plants in the Seattle area, and other related resources were recognized as installations which needed additional protection. The attack on Pearl Harbor underscored the importance of plans to modernize the harbor defenses of Puget Sound. After the attack, military planners moved quickly to put these plans into action.

Fort Ebey, on Whidbey Island, was established in 1942 with the primary purpose of supporting the harbor defense of Puget Sound. The installation was completed on February 1, 1944. Barracks, a barbershop, library, and a bowling alley were located near where the current park office is located today. An elevated 100,000-gallon wooden water tank was also constructed. The remains of the tank can still be seen from one of the many trails which have been constructed around the old fort.

The fort was named for Colonel Isaac N. Ebey, a Whidbey Island pioneer, who had been killed by Native Americans. Fort Ebey joined the company of Forts Flagler, Casey and Worden which had been constructed in the late 1890s. Fort Ebey was the only coast artillery post that was developed exclusively for military defense during the World War II era.

The design of Battery 248 at the fort was planned to provide a counter to aerial and chemical attacks. Positioned to have a perfect view out to the Strait of Juan de Fuca and the open ocean, it provided observation posts to watch for incoming ships and aircraft. Observers were stationed along the bluffs and used telescopes to provide initial information and location. This information was then passed to plotters inside Battery 248.

The fort used radar and camouflaging techniques to protect against aerial attack, and used existing trees around the guns as part of its camouflage measures.

One of the most interesting things about Battery 248 was its tree wells. When dirt was spread over the battery, the health of the trees was placed in jeopardy. Brick walls were built around some of the trees to help capture water to help ensure the trees would stay alive. The trees helped provide camouflage for the fort. Ivy was also planted to help hide the installation.

The guns included two 6-inch guns and eight 50-caliber machine guns. The guns and crew proved to be accurate, as evidenced by their winning an international shooting competition. Major Samuel C. Kelley, Jr., Commanding Officer, noted, "Firing at 14,000 yards on a towed target simulating a destroyer . . . We scored 22 hits in 18 rounds. (A hit within an area 5 yards square counts as two hits, a broadside and a bow hit.)" The Naval Model 1905A2 guns had a range of approximately 15 miles. The barrels were 26 feet long, and required 26 men to load and fire.

The battery, comprised of a powder room, plotting room, spotting room, and power room, also had a chemical warfare service room. The room was gas-proofed to help protect the forces in case of a chemical attack, being pressurized with filtered air.

The guns were manned 24 hours a day from 1943 to late 1945 by members of the Army's Coast Artillery Corps. The 248th Coast Artillery Regiment of the Washington National Guard, concentrated at Fort Worden, saw duty at Fort Ebey, as well as other nearby posts.

Military tactics and technology, however, changed quickly as the war continued. Long-range bombing, missiles, and a diminished naval threat rendered the installation obsolete. Fort Ebey's utilization as a fort had been short-lived and the facilities were abandoned in 1946 following the conclusion of World War II. The Army Corps of Engineers utilized the fort for approximately two years at the conclusion of the war. The Navy also occupied the property for a short period of time.

In 1947 the property was declared surplus. The guns were cut up and ultimately melted down for scrap. The fort was acquired by Washington State Parks in 1968. It was opened to the public in 1981. As part of the park, interpretive signs provide an insight into the history of the fort.

Fort Ebey is easily accessed and provides beautiful views of the Strait of Juan de Fuca, and the Port Townsend area, and on clear days it is possible to see Vancouver Island.

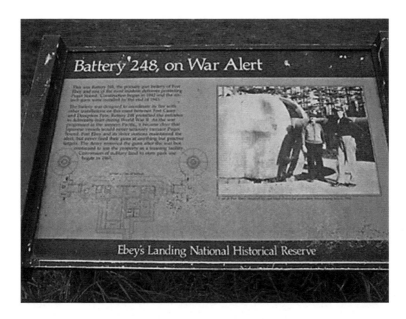

Interpretive sign at Fort Ebey. Photo by Author

Battery 248 service entrance. Photo by Author

Red Bluff Lighthouse

Red Bluff Lighthouse. Photo from National Archives

Current lists of lighthouses in the Puget Sound area rarely include the Red Bluff Lighthouse. Some accounts refer to it as Washington's most forgotten light. Today, although it served mariners for over 49 years, little remains at the site.

A marine survey in 1857 recommended to Congress that two lighthouses be constructed on Admiralty Inlet. One of the recommendations was for a light to be placed at Point Wilson near Port Townsend. The other was to put a light on a ninety-foot bluff, called Red Bluff, near Coupeville. Property, approximately ten acres was purchased from Dr. John Coe Kellogg by the Lighthouse Board for $400. Upon its completion in 1860, Red Bluff was the sixth lighthouse and first wooden lighthouse to be built in Washington Territory.

The light was essentially a square wooden tower which was placed on top of the keeper's quarters. The white tower was 108 feet above sea level and was equipped with a fourth-order Fresnel lens. This lens directs light through prismatic rings to a central prism, and a concentrated beam of light comes out of the convex lens. Red Bluff light was turned on in January 1861. It could be seen for over 16 miles.

Captain William Robertson was Red Bluff's first keeper. He and his wife Mary lived at the lighthouse. Robertson was also the Island County Coroner. A former east coast sea-captain, he sailed around the Horn and found his way to San Francisco. He sailed up and down the west coast carrying supplies for the new settlers in the area. He staked a homestead claim on Whidbey Island and settled on the west side.

Local natives felt crowded with the arrival of the white settlers, and the settlers on Whidbey Island were a bit uneasy. Threats turned into action when a band of Haida natives from British Columbia attacked and burned the Robertsons' cabin. The Robertsons built a new cabin, and Captain Robertson put a ship's cannon in the yard to help deter future attacks.

Rather than leaving his family to go back to sea, Robertson allowed his business partner to take his ship, the *Tarquina*, to embark on more resupply and trading voyages. That was the last he saw of the ship. The partner sailed the ship out of the harbor, apparently forgot about Robertson's interest, and effectively, although unilaterally, terminated the partnership. Appointed by President Buchanan, Captain Robertson took on the responsibility of the new light and served until 1864.

The second keeper, Daniel Pearson, came to Washington Territory from Massachusetts. He served as keeper at the facility for fourteen years. When he resigned in October of 1878, he moved to a small farm near Coupeville. Pearson was followed by Lawrence Nessels in 1878, although he was not officially appointed for another two years.

Joseph Evans, assumed responsibility of the light in 1887. When Evans' teen-age son, Henry, drowned in a boating accident, Evans left the facility and took a lighthouse post in Clatsop County, Oregon. He returned to Washington State in 1912, and was appointed as the keeper of the Smith Island Light Station. While on a trip to visit friends in Port Townsend in 1913, he died of a heart attack. He was buried with full military honors at Laurel Grove Cemetery in Port Townsend.

Charles Davis, who had once been a river boat captain, was appointed in January 1900. He was to be the last keeper of the wooden lighthouse.

The lighthouse facility had several enhancements during

these years. A water cistern was added in 1868. In 1880, a winch was installed to hoist supplies from the beach to the lighthouse. A tramway for launching boats was built in 1882 and water tank was added in 1890.

With the onset of the Spanish-American War, the entrance to Admiralty Inlet became a strategically important site. As the entrance to Puget Sound, it required fortifications to protect what was to eventually become the Puget Sound Naval Shipyard. The light at Red Bluff was sitting exactly where Army plans called for a 10-inch disappearing gun.

In 1903 the lighthouse building was moved to the north to make way for the construction of the gun emplacement. The wooden facility was replaced by a masonry lighthouse, which became known as Admiralty Head. The wooden structure itself was used to house non-commissioned officers, and then, for a short period of time, functioned as a temporary medical clinic. In 1928, it was torn down and the lumber was recycled into a house on Whidbey Island. The lens of the light was removed and re-installed in the new lighthouse facility at Admiralty Head.

Admiralty Head Lighthouse

Admiralty Head Lighthouse. Photo by Author

Admiralty Head and Point Wilson, facing one another across Admiralty Inlet, define the entrance into the waterways of Puget Sound. Lighthouses were placed on both points to help guide outbound shipping into the Strait of Juan de Fuca and inbound into Puget Sound. The light at Admiralty Head was built first, followed by Point Wilson's beacon some 19 years later.

The new lighthouse was built in a Spanish style and included a dwelling for the lighthouse keeper. It was constructed of stucco-covered brick walls, 18 inches thick to withstand the concussion from the new guns at Fort Casey. The lighthouse was painted the traditional white with green trim and a red roof. Three bedrooms were located upstairs, while the kitchen, dining room, and a living room were downstairs. It was activated in 1903.

By the early 1920s, maritime traffic was being powered by steam, allowing ships to travel closer to the west side of Admiralty Inlet. As a result, the need for Admiralty Head Lighthouse was diminished. The light went out in 1922 after only nineteen years of service. In 1927, the lantern room was removed from the structure and shipped to the New Dungeness Lighthouse in Clallam County. The lens was also removed, with no record of what happened to it.

In 1939, the Coast Guard merged with the Lighthouse Service and assumed responsibility for all aids to navigation, including the nonfunctional Admiralty Head Lighthouse.

The facility was vacant until World War II, when Fort Casey was reactivated. At that point it was painted an olive drab color and was used as living quarters for the K-9 Corps assigned to Fort Casey, which actively patrolled beaches every night.

After the war, the building stood empty. Vandals, weather, and neglect resulted in major deterioration. In the 1950s, Fort Casey, including the lighthouse, was declared as excess property and was transferred to the General Service Administration. In 1955, Washington State Parks acquired 100 acres of Fort Casey.

The Island County Historical Society and Washington State Parks initiated a joint, coordinated restoration effort of Admiralty Head Lighthouse in 1957. The lantern room and the lighthouse building underwent painstaking restoration. A fourth-order Fresnel lens was relocated from the Alki Point Lighthouse in Seattle in 1962. Stucco was reapplied to the structure and it was painted white again.

In 1973, both Admiralty Head Lighthouse and Fort Casey State Park were incorporated into the National Register as part of the Central Whidbey Island designation as an Historic District. The Central Whidbey Island Historic District is approximately 25 square miles and includes the interesting town of Coupeville as well as the fort and the lighthouse. Over 100 National Register of Historic Places structures are

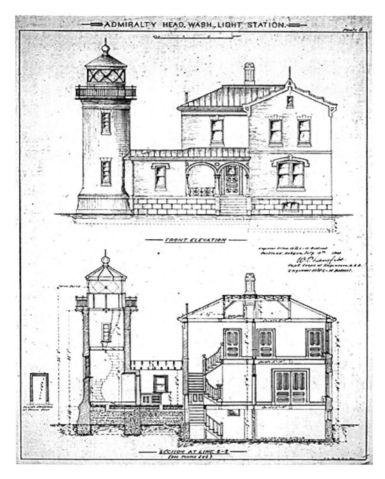

Original plans for the Admiralty Head Light, by the U.S. Army Corps of Engineers

located within the district.

In 2003, the Coast Guard loaned a fourth-order Fresnel lens to the lighthouse museum. It had been found in storage at the Coast Guard Station in Port Angeles and was identical to the original Admiralty Head lens.

Today, the lighthouse is home to a gift shop, an interpretive center and a museum administered by Washington State University Lighthouse Docents. Free tours, a climb of the tower, and a close look at the lenses are available. Donations and gift shop sales enable the efforts of volunteers to keep the lighthouse open and available for tours.

Although decommissioned in 1922, the Admiralty Head Lighthouse received national recognition in 1990 when the U.S. Postal Service selected it for a collection of five commemorative lighthouse stamps honoring the U.S. Coast Guard's bicentennial.

Crockett, Davis, Ebey and Alexander Blockhouses

In the mid-1850s, settlers on Whidbey Island were beginning to feel threatened by natives coming from the north. In addition, the treaties that had been imposed upon Washington area natives were being recognized as being unfair. As a result, settlers were becoming nervous about future reactions from local natives including the Skagit, Snohomish, and Stillaguamish. Citizens on Whidbey Island banded together to build blockhouses. Four of these blockhouses remain. While they were not military sites, these blockhouses made a significant contribution to the peace of mind and safety of early Whidbey Island settlers.

Crockett Blockhouse. Photo by Author

Crockett Blockhouse stands about 2.5 miles south of Coupeville near the intersection of Fort Casey and Engle Roads. William Crockett, who came west in 1854, built the blockhouse on his property. Today, the blockhouse is open to the public, although the adjacent farm is not.

The **Davis Blockhouse** is a two story blockhouse, built on the donation claim of three brothers, John, James and Thomas Davis. It was built in November-December 1857 as a response to the August murder of Isaac Ebey by hostile local natives. The claim was subsequently sold to Cyrus and Sarah Cook at auction in 1868. At various times, the blockhouse was referred to as the **Cook Blockhouse**. The Cook family donated the structure and property to the local Ladies of the Roundtable, who began restoration efforts in 1922. Restoration was completed in 1931. Island County took ownership of the property as part of the adjacent Sunnyside Cemetery.

The Ebey Blockhouse was built in 1855. It was originally one of four structures which were connected by a 12 foot stockade. Built during the Yakima Indian War (1855-1858) the blockhouse was sited on a ridge which overlooked what was then Sunnyside Farm.

Colonel Isaac Ebey was killed in 1857 by a party of Haida from Canada. The Haida selected him as the "chief for a chief," the man who would be killed in retribution for the murder of one of their chiefs in 1856 near Port Gamble. The Haida knocked on his door, and asked him to come out of the house. Without any warning they shot him, beheaded him, and left his body in the front yard. His wife and children ran to the blockhouse.

Revenge had been achieved and the family was not harmed. Emily Ebey, not willing to remain there, left forever with her daughter Anna. Relatives raised the remaining two sons and later divided the farm between them.

The **Alexander Blockhouse** was built in 1855 by landowner John Alexander. It was a two-story log blockhouse which was originally surrounded by a high double-log stockade. After hostile natives were forced from the area, the blockhouse was abandoned in 1856. The structure was moved from its original location on the west side of Coupeville to the center of town in the 1930s. The blockhouse is an interesting adjunct to the Island County Historical Museum.

The Davis Blockhouse, built in 1857, is located off of Cemetery Road, southwest of Coupeville. Photo by Author

The Ebey Blockhouse is located adjacent to the Jacob Ebey House, Ebey's Landing National Historic Reserve. Photo courtesy National Park Service

The Alexander Blockhouse is currently located between the canoe shed and the Island County Historical Museum in Coupeville. Photo by John Stanton

Fort Nugent

From 1855 to 1856, Western Washington natives were subject to strong persuasion to sign treaties which essentially gave their lands to the new settlers. Hostility grew both on the east side of the state in the Yakima Indian Wars and in general unrest on the west side of the state. Governor Stevens ordered Washington Territorial Volunteers to build forts for settler protection. The forts would be a refuge that they could retreat to during Indians attacks.

The term "fort" for many of these shelters is misleading as most were only a blockhouse. Some had stockade fences and hut housing. There were no barracks, mess halls, parade grounds, or other traditional features of United States forts. In addition to the Washington Territorial Volunteer forts, the U.S. Army constructed posts to support operations against the Indians. Also, in some cases the local settler community or individual families erected blockhouse defenses. Unnamed, locally-built blockhouses went up in many communities.

Located west of Oak Harbor, Fort Nugent was a log fort which provided settlers safe haven during native uprisings. Today, the site is a municipal park. Nothing remains of the original structures.

Deception Pass:

West Beach, Reservation Bay, Reservation Head, Gun Point

In 1866, approximately a thousand acres was acquired by the federal government to help protect Saratoga Passage into Puget Sound. Land was acquired on both sides of Deception Pass. As a result of this acquisition, what is now known as Lighthouse Point was originally called Reservation Head. Bowman Bay was once known as Reservation Bay. Older maps often include these former names.

The only time the area was utilized by the military was during World War I. At West Beach, a searchlight was mounted on the most westerly point. The concrete platform for the light is still there. Gun Point at North Beach received its name for a rapid-fire gun, which was established on the rock just west of the Deception Pass Bridge.

Virtually nothing remains of these sites, although visitors

will be struck by the natural beauty of the pass, the Deception Pass Bridge, and the surrounding area.

Bush Point Lighthouse

Bush Point is located on the west side of Whidbey Island, directly across from Marrowstone Island. Its location helps mark the narrowest entrance to Puget Sound.

The Farmer family, early settlers of Whidbey Island, operated a private light by hanging a lantern on a wooden structure. In 1894, the Lighthouse Board installed a post light on the Point. In 1921, the Bureau of Lighthouses sought an appropriation of $46,000 from Congress for a light and fog signal. It took nine years before $10,000 was made available for an automatic acetylene light.

Construction began with the hopes that it would be completed in 1931. The twenty-foot tower was not completed until 1933. The tower was operated by commercial electric power and controlled from a resident caretaker's quarters located nearby. The total project cost approximately $6,200.

The site is maintained by the U.S. Coast Guard, and is not open to the public.

Bush Point Light. Photo courtesy U.S. Coast Guard

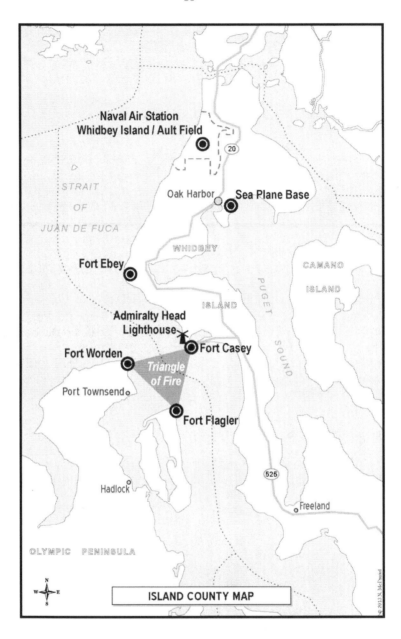

Chapter 6
King County

Fort Lawton

As early as 1891, planning for placement of west coast military installations resulted in keen competition between Congressional representatives. U.S. Senator John B. Allen presented his case before his Washington D.C. Congressional colleagues (especially those from California and Oregon) for establishing a Navy yard on Puget Sound. Port Orchard Bay was selected for what would become the Puget Sound Naval Shipyard at Bremerton. As a result, protection of this new asset with additional military installations became a high priority. Military planners considered defense of the area a high priority because:

- enemy vessels might easily harbor in Puget Sound;
- the growing commercial centers of Seattle, Everett, and Tacoma could become targets;
- plans were in place to build a ship canal from Shilshole Bay to Lake Union large enough to accommodate warships.

In 1896, the Secretary of War selected land adjacent to Seattle, which would later be named Fort Lawton, for construction of an artillery battery. The installation was intended to defend Seattle as well as waters south to Bremerton from naval attack.

Local government, concerned citizens, and the early Seattle Chamber of Commerce began a campaign for donations of land and cash which could help strengthen the case for establishment of this new military installation. In 1898, the first 703 acres of land was turned over to the U.S. Army. A water line was built in 1898 to supply water to the new installation. This was the first system to run outside of the Seattle city limits. Building and road construction began in late 1898, and soldiers arrived in December of 1899. The fort was officially opened on 9 February 1900 on a site comprised of 1,100 acres.

The installation was named for Major General Henry Lawton, U.S. Volunteers, who was killed in action at San Mateo, Philippines, in December 1899, the highest ranking officer to be killed in the conflict. He had been a veteran of the Civil War and the Indian Wars.

While the fort was originally slated to be a coastal protection facility, the first Coast Artillery unit did not arrive until July 1901. Temporary guns were put in place and the installation was poised to intercept enemy ships heading south.

Major General Lawton in the Philippines, 1899. Photo courtesy of the National Archives

Fort Worden and Fort Flagler near Port Townsend and Fort Casey on Whidbey Island, provided the first three defensive installations protecting Puget Sound. Fort Lawton's first role was to serve the nation as a fourth defensive installation.

In 1902, the fort became an Infantry post. It had been designed to accommodate the 3,500 men comprising a full regiment, but only rarely did it have more than a headquarters unit and one battalion. In 1909, 900 men of the U.S Army's 25th Infantry Regiment arrived from the Philippines. The 25th was one of four African-American units in the Army; the unit was also known as the "Buffalo Soldiers."

Fort Lawton and Fort Worden showcased the latest technological accomplishments of the time. The March 6, 1906 edition of the *Port Townsend Daily Leader* (page 4) describes the installation and implementation of a telephone connection between the two forts. "The line is remarkable from the fact that it utilizes a submarine cable as a circuit and is probably the longest distance over which submarine telephony has been completed on the Pacific Coast if not in the entire country."

John Olmsted, the noted landscape architect, had done significant work in the design of parks and in city planning throughout the Northwest. He was asked by the City of Seattle to look at Fort Lawton as part of his work on Seattle City Parks. He suggested a number of design ideas which would improve the property for the Army but also serve as an extension of open areas on the fort which could be utilized by residents of the City of Seattle. He prepared a design for the Fort in 1910 which resulted in newly-sited housing for enlisted and officers.

1st Cavalry tent encampment, Fort Lawton, Washington, July 28, 1900. Photo by H. Ambrose Kiehl, KHL001 Special Collections, University of Washington Libraries

Shortly before World War I, Camp Lewis was established just south of Tacoma. With this new army post, later to become Fort Lewis, the Army's focus on Fort Lawton as a key installation began to diminish. During World War I, Fort Lawton was used as a base for embarkation, and it also served as a training facility for the Army Reserve and the National Guard. In 1914, the fort was garrisoned by a four-company battalion of the 14th Infantry Regiment, and also served as the regimental headquarters. By 1915, the fort was the headquarters for the 7th Infantry Brigade.

Barracks, Fort Lawton, Washington 1900. Photo by H. Ambrose Kiehl. KHL016, Special Collections, University of Washington Libraries

Fort Lawton Officers' Residences, January 23, 1934. Photographer unknown, UW14819 Special Collections, University of Washington Libraries

During the Seattle General Strike of 1919, an Army unit was sent to Fort Lewis to provide an armed presence should the strike become violent; the 1st Battalion, 1st Infantry Regiment, was deployed to Fort Lewis as a reserve unit. Each of the soldiers was armed with 120 rounds of ammunition to utilize if necessary. No shots were fired, but the fort provided a sense of security for Seattle residents. Soldiers of the 44th Infantry Regiment, less Company C, garrisoned Fort Lawton in 1919.

In 1927, the fort was converted to an Army Corps of Engineers installation. In 1938, the Army offered to sell Fort Lawton back to the City of Seattle, but the city declined. High costs to maintain the installation were cited by the Army as the reason for the planned closure or reutilization.

Captain's Quarters, Fort Lawton, Washington, May 19, 1900. Photo by H. Ambrose Kiehl, KHL031. Special Collections, University of Washington Libraries

During World War II, Fort Lawton became a part of the Port of Embarkation, San Francisco. A total of 1.1 million troops passed through Fort Lawton both during and after the war. The installation was also used as a prisoner of war (POW) camp. More than 1,000 Germans were imprisoned there, in addition to approximately 5,000 Italians, who were housed temporarily on their way to facilities in Hawaii.

On the night of August 14, 1944, an all African-American port company was under orders to ship out the following morning to a Pacific war zone. Deep segregation was a part of Army life during World War II. All-African-American units were common throughout the Army. This particular unit was part of the US Army's Transportation Corps. Port companies were responsible for ensuring that thousands of tons of military supplies were packed, unloaded, and delivered to the front lines.

The story, as told to investigators, was that an intoxicated soldier and three of his companions, got into a verbal altercation with three Italians. Italian soldiers were allowed privileges to attend dances and social events. In some cases, the Italians had more privileges than the African-American soldiers. Words were exchanged and the confrontation escalated into a fist fight. An Italian knocked out the American soldier with a single punch.

Word spread quickly that American soldiers had been attacked by Italian prisoners. A small contingent of American soldiers ran after the Italians. Hearing a commotion, more American soldiers joined the fight. Rumors quickly spread that an American had been killed. Dozens of the American unit headed into the Italian area with rocks, boards, and knives. American and Italian soldiers alike were injured.

More than forty minutes passed before a contingent of military police arrived. Private Clyde Lomax, a military policeman, was allegedly involved in the fighting rather than trying to stop the altercation. After finally taking the injured Americans to the post hospital, the story is that Private Lomax disappeared for a couple of hours. At 5:00 a.m. the next morning, Lomax drove his patrol jeep to a gully at the base of Magnolia Bluff, and there discovered the body of Guglielmo Olivotto, lynched from a noose on an obstacle course facility.

German prisoners at Fort Lawton, Seattle, 1945. Photo courtesy of Seattle Post-Intelligencer *Collection, Museum of History and Industry*

The lynching quickly became national news. Fear that U.S prisoners of war could receive brutal treatment or even be killed in retaliation for this tragic event permeated the news, government, and military units.

What actually happened was suppressed at the time: the Army classified its investigation, and newspaper stories were based on hearsay gathered in a bar days later. The ensuing court-martial resulted in the conviction of 28 American soldiers, including two for manslaughter. Several others were charged with rioting. The trial was the largest and longest court-martial of World War II.

In 2005, the Army court of appeals was convinced by the book *On American Soil* by Jack Hamann (Chapel Hill: Algonquin Books, 2005) that the lead prosecutor, Lieutenant Colonel Leon Jaworski, had committed some critical errors in the prosecution of the case. The case was reopened. All convictions were reversed. President George W. Bush signed legislation in 2008, allowing the Army to disburse back pay to the defendants or their survivors. Leon Jaworski would go on to be part of some of America's most highly profiled litigations, including the investigation of President Nixon's involvement in the Watergate break-in. Today, Olivotto's headstone stands outside the perimeter of Fort Lawton's military cemetery.

Broken column headstone of Guglielmo Olivotto, Italian POW. Photo courtesy of Janell Brown

After World War II, Fort Lawton was used as an Air Force radar site, a surface-to-air Nike missile site, a training center, and as the home for a Federal Aviation Administration long range radar site. During the Korean conflict, Fort Lawton experienced heightened activity as troops processed out or returned from Korea. In 1953, however, the outbound portion of this mission was transferred to Fort Lewis while troops returning from Korea continued to process back to the United States through Fort Lawton.

In the late 1950s, Nike anti-aircraft missiles and radar were in use at Fort Lawton. Of the 47 Nike units in the nation, five were in the state of Washington, and two were at Fort Lawton. In 1968 the site was rejected for proposed defense upgrades. The Army surplused the remaining acres in 1971, and gave the land back to the City of Seattle in 1972. It was dedicated as Discovery Park in 1973 in honor of Captain George Vancouver's HMS *Discovery*.

Public viewing of Nike Defense Missile at Fort Lawton, Seattle, 1955. Photo courtesy of Seattle Post-Intelligencer Collection, Museum of History and Industry

West Point Lighthouse

Located on the grounds of what was once Fort Lawton, Discovery Park is the site of West Point Lighthouse. At the base of Magnolia Bluff, West Point Lighthouse has sent out alternating red and white flashes for over 100 years. Although a modern beacon replaced the fourth-order Fresnel lens, the lens is still located in the tower.

West Point Lighthouse began operation in 1881, and served to guide vessels into and out of Elliott Bay. The completion of the Lake Washington Ship Canal in 1917 provided a link between Puget Sound and Lake Washington. The lighthouse served as a marker for the canal.

One of the first keepers of the light was George Fonda. It was during his watch that the Lighthouse Board prescribed a standard uniform for lighthouse keepers. The uniform consisted of navy blue trousers topped by a double-breasted coat, and a billed cap.

West Point Lighthouse. Photo courtesy of U.S Coast Guard

The first fog signal at West Point Light was a bell which had been once located at Cape Disappointment on the Washington coast. In 1887, the bell was replaced by a steam whistle, which was then upgraded to a Daboll trumpet. The bell finally ended up at the Warrior Rock Lighthouse in Oregon, where it still resides today.

In 1979, the station was programmed to be automated, but then-keeper Marvin Gerber asked that it be manned until its centennial in 1981. On November 15, 1981, Gerber climbed to the tower and celebrated one hundred years of operation by dousing the tower with a bottle of champagne.

The West Point Lighthouse was finally automated in 1985. Two lighthouse keeper's residences still stand near the light.

In 2002, the Lighthouse was declared surplus by the federal government under the National Historic Lighthouse Preservation Act of 2000. This program enables federal agencies, local and state governments, non-profit preservation associations, or community development organizations to acquire surplus lighthouses for restoration and eventual incorporation into public access facilities. The City of Seattle owns the lighthouse. The Seattle Parks and Recreation Department has plans to restore the facility and eventually open it to the public.

Alki Point Lighthouse

Alki Point Lighthouse. Photo courtesy of U.S. Coast Guard

Alki Point Lighthouse marks the southern entrance to Seattle's Elliott Bay. The lighthouse is one of the most important in Puget Sound. It can easily be seen from the Seattle-Bainbridge and the Seattle-Bremerton ferries. The word "Alki" became the Washington State motto and is a Chinook Indian Jargon word meaning "by and by."

Alki Point is the site of one of the first settlements in the Seattle area. In 1851, the schooner *Exact* landed with twenty-four passengers. The settlers called their new settlement New York, and then New York-Alki. Today it is known as Alki. A monument honoring this first community is located at the intersection of Alki and 63rd Avenues.

In 1887, the Lighthouse Service recognized the need for an official light and placed a lens-lantern on top of a wooden post at the point. Prior to that, however, two settlers by the names of Hans Martin Hanson and Knud Olson lighted a lamp on the point as an aid to mariners.

Hanson was hired to take care of the new light and received $15 a month for his services. A lighthouse tender would bring several barrels of coal-oil twice a year to fuel the light. Hanson passed away in 1900, and his son Edmund Hanson took on the duties.

In 1911, the Lighthouse Service purchased 1.5 acres from Edmund Hanson for the sum of $9,999 in order to upgrade the light and add a fog signal. The present concrete fog signal building and the octagonal tower at the site were completed in 1913.

The fourth-order Fresnel lens used in the tower was manufactured in Paris and contained multiple bulls-eyes. Rotation of the lens was accomplished with a clockwork mechanism which was powered by suspended weights. A Daboll trumpet fog signal was installed and on foggy days and nights two engines filled a tank of compressed air which was then directed over reeds on three sides of the lighthouse (north, east, and south sides). The Fresnel lens is now on display at the Admiralty Head Lighthouse. The compressors and generators for the fog signal, long since replaced by electric horns, remain in excellent condition in the fog signal building.

Charles Elliott, one of the head keepers, was purported to have a hobby of researching and collecting the works of Walt Whitman. He often commented that the long hours watching the light on a foggy night were filled with reading in his library and furthering his study of Whitman.

When the Coast Guard assumed control of lighthouses in 1939, keepers had the choice of joining the Coast Guard or staying on as civilian keepers. Alki Point was one of the last two civilian-operated lighthouses along Puget Sound when Albert Anderson retired in 1970.

After the lighthouse was automated in 1984, one of the two keeper's houses was remodeled to serve as the residence for the Commandant of the 13th Coast Guard District. The Commandant has since relocated; however the dwelling is still available for Coast Guard senior officers.

In 1976, the lighthouse was designated as an historic place and was listed on the Washington Historic Register. The lighthouse is open to tours on weekends during the summer months.

Aerial view of Alki Point Lighthouse. Photo courtesy of U.S. Coast Guard

Nike Missile Locations
Seattle Defense Area

During the Cold War, Seattle was viewed as a potential target. Home of Boeing Aircraft, the Puget Sound Naval Shipyard, and strategic military sites, the area was an important component of the military industrial complex. As a result, a ring of Nike missiles was established around the city.

Each site generally consisted of two separate areas. The radar control site was one of the areas. The other, the launch site, was where the missiles were kept. The Nike system required three separate radars which were linked by a central computer. The Acquisition Radar could locate the enemy aircraft at a long distance. The Target Tracking Radar locked on to the potential "attacker" and stayed locked on even with evasive maneuvers. The Missile Tracking Radar was used to track and control the launched missile and direct it to the attacker. The computers which linked the radars are thought to have been the ancestors of the internet.

These defenses were manned by both the Regular Army and Washington National Guard units. Acquisition of the land, design, and the construction of the sites was handled by the Seattle District of the Corps of Engineers.

The first missile sites were activated in 1956. By 1959, there were ten missile sites around the area. Batteries S-13/S-14 and S-32/S-33, built at Redmond and Lake Youngs in Renton, were double sites. Other batteries and designations and locations were:

S-03	Bothell / Kenmore
S-62	Olalla
S-20	Cougar Mountain / Issaquah
S-81	Poulsbo (Kitsap County)
S-43	Kent / Midway
S-82	Winslow / Bainbridge Island (Kitsap County)
S-61	Vashon Island
S-92	Kingston (Kitsap County)

Headquarter facilities were located at McChord Air Force Base, Fort Lawton, Redmond, Phantom Lake, O'Brien, and Kent. A radar section was posted at Fort Worden, near Port Townsend.

The Army units manning the Nike Ajax batteries were regarded as tops in the nation. These units earned the Army Air Defense Command Commander's Trophy in 1956, 1957, and 1958 as a result of the high scores achieved in national competitions.

By 1960, Nike Ajax sites were beginning to be phased out. Sites at S-13 (Redmond), S-61 (Vashon Island), and S-92 (Kingston) were upgraded to launch Nike Hercules missiles and were active until 1974. A "Missile Master" command and control center was built at Fort Lawton.

The sites located in King County are described below and shown on the adjacent map:

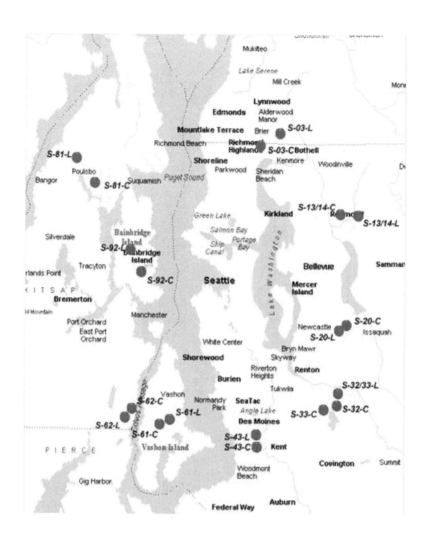

S-20, Cougar Mountain / Issaquah Site

The site on top of Cougar Mountain in the Cascades transitioned from a World War II lookout post for Japanese-launched incendiary balloons to what was an extremely high-technology missile site. Nike Ajax missiles replaced radar-guided anti-aircraft guns. A radar system called LOPAR acquired the target. The guidance system was controlled by computers (with vacuum tubes). The Nike Ajax system could handle a single target at a time, and could generally fire a missile every 45 minutes.

The missile site at Cougar Mountain came on line in 1957. It was designated as S-20. The launch site was built just east of 166th Way Southeast not far from the Bellevue neighborhood. The fire control area was on top of the mountain, along with barracks, offices, and a cafeteria. The site was secured by high chain link fences, and was patrolled by soldiers and military dogs. The buildings were primarily "Butler Buildings." Neighbors knew the site was there, but generally regarded it as a "necessary evil."

The team consisted of approximately 100 men who resided and worked in the buildings on the mountain. Each year, the team would travel to White Sands Missile Range in New Mexico to participate in live fire exercises.

In 1964, as the technology and the threat changed, the Issaquah site became obsolete. Other Nike Ajax sites (Kingston, Redmond, and Vashon Island) were upgraded to handle the new Nike Hercules missile.

The Issaquah site was deactivated in 1964 and the process began in 1965 to transfer the property to King County. Buildings loaded with asbestos were removed. The underground missile storage facility was welded shut as the transformation got underway to change the facility from a military installation into a county park.

The site is now an open field. Only remnants of concrete pads and sidewalks remain at the site. Renamed as Radar Park, interpretive signs indicate where buildings were located when the site was active.

S-03, Bothell / Kenmore Site

The S-03 site in Bothell / Kenmore was an eight-launcher Ajax site. Operations were closed out by the Washington National Guard's A/2/205th in March 1964. The Army

Reserve now has a center on the site which is new construction; the launch area is now utilized by the Federal Emergency Management Agency (FEMA) as its Region X Headquarters.

S-13/14, Redmond

Redmond was a major site, with six magazines and 24 launchers, and served as a headquarters and Hercules site until shutdown in 1974. The control area is located on top of a hill in northeast Redmond, at the end of 95th Street, off 171st Avenue NE. The site is partially intact, with multiple buildings and two of the radar plats and is privately owned

S-32 / 33, Lake Youngs / Renton

Established in 1956 and closed in 1961, site S-33 shared a launch facility with S-32. The Lake Youngs site is now the campus of Maple Valley Elementary School.

S-33C, Renton

S-33C is located southeast of Renton at 14631 SE 192d; current owner is the Army Reserve. The buildings are intact and the locations of the radars are easy to determine.

S-43 Kent / Midway

The site is now partially used as an off-leash dog park and partially by the Kent School District. The Nike site was closed in 1963.

S-61 Vashon Island

Located on Vashon Island, the site was established in 1956 and closed in 1974. It is partially intact. Some of the buildings remain; however, at present the Vashon Island Equestrian Park occupies the space (Nike Site Park).

The Oozlefinch

if it flies...
it dies

The Oozlefinch was a mythical bird which had a long association with Army artillery, the Coast Artillery Corps, and the Nike Missilemen. It was described as a completely featherless bird which could fly at supersonic speeds, fly backwards if necessary and was especially adept at picking off Soviet bombers. The Oozlefinch has a special place in the hearts and memories of Nike Missilemen

Coast Guard in Seattle: Pier 36
Base Support Unit Seattle
Integrated Support Command (ISC) Seattle

The first Coast Guard cutters came to the Seattle area during the 1850s; however, they were home-ported in Port Townsend and in Port Angeles. In the late 1800s as Seattle began to grow, cutters were a common sight along the waterfront.

Through World War II, cutters were homeported in numerous places along the Seattle waterfront. Following World War II, cutters still tied up at Pier 70 and at Pier 91, the Navy Pier. They also tied up at the old "North Base" near the Ship Canal. With the integration of the Lighthouse Service in 1939, the Coast Guard presence in Seattle was extremely prominent.

Pier 36 — Seattle

The Seattle waterfront has long been a site for various military units, ships, and activities. Shipbuilding and maritime operations in support of military activities became increasingly active with World War I. In September 1916, the United States Shipping Board was created to support war efforts. The Emergency Fleet Corporation was soon established by the Shipping Board. Within two years after the United States entered the war, the Emergency Fleet Corporation doubled the number of vessels operating under the American flag.

In 1917, Skinner & Eddy Corporation expanded its shipbuilding operation along the waterfront. The area was soon to become Skinner & Eddy's Plant No. 2. Later it would become known as Piers 36, 37, 38, and 39. By the end of World War I, Skinner & Eddy shipyards had broken national production records by cutting ship production time to 42 days from keel laying to launch. The company also produced more ships for the Emergency Fleet Corporation than any other shipyard in the nation. The company built 75 ocean-going vessels and was one of the largest shipbuilding companies in the nation.

World War I was an economic boon to Puget Sound shipyards. These facilities constructed more than 25 percent of the U.S. Shipping Board's fleet. In 1918, there were more than 20 shipyards in Seattle employing 35,000 workers. When the war was over, however, America sank into a severe depression as production wound down to a peacetime economy. Shipyards were among the first businesses to close.

Skinner & Eddy closed their doors in 1920 and the United States Shipping Board acquired the Seattle properties. In 1923, the Port of Seattle started negotiations for the property (now Piers 36-39). The bloc was acquired for $600,000. By 1924, the Pacific Steamship Company purchased Skinner & Eddy's Plant No. 2. Shipping, however, began to drop off in European markets when the Great Depression began in 1929, and shipping activity along the Seattle waterfront came to a near standstill. By 1940, the Pacific Steamship Company was sold to the government.

The property around the shipyards turned into shacks made out of scrap lumber, cardboard, and tarpaper. Known as Hooverville, the area was home to approximately 1,000 homeless and jobless. In 1935, the Works Progress Administration began construction of the seawall along the Seattle waterfront. Some "Hooverville" residents found jobs and left the area.

In 1940, the Army Quartermaster Corps was looking to expand operations and build a larger supply depot on the waterfront. Assets were readily available and the Army looked to the former Pacific Steamship Company terminals at the foot of Atlantic Street.

By 1941, the City of Seattle ordered "Hooverville" to be torn down in order to make room for the growing defense activities. The Army built a four story warehouse, and contracted to have a new pier built (Pier 37). By November of that year, the Seattle Army Depot at Pier 37 was the Quartermaster Corps' largest depot under one roof. It had approximately 1,000,000 square feet of space. At the same time, the depot became part of the Army Transportation Service (ATS), San Francisco Port of Embarkation. By January 1942, it was no longer under the control of San Francisco and was made a permanent Port of Embarkation. Two more piers were added to the depot (Piers 38 and 39).

Technology was changing, however. By 1956, the Military Air Transportation Service (MATS) was transporting more and more supplies by air. Air transport was faster and cheaper. In June 1957, the Department of Defense informed Seattle leaders that the Army Terminal would be closing and West Coast operations would be moving to Oakland, California.

In 1964, the Department of Defense declared Piers 36-39 as surplus. The Port of Seattle purchased the property, buildings, and the four piers from the United States General Services Administration for $4,000,000. In 1973, the Port leased Pier 36 and the apron of Pier 37 to the Coast Guard for $1 a year. The Coast Guard had been using Navy facilities (Piers 90 and 91), and took the opportunity to consolidate their activities and move to a new base.

Piers 90 and 91, adjacent property which had been owned by the Navy, and the former Coast Guard properties, were once again acquired by the Port of Seattle.

Pier 36 became the Coast Guard Integrated Support Command. The Steamship Terminal Office Building is the administrative office for the Coast Guard's Captain of the Port, the Vessel Traffic Safety Office, and other offices critical to vessel traffic movement throughout Puget Sound. The Army Quartermaster Corps warehouse became the Federal Warehouse Building.

The Port of Seattle made the waterfront area north of Pier 36 to Pier 46 into one of the largest container loading stations in the world. With the designation of Terminals 37, 42, and 46, the facility provides services to several major shipping companies.

Today only a few commemorative plaques mark the military and support activities that took place on the waterfront of Seattle. The only recognizable landmark that remains is the Pacific Steamship Terminal Office Building, built in 1925.

Piers 36 - 38, ca. 1925. U.S. Navy photo

Coast Guard Museum Northwest

The Coast Guard Museum Northwest at Pier 36 in Seattle features thousands of historical items recalling the Coast Guard's contribution to Pacific Northwest maritime history. Exhibits include large, detailed models of Revenue Cutter Service and Coast Guard cutters, and the ship's bell from the steam tug *Roosevelt*, which was Admiral Robert E. Peary's ship during his exploration of the Arctic Ocean. Visitors also discover a Revenue Cutter Service ensign from Captain "Hell-Roarin'" Mike Healy's *Bear*, which also sailed the waters off Alaska.

The museum is on the grounds of the U.S. Coast Guard Station in downtown Seattle, home port of the icebreakers *Polar Star*, *Polar Sea*, and *Healy*, as well as the endurance cutters *Mellon* and *Midgett*. The museum's collection includes a few non-Coast Guard items, such as the sextant from a German Navy U-boat captured by the Coast Guard-manned USS *Durant* during World War II. Items from the German trawler *Externsteine* captured by *Eastwind* off Greenland in

World War II are exhibited along with thousands of photos and slides of cutters, aircraft, lighthouses, crews, and stations. Three thousand books on Coast Guard and maritime history round out the collection.

U.S. Coast Guard Museum. U.S. Coast Guard photo

Coast Guard related exhibits include thousands of uniforms, several lighthouse lenses, a piece of the HMS *Bounty,* and what is purported to be the largest public collection of Coast Guard patches. Research resources are also available in well over three thousand books and periodicals dedicated to Coast Guard and Northwest maritime history. Highlights of the exhibit are found in cases housing several intricate, accurate models of Coast Guard ships. Thousands of photos and slides are available depicting cutters, lighthouses, people and Coast Guard stations.

The Museum is open to the public and admission is free. Staffed entirely by volunteers, the museum is generally open on Monday, Wednesday and Friday. The museum is behind a secure gate, so a picture identification card will be necessary to gain access to the base.

Naval Air Station Seattle / Sand Point Naval Air Station

Sand Point, a peninsula that juts into Lake Washington in North Seattle, has been identified under a variety of official designations. It served for nearly 50 years, however, as an air base, aviation training center, and as a critical aircraft repair depot for the U.S. Navy.

Before World War I began, the U.S Navy was searching for an aircraft facility to create an oversight base for the naval bases and yards throughout Puget Sound. Captain Luther

Gregory was given the assignment of finding a suitable site and he selected Sand Point as his top candidate. The only available landing field at that time was, in fact, not a landing field but was the Jefferson Park Golf Course, which had been used on a Liberty Bond tour as a landing site for Army aircraft.

World War I was over before the Navy made a decision. A group of veterans began to lobby King County for an airport at Sand Point. At that time, Sand Point was outside of the Seattle city limits. The lobbyists noted that the following advantages existed at Sand Point:

- it was discernible from the air
- it was not subject to flooding and not affected by tides
- there were no buildings nor power poles which could obstruct takeoffs and landings
- it was accessible by rail and by sea
- it had favorable prevailing winds.

The King County commissioners began to acquire the small farms which occupied the site. On June 19, 1920, the Navy and local King County officials had a symbolic tree-cutting ceremony and groundbreaking on the site.

The site, however, was still not an official site. Congress had yet to adopt it as an air field. A Congressional committee visited the property and reported that the site was probably the best base for "heavier-than-air equipment."

Supporters of an Army air field just north of Camp Lewis argued the site should not be in north Seattle. Competition between Seattle and Tacoma as to which city should be the focal point on Puget Sound fueled the competition and the argument. King County commissioners went on to authorize the construction of an air strip and on October 8, 1921, Major Henry Muhlenberg flew a Curtis JN-4H "Jenny" from Camp Lewis and made the first military landing on the fairly unimproved 500-foot dirt strip. King County officials found a prefabricated Army hangar in California and arranged to have it shipped to the Sand Point location. Pilots arranged to have the runway seeded with grass to make a more stable, firm surface.

It took until July 1922 for the Navy to accept 268 acres from the county on a ten-year lease at $1 per year. Funds in the amount of $800,000 were authorized for the initial development of a joint Army and Navy airfield. The first permanent hangar was completed in April 1923.

Sand Point became part of the history books when it was chosen as the beginning and ending point for the first circumnavigation of the globe by air. Four Douglas biplanes took off for Alaska on April 7, 1924, and then continued around the world. Fifty thousand people came to Sand Point to greet the three aircraft that completed the journey on September 28, 1924.

In May 1925, the Chief of Naval Operations formally established a Naval Air Reserve unit at Sand Point. A year later, Congress authorized the Navy to accept "without cost," fee simple, 413 acres which would be used as a naval air station. At this time, it was one of only five naval air stations in the nation. The Navy received this gift from King County, which had spent $500,000 in the acquisition and the development of the property.

By 1926, improvements were not extensive and not as complete as King County leadership would have liked. The station commander worked out of an old farmhouse. A field served as a runway. Naval Reservists met there one evening a week for drills and they flew on Sundays. Naval Aviation Cadets were housed in an old chicken house and the supply officer ran his operations out of a kitchen. The base's turf runway made it unreliable throughout much of the year. The facility's principal mission was to train reservists. These reservists, however, provided valuable contributions through aerial mapping of Alaska and Washington over the next few years.

Officers' quarters, Sand Point, ca. 1935. Real Photo Post Card, Author's collection

In 1931, the number of full-time personnel numbered 31 Marines and eight Navy personnel, who operated 14 airplanes. Five Navy active patrol squadrons were assigned to the base. Aircraft at that time included multi-engine flying boats which were used for long-range reconnaissance and attack missions. With the arrival of these aircraft, overhaul facilities were also constructed. More than 600 sailors supported the overhaul and patrol squadron missions.

With the deepening of the Great Depression, funding was difficult to obtain. Improvements were slow in coming during these years but by the close of 1935, the Navy had increased the number of buildings to seventeen. Commercial airlines were also utilizing the newly paved runway. In 1939, Pan American Airways began Clipper service to Alaska from nearby Matthews Beach, a county park just north of the Naval Air Station. They also used the Sand Point hangars and runways.

Aerial view of the U.S. Naval Air Station Sand Point, Seattle, Washington, in the 1940s. U.S. Navy photo

The year 1939 brought increasing tension throughout the world. President Roosevelt declared a national emergency in response to the outbreak of World War II. In July 1940, Congress authorized $4 million to improve what was then known as Naval Air Station Seattle. By June 1941, naval schools at the station were training radiomen, aviation metalsmiths, and machinists. At the same time that the base was growing, Seattle was also growing. City of Seattle officials requested that aircraft no longer carry live bombs and Naval Air Station Whidbey Island was established to handle the arming of combat aircraft.

The numbers of operations and staff ballooned during the war years. At the height of its service, Sand Point had five runways providing eight landing directions. The daily population of the base grew to 8,000 civilian and military personnel. Other functions including a weather center, a communications center and an overseas terminal for the Naval Air Transport Service were located at Sand Point. While shipyards in Tacoma and Vancouver produced aircraft carriers (50 in three years), Sand Point provided supplies ranging from parachutes to propellers.

The Navy began to utilize the Washington State ferries in 1943 as mock "targets" for torpedo bombers of Air Group Ten assigned to Sand Point Naval Air Station. Using radar, the pilots would identify a ferry crossing Puget Sound as a target and practice low level, night attacks on it.

NAS Sand Point control tower in the 1950s. U.S. Navy photo

Magnuson Park, World Flight Monument. Photo by Author

By the time World War II was over in 1945, Sand Point Naval Air Station base found itself with a much reduced mission. In 1946, only approximately 3,000 staff members were located at the base. Base personnel responsibilities diminished to the preservation of 89 flying boats in Renton. The Navy announced that the base would be closed permanently in the fall of 1950.

With the beginning of the Korean conflict, base closure plans were delayed and then subsequently canceled when the base began 6-day work weeks as the missions of overhauling wartime aircraft, training reservists, and support of Whidbey Island Naval Air Station became more critical. In 1953, the Korean efforts were over and so was the station's responsibility for aircraft maintenance. The facility returned to its original role of training Naval Reservists.

As Whidbey Island facilities expanded, Sand Point became excess capacity. Flight operations at Sand Point ceased in 1970. Several federal agencies by this time had found a home at Sand Point. The U.S. Fish and Wildlife Service, Civil Air Patrol, U.S. Postal Service, some small Army units, and the U.S Public Health Service occupied the facility. Sand Point became known as Naval Station Seattle.

In 1970, when the Naval Station was officially deactivated, the real battles for the property began. Long, bitter debates over uses of the land ensued. The City of Seattle claimed a little over 195 acres for what would eventually become known as Warren G. Magnuson Park, named in honor of a former Senator representing the State of Washington. Approximately 100 acres became the Seattle headquarters for the National Oceanic and Atmospheric Administration (NOAA). Debates over whether light aircraft should be able to use the runways raged. Entities including the Muckleshoot Indian Tribe, dog owners, advocates for the homeless, and Sand Point neighbors were all involved in a struggle over control and land use.

At present, recreation and arts are the missions of Sand Point. An exhibit of surplus submarine vanes continues to tie the present uses of the property to its previous missions of military training, aviation, and support.

Remaining buildings at Sand Point 2011. Photo by Keppie Keplinger

Museum of Flight

While not a military installation nor a support facility, the Museum of Flight does house an extensive collection of military aircraft. The Museum's collection includes more than 150 historically significant air- and spacecraft, as well as the Red Barn®—the original manufacturing facility of The Boeing Co. The Museum's aviation and space library and archives are the largest on the West Coast.

Accredited by the American Association of Museums, its holdings and exhibits are extensive and presented in an exemplary manner. In addition to aircraft, the Museum of Flight collects and preserves all types of aviation and space artifacts. Some of these are on exhibit, while many more are stored, awaiting research, loan, or future display. All are carefully indexed, photographed, and conserved. Highlights of the object collection include nearly 6,000 garments, including flight attendant uniforms, military uniforms, and insignia.

The Red Barn, Boeing's original aircraft factory. Photo by Author

Aircraft on display include both military and civilian planes from all over the world. Many are on exhibit at the Museum; others reside in storage or are being refurbished at the Museum's Restoration Center at Paine Field in Everett.

With the downsizing and reorganization of the National Air and Space Administration (NASA) and the cessation of the space shuttle programs, many assets were dispersed to museums and facilities around the country. The Seattle Museum of Flight was fortunate enough to be named the recipient of the Full Fuselage Trainer (FFT). The FFT is an interactive display and is a critical and integral part of helping tell the story of the United States' space program.

The Museum of Flight is located South of downtown Seattle, at the south end of Boeing Field / King County Airport; Exit 158 off Interstate 5.

Boeing Airplane Company, Seattle

Boeing's contributions to World War II are legendary. By March of 1944, Seattle plants were rolling out 16 planes in 24 hours. A total of 12,731 B-17s were produced around the country. Boeing built 6,981 of these at the Seattle and

Wichita, Kansas, plants. Similarly, the B-29, which entered production less than two years after its first flight in 1942, was also produced at record rates at Seattle plants.

Boeing's contribution to the war effort through its bombers was highly regarded by wartime leaders. General Andrew Spatz, Commanding General of the U.S. Army Air Forces, recalled in 1947 the importance of the Pacific Northwest's achievements, advancements, and production records in critical military aviation assets for the war. "To an airman, the Pacific Northwest is the home of the long-range heavy bomber, which has changed the character of war and the meaning of peace."

The plants were obviously critical to wartime production, and protection of the plants from aerial bomb attacks was extremely important. Hiding an entire factory was a challenge. Boeing brought in a Hollywood set designer, John Stewart Detlie, to use movie set techniques to hide the plants. Invasions by air were a continuing perceived threat, so disguising the plant as it would be viewed from above became an imperative. The solution was the fabrication of a fake housing development which was built on the roof top of the plants.

Plywood houses and bushes and trees made out of netting created an entire residential neighborhood on the roofs of what would otherwise have been easily identifiable factory roof tops. Chicken wire and burlap formed the vegetation which made the plant look from the air like a peaceful Pacific Northwest neighborhood complete with trees, houses, streets, and backyards just like adjacent neighborhoods.

The effectiveness of these efforts was never tested because no Japanese aircraft got anywhere near the plants. The efforts did, however, reinforce the collective war efforts of the military, industry, and civilians throughout the area.

The Boeing plant in Renton was originally built to produce the XPBB-1 Sea Ranger for the Navy, but after the Battle of Midway, the emphasis on land-based bombers gained more support. The mission changed and the plant was traded to the Army to produce the B-29. As a result, only one of the Sea Rangers was built before the production line changed.

Boeing B-17B ca. 1940. Real Photo Post Card, Author's collection

Battle of Seattle (1856)

In 1856, the settlement of Seattle was located in the area of what is now Seattle's Pioneer Square. Settlers in the area were becoming increasingly nervous after a series of angry encounters with Native Americans in the area, and erected blockhouses and stockades throughout the area to help preserve their safety in the face of this unrest.

Native Americans had, in reality, been forced to enter into treaties beginning in the fall of 1855. These treaties drove them off of their traditional hunting and fishing grounds and onto reservations which were woefully inadequate to handle the population and the varying tribal cultures. Between the time that Territorial Governor Isaac Stevens arrived in the area in the fall of 1855 and January 1856, treaties had been "signed" by virtually all tribal entities in the area. However, treaty promises were not kept by the U.S. Government. By 1856, Native Americans were angry as they discovered how they had been misled.

Five days before the "Battle of Seattle" on January 26, 1856, Governor Stevens declared a "war of extermination" upon the natives. The sloop *Decatur* had earlier been called to Puget Sound because of the troubles with local natives and to deter raids coming from natives in what is now Canada. From January 19, the *Decatur* was anchored in deep water in Elliott

Bay with 16 32-pounder guns which could fire fuzed shells trained on the shore. The ship also carried two nine-pounder cannons which could be deployed ashore. Captain Isaac Sterret of the *Decatur* contributed Marines and these cannons to assist in the effort. A two-story, two-gun blockhouse, called Seattle Blockhouse and later Fort Decatur, was built by the Marines and armed with the nine-pounders. The site was located at what is now 1st Avenue and Cherry Street in downtown Seattle.

Lieutenant T.S. Phelps, in a memoir of the engagements, noted that the hostile warrior natives were from various tribes. These tribes are now regarded primarily as the Klickitat, Spokane, Palouse, Walla-Walla, Yakima, Kamialk, Nisqually, Puyallup, and "Lake" (Duwamish-related, living near Lake Washington), as well as various other tribes.

Significantly, many of these tribes were from east of the Cascades. The number of warriors was estimated by Phelps at 6,000. Other historians now estimate the forces at no more than 150. They were under the command of three chiefs, Coquilton, Owhi, and Leschi. This warrior contingent failed to recruit several tribes from the Olympic Peninsula, nor did they succeed in enlisting the support of the Snoqualmie and Snohomish to their cause. Patkanim, who was regarded as a leader of both the Snoqualmie and the Snohomish, decided it was more expedient to stay out of the attacks.

Two of the chiefs disguised themselves as friendly natives and came into Seattle on the evening of January 25, apparently to size up the situation. The native attack on the Seattle settlement was originally planned to begin at around 2:00 a.m. The disagreement amongst the native forces resulted in a new plan for a mid-morning attack using a small decoy force to draw the *Decatur*'s men out of the better defended areas to do battle on what is now known as Seattle's "First Hill."

Based on warnings received, the Marines were ordered ashore early on the morning of January 26. Gunners from the *Decatur* lobbed a shell at a house at the crest of First Hill which was believed to be a shelter for hostile natives. Raiders answered with gunfire, and settlers found shelter in the two blockhouses in the settlement. Friendly natives, along with some settlers' wives and children, sought shelter along the beach.

The *Decatur* fired solid shot, shells, grape shot, and canisters into the trees where 3rd Avenue is today. Sporadic fire was exchanged until approximately 11:45 a.m., when the natives paused the action to eat. Settlers took that opportunity to evacuate women and children to the *Decatur* and another ship, the *Brontes*. Exchanges continued throughout the afternoon. Natives were preparing to set the villagers' homes on fire. The *Decatur* shifted fire in the direction of the approaching natives to prevent the further destruction of the village. By 10:00 p.m. all firing had stopped.

By the next morning, the attackers were gone, along with whatever stock, food, blankets and other possessions they could carry off. Two settlers had been killed. The estimate of natives killed varied widely. No bodies of Native Americans were found at Seattle after the one-day war.

Following the war, Snoqualmie and Snohomish leader Patkanim offered a bounty for the heads of those who had attacked Seattle -- $80 for a chief and $20 for a warrior. Historians report that during the month of February several grisly trophies were received in Seattle and then sent to Olympia. Governor Stevens blamed the attack on Chief Leschi and Chief Owhi of the Klickitat / Yakima tribes. Leschi eluded capture for several months but was subsequently captured. Settlers came to his defense and insisted that he had been falsely accused of unrelated murders. A year-long defense to save his life ensued, but he was subsequently hanged at Fort Steilacoom on February 19, 1858.

Stevens also implicated Kitsap of the Muckleshoot and Squamish as an instigator of the violence, but settlers did not agree. Later, residents named the new county on the west side of Puget Sound Kitsap.

A plaque commemorating the Battle of Seattle is located on the waterfront in downtown Seattle. An additional plaque is located in a park bordering the King County Public Safety Building. The former battlefield is now a small walking and sitting space filled with grass, trees, benches, small tables, and chairs where the plaque and a small oak recall the 1865 Battle of Seattle.

Sites of Blockhouses

Several blockhouses were built to help protect settlers from attacks by Native Americans in and around King County. In most cases, nothing remains of these sites. These blockhouses included:

- **Fort Lander** (1856): The first structure to be known as Fort Lander was a blockhouse built by Washington Territory Volunteers on the Duwamish river. The defensive site later moved upriver to the south bank of the river. The blockhouse was enclosed by a 98 x 58-foot stockade. It was named for Captain Edward Lander, Washington Territorial Volunteers. The site is located one-quarter mile south of the King County Airport Administration Building. (Sea-Tac)
- **Black River Blockhouse** (1856): A federal blockhouse built on the Black River. The exact location is undetermined. (Sea-Tac)
- **Fort Dent** (1855): A federal blockhouse. Fort Dent Park in Tukwila was once a winter village for the Duwamish Indian tribe. After being partially vacated following the signing of the 1855 Point Elliott treaty, the site briefly became home to a small military blockhouse. A marker exists at the site. The former blockhouse site has been operated by the city as a park since 2002. (Tukwila)
- **Fort Henderson** (1856): A temporary blockhouse built by Washington Territory Volunteers. The site was located on the Snoqualmie River at Patterson Creek. The blockhouse was also called **Fort Patterson**. (Near Fall City)
- **Fort Tilton** (1855 - 1856): A temporary blockhouse built by Washington Territory Volunteers. Used as Northern Battalion headquarters during the Indian Wars. Site located three miles below the Snoqualmie River Falls. (Near Fall City)
- **Fort Alden** (1856 - 1857): A temporary blockhouse built by the Washington Territory Volunteers, located above the falls of the Snoqualmie River. Jeremiah Borst used the blockhouse as his home in 1858. Borst accompanied Seattle pioneer Arthur Denny over what is now Snoqualmie Pass, and as a result became one of the first non-natives to make the trip. In 1868, he took charge of building the first road through the pass. The blockhouse was also known as **Fort Alder**. (Snoqualmie)
- **Fort Thomas** (1855): Temporary two-story blockhouse. Located on the Green River opposite Kent, near the community of Thomas on the south bank of the river, this establishment was built by regular Army troops during the Indian Wars of 1855-56. It was named in honor of John

M. Thomas, who owned the land where the fort was built. (Kent)

- **Fort Duwamish** (1855): A settler's blockhouse located on property owned by Luther Collins at the base of the peninsula just south of the settlement of Seattle. Records indicate that a palisade stretched cross the peninsula. (Seattle)

- **Fort Slaughter** (1856-1857): A federal stockade and blockhouse located on the White River northeast of Lake Tapps. It was also known as **Camp Muckleshoot Prairie**. The fort was named for Lieutenant William Slaughter, commander of Company C, 4th Infantry, Washington Territory Volunteers, who was killed near the Puyallup River. (Muckleshoot Reservation)

Lieutenant William Slaughter. National Archives photo

Lend-Lease Depot, Auburn

When World War II broke out in Europe in 1939, the United States originally chose to remain neutral. However, as Nazi forces started to win important victories throughout Europe, President Roosevelt began to explore ways to support Britain's war efforts while still remaining out of direct conflict. As the war escalated and allies were being threatened, President Roosevelt declared large amounts of weaponry and ammunition as "surplus" and authorized their shipment to Great Britain in mid-1940.

Under the Destroyers for Bases Plan, President Roosevelt entered into negotiations with Prime Minister Churchill to exchange Navy ships for bases in British holdings including the Caribbean and the east coast of Canada. When Hitler attacked the Soviet Union in 1941, Roosevelt pledged aid to Russia as well. Eventually the Lend-Lease Act was extended to countries fighting the Axis powers. Great Britain and Russia were the biggest recipients.

By 1943, outbound supplies and equipment were stacking up at U.S. ports. A better logistical system was needed to keep supplies moving. At this point, the largest Holding and Reconsignment (H&R) depot in the nation was constructed in Auburn.

H&R depots were designed to hold supplies until they could be promptly moved to the ports and on their way to intended Allied recipients. Military strategists were concerned that western seaports were subject to attack, so the H&R depots were located inland. In June 1943, the government purchased 600 acres a few miles southwest of Auburn. The site's proximity to transcontinental railway lines and its location near Seattle, Tacoma, and Portland ports were the primary reasons for its selection as a site. Reports indicate that the land had been agricultural land. Many of the 72 tracts had been originally owned by Japanese farmers who had been relocated to internment camps for the duration of the war.

Since War Department funds were unavailable, construction of depots was undertaken with Lend-Lease revenues. By February 1944, approximately $43 million had been expended to construct depots. Ten depots were established—the two in Washington State were at Pasco in eastern Washington and the Auburn installation, south of Seattle. In addition, storage facilities for export ammunition and explosives were constructed in Marysville, near Everett.

Within a few weeks after the Auburn property was purchased, contractors immediately began to construct the H&R facilities including warehouses, platforms, and railroad spurs. By October 1943, twelve large warehouses had been built which provided 27 million square feet of covered storage area. Railway tracks and platforms ran along the entire length of the warehouses. The site was two-and-a-half miles long and a half-mile wide.

The twelve warehouses were arranged in a north-south pattern. Internal lighting was provided by incandescent light fixtures with mirrored glass or steel reflectors and by daylight through the roof monitors. Exterior elements, such as doors and windows, were also simple and constructed of common, easily-obtainable wood materials. Except for the roof, the buildings were un-insulated.

Above each of the side aisles of a warehouse, wood catwalks provided a two-foot wide continuous maintenance access along the clerestory windows. The catwalks were supported by the roof trusses and accessed with fixed wood ladders.

Construction of the depot provided employment for 1,200 men and operation after it was completed provided employment for 2,000. Auburn had a population of approximately 4,000 people prior to the war. The addition of the depot changed the profile of Auburn.

The facility was dedicated in early December 1943 and the event attracted military personnel, businessmen, and school children. Lend-Lease officials from Great Britain, Russia, and China were key participants in the celebration.

The initial purpose of the sites was specifically for Lend-Lease cargo, but as the war continued general Army shipments intended for overseas deployments were also stored there. Later on in the war effort, however, the policy evolved to ensure these sites could only be used to temporarily house freight designated for overseas shipments and not just for general storage.

Portland became the primary point for shipment of Lend-Lease materials to Russia from the Auburn depot. Goods moving across the Pacific were transported on Russian flagships, since Russia was officially neutral in the war in the Pacific. Other supporting ports included Longview, Kalama, and Vancouver.

After the dedication, the depot was closed to the public and security concerns made further articles in the local newspapers subject to wartime censorship. References to the center named it only as "the Point." Even though it was the largest employer in Auburn it received only a few cryptic references in the press.

Labor shortages at the Point resulted in a group of Italian Prisoners of War being brought in to work there. In August 1944, the *Auburn Globe-News* article had a headline reading: "Italian Prisoners Employed at Point." The group consisted of four Italian officers and 215 men. One American officer and six soldiers provided supervision for the Italians. The POWs were housed at the site, and received the $24 per month which had been allotted to all POWS. Some of the pay was in cash, while the rest was in coupons which could be redeemed at a branch of the Fort Lewis post exchange which had been established at the Point.

Italian detainees were also employed at the site after the

war ended in the Pacific. Teamsters Union representatives protested to the War Department that these men were taking jobs away from Americans, especially those returning from the war. Italian POWs were apparently not used at the Point after 1945.

An all-civilian force, under civil service regulations, would be used instead. Newspaper reports indicated that approximately 575 people, 35% of whom were women, were employed at the end of the war. Army Transportation Corps recorded that the Auburn facility handled approximately 575,000 short tons of cargo in 1944 and approximately 243,000 short tons in 1945. This was below the average of the other facilities. Much of the cargo from shipped from Auburn was destined for the Pacific. Following the Japanese surrender, the workload significantly dropped.

In 1946, the Auburn depot was designated as the center to receive war dead from the Pacific and served Washington, Oregon, and Northern Idaho. Approximately 5,000 casualties were received in Auburn and subsequently delivered to next of kin.

The facility was instrumental in shaping the profile of Auburn and surrounding communities. Employment opportunities were created in its construction, operation, and in the transition to peacetime operations.

The depot went on a base closure list in 1960, and was recommended, although unsuccessfully, as a site for the 1962 World's Fair. When the General Services Administration (GSA) proposed building a supply warehouse at Sand Point Naval Air Station in Seattle, Congressional staff members pointed out that the Auburn depot had excess storage space. The Sand Point proposal was dropped and the GSA took over 31 buildings at Auburn. Two years later portions of the depot were sold to private interests and six acres of the facility were donated to the City of Auburn for a park.

Only portions of the Auburn Point exist today as a General Services Administration Depot. The site is also occupied by the Boeing Company and many other businesses. Discerning which facilities were part of the original site is difficult.

Note: An article by William E. Saxe in the *The Columbia Magazine,* Summer 2006, Volume 20 No.2, provides more details on this little-known World War II resource.

Submarines and Naval Shipbuilding in Puget Sound

Submarines

On the morning of the 6th of January 1912, 500 people gathered at Robert Moran's shipbuilding yard in downtown Seattle (area south of Yesler Way) to witness the first launch of a submarine on Puget Sound. The submarine was a new addition to Navy platforms. Considered to be somewhat a secret weapon, the new boats were at the forefront of technology. Naval opinion was skeptical about their real value. Admiral George Dewey, however, had become an enthusiast and was ready to support the exploration of this new idea. He noted that if the Spanish had possessed and utilized submarines in Manila, the outcome of the war in the Philippines would have been totally different. He indicated that his fleet at the time could never have countered this threat. As the result of such strong proponents, Congress authorized 52 submarines between the period of 1900 to 1914. (The Navy had requested only 23.)

Public pressure to have naval defense located along the West Coast increased as trade grew, and as world conditions changed. The Philippines, Hawaii, the Canal Zone, Alaska, and ports up and down the West Coast needed protection. Meanwhile, Germany had completed a large naval base at Tsingtao on the China coast. The Japanese victory over Russia in the Russo-Japanese War (1905) highlighted Japan as a "probably enemy."

In the early 1900s, the Seattle Chamber of Commerce, along with Chambers of Commerce in Bellingham, Everett, and Port Townsend, forwarded resolutions to Congress indicating their desire for protection along the West Coast.

Four submarines, F-boats, were designated as West Coast boats to be built on the West Coast. Seattle got two of the four boats at $454,740 each. They were single-hulled boats, 142 feet-6 inches long with a beam of 15 feet-five inches. The hull contained three compartments—the torpedo room with four torpedoes, the control room, and the engine room which had two diesel engines. The two engines were connected to a common shaft that turned motors that could act as generators for charging the batteries. The battery was an array of cells in rubber-lined, open-topped jars.

F-3, circa 1912. Courtesy navypedia.org

- The F-boats were the fastest submarines when submerged of all the US submarines prior to nuclear-powered vessels.
- They were the first class of vessels laid down for the U.S. Navy with diesel engines.
- They were the first diesel-powered submarines constructed on the Pacific Ocean.
- F-3 was the first diesel-powered vessel of any type launched in the Pacific Northwest.
- F class submarines, were the first U.S. Navy submarines suitable for autonomous operations near the coast. They were prototypes for the basic classes of U.S. submarines in the First World War.

The submarine contracts placed Seattle as one of the most important shipbuilding sites on the West Coast.

While the operation, testing, and war records of these boats is beyond the scope of this book, the submarine history in Puget Sound remains as an important contribution to military history in the area.

Note: Recommended reading on historical aspects of submarines in Puget Sound:

Beneath the Surface: Submarines Built in Seattle and Vancouver 1909 - 1918. Bill Lightfoot, with a foreword by Roland H. Webb. Cordillera Books, Vancouver, British Columbia, 2005.

Navy Ships

Shipyards in Seattle trace their history back to 1882 when Robert Moran had a marine repair facility at Yesler's Wharf. The Moran Brothers Company had been successful in building pumps for Navy vessels and had built boats to be used in the Gold Rush in the Yukon and Alaska. When the Navy asked for bids on a Virginia class battleship, company President Robert Moran (mayor of Seattle in 1888-1890) submitted the lowest bid to build the new *Nebraska*. The bid was still more than the Navy wanted to pay. To help the company win the contract, 536 Seattle citizens pledged a total of $100,000 to offset the cost.

On October 7, 1904, the battleship USS *Nebraska* was launched from Moran Brothers shipyard in Seattle. It is still the only battleship built in Washington State. Fifty-five thousand people attend, including 40,000 along the wharves and shoreline and 15,000 in boats across Elliott Bay.

The USS *Nebraska* joined the Great White Fleet and sailed to locations around the world. When World War I broke out, she was undergoing repairs at the Boston Navy Yard. She soon joined the active service again and was used for maneuvers and battle practice primarily along the east coast. Following World War I, she saw duty on the west coast with the Pacific Fleet. Following her decommissioning in 1920, she was sold for scrap in 1923.

Shipbuilding continued in Seattle. By the end of 1911, the Moran Brothers Shipyard became the Seattle Construction and Dry Dock Company. Other shipyards sprang up in the Seattle area, producing ships of various kinds. In 1916, the William H. Todd Corporation merged with Robins Dry Dock and Repair Company of New York and several other shipbuilding corporations in New Jersey to become Todd Shipyards.

In the years following World War I, the Navy's assessment of the potential global threats compared with the inventory of available Navy ships resulted in contract awards for additional ships. In 1939, the Todd Shipyards and the Kaiser Shipbuilding Company in Tacoma began building ships with the aid of some $15 million in capital provided by the US Navy, for the production of vessels in anticipation of possible US entry into World War II. Todd and Kaiser Shipbuilding produced a significant number of ships including escort carriers, destroyers, and merchant marine ships.

In 1942 Todd bought out Kaiser's holding and thereafter the company was reabsorbed into Todd Dry Dock & Construction, which eventually became Todd Pacific Shipyards. During the war, the Seattle Division of Todd Shipyard's facilities produced over 126 ships of six different classes during a 36 month period during the war.

Harbor Island, at the mouth of the Duwamish River across Elliott Bay from the Seattle downtown waterfront, was created in the early 1900s by filling in tidal flats with the tops of some of Seattle's major hills. When it was completed in 1909, it had become the world's largest artificial island.

Seattle-Tacoma Shipbuilding started construction of a facility on Harbor Island, dedicated to destroyer production, in 1940. By 1941, the "Sea-Tac" Harbor Island yard was ready to lay keels for the *Gleaves* class destroyer. Ships were launched from this facility at an average of one ship each 324 days and commissioned in an average of 653 days.

While production was still underway on the *Gleaves* class destroyers, the yard retooled and also began to produce the *Fletcher* class. Without a pause in production the yard also began to produce *Sumner* and *Gearing* class ships. Five of the ten *Gearing* class ships were completed before the end of the war. The final, and tenth ship (the *Seaman*, DD 791) was never completed.

USS Nebraska *ready for her voyage with the Great White Fleet, May 1908. U.S. Navy photo*

Approximately 17,000 people were employed at the ship building facilities on Harbor Island. The ability to handle as many as ten hulls on the yard's slipways at one time made it extremely valuable to the war effort. As a result, the shipyard's wartime total of 40 destroyers was the third-largest in the country. Efficiencies in construction also contributed to the shipyard's outstanding contributions to the war effort. Employees at Harbor Island were able to trim the time to launch down to an average of 243 days by the end of the war,

Seattle's long connection to Navy ships and aircraft extends to the annual Seafair celebration held during several weeks in July and early August of each year. Navy ships often visit the harbor and provide the opportunity for tours. The Navy's Blue Angel aircraft demonstration team has been a regular visitor at Seafair over the years.

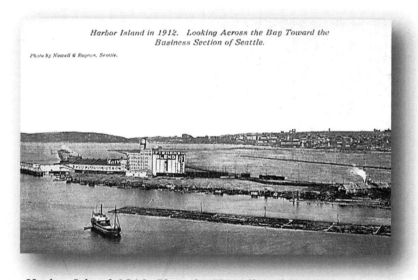

Harbor Island 1912. Photo by Newell and Rognon, Seattle, Real Photo Post Card, Author's collection

Jefferson Park, Highland Park, Laurelhurst Playground, Froula Playground, Delridge Playground, Grand Army of the Republic Cemetery near Volunteer Park, Sears Building in Downtown Seattle

Boeing Airplane Company and Todd Shipyard made Seattle a prime target for enemy attack in World War II. In January 1942, following the attack on Pearl Harbor, Army anti-aircraft guns were placed in several Seattle city parks including the Highland Park playground. In addition to guns, the 63rd Coast Artillery Regiment (Anti-Aircraft) established searchlight and barrage balloon emplacements in several locations. Barracks and messing facilities were also constructed.

Now a golf course and recreational area, Jefferson Park Golf Course on Beacon Hill was used as a site for anti-aircraft defense. It was also used as an Army recreational camp. The park is a 52-acre recreational facility bounded on the east by 24th Avenue South and 24th Place South, on the west by 15th Avenue South, on the north by South Spokane Street, and on the south by Cheasty Boulevard South. Guns, searchlights, and barrage balloons were positioned on these grounds to help defend Boeing Field and surrounding shipyards.

The Army requisitioned the rest of the park west of Beacon Avenue for a recreation center. Tents housed up to 1,000 soldiers, who utilized the recreation facilities and a gymnasium. Wives could stay in tent cabins at the park for two nights.

The park returned to city control after the war. Some of the remaining Army facilities were used for park maintenance facilities.

Searchlight batteries were placed in Woodland Park, Fort Lawton, Froula Playground, and at the Grand Army of the Republic Cemetery near Volunteer Park.

Army troops occupied Laurelhurst Park's playfield across the street from Laurelhurst Elementary School. Tents and a permanent barracks provided housing for the troops. In order to get to school, students had to walk around the installation. Ground rules for baseball games at the school during the war ensured an automatic double if anyone hit a ball into the machine gun installation at the park. The Army's occupation of the site ended when World War II concluded.

The parks were fenced off with barbed wire and were guarded by sentries. Guns and bunkers replaced lawns and flower beds. Public restrooms and sports facilities provided troops with showers and toilet facilities. Soldiers were often invited to neighborhood homes for Sunday dinners. Neighbors regretted the temporary loss of their parks, but they appreciated the feeling of security the local installations offered. At the end of the war, the Army reimbursed the city of Seattle for damages to the parks.

The Sears Building on 1st Avenue South in downtown Seattle also became the site for a 40 mm gun on the tower. Today, the building houses Starbucks Center

Starbucks Center, Seattle. formerly known as the Sears Building. Photo by Author.

Barrage Balloon Causes Air Raid Scare

During World War II, barrage balloons were tethered around potential air attack targets in Seattle. The idea was that the balloons and their cables would force enemy aircraft to fly at higher altitudes and would interfere with the ability to drop bombs.

World War II Barrage Balloon. U.S. Marine Corps photo

The balloons were tethered in various places around the city. From time to time, the balloons would get loose. On the evening of January 12, 1942, one of the balloons did so and dragged its trailing steel cables across power transmission lines north of the city. Electrical power went out immediately.

The United States had entered the war just five weeks earlier. Citizens were convinced that the sudden blackout was the result of the need to put the city into a total blackout because of approaching enemy aircraft. On Queen Anne Hill, a planned test of the air raid siren added to the confusion and to the frayed nerves of Seattle citizens. Commuters were trapped in elevators and on trolleys. Radios were silent. Citizens of Seattle were certain they were being attacked. The outage lasted from a few minutes to several hours depending on the part of the city.

The balloon descended and landed in the water just off of Richmond Beach.

As a result of the incident, Seattle City Light launched a new campaign to stop children from playing with toy balloons near power lines.

Two Airports: King County Airport & Seattle-Tacoma International Airport

In 1926, as the Navy began to use Seattle's Sand Point airfield as a base, William Boeing threatened to move his airplane business unless King County built a new airport which Boeing Aircraft Company could use. Boeing Aircraft was the largest civilian employer in the county. Losing that business would have been a severe economic blow to Seattle, as well as to the remainder of King County.

Within two years King County voters approved a plan to build a municipal airport at a cost of $950,000. The airport was originally named Boeing Field in honor of William Boeing.

Today, King County Airport (also still known as Boeing Field) serves private aircraft owners, passenger airlines, helicopters, corporate jets, military aircraft, and is home to Boeing Company's 737 flight test program. It also serves as the landing facility for Air Force One when the President of the United States visits the Seattle area.

On December 6, 1941, a day before the attack on Pearl Harbor, the field was closed to the public and was taken over by the federal government to better provide security to the Boeing production center. In early 1941, the federal government had provided $223,000 to pave the runway. Further improvements included extending the runway to over 7,500 feet in 1944. During World War II, the airport was instrumental in the production of thousands of B-17 and B-29 bombers. At this time, civilian aviation could not compete with the mission to produce military aircraft; Boeing Field was dedicated to military aircraft production. In January 1942, the Civil Aviation Authority offered one million dollars to any local government which would take on the mission of building a new regional airport. Within a month, the Port of Seattle accepted the challenge.

Two areas were on the short list for the new airport. Lake Sammamish was an early favorite since it offered the opportunity for seaplane landings for increasingly popular Alaskan flights. Safety concerns because of its proximity to the Cascade Mountains forced the Port to look south to an area at Bow Lake, approximately midway between Seattle and Tacoma on Highway 99. The site already had a small private airfield. Tacoma and Pierce County offered an additional $100,000 to build the airport there.

The site was approved in early 1942. Finished in the fall of 1944, it did not provide civilian service right away. The Army Air Force took control of the new airfield for transshipment of bomber aircraft. Two of these B-29 bombers would drop the atomic bombs that ended World War II in August 1945.

Seattle Tacoma Airport, ca.mid-1950s. Real Photo Post Card, Author's collection

Today, Sea-Tac Airport is ranked as the 17th busiest airport in the United States for passenger travel. Nearly 33,000,000 air travelers pass through it each year.

Naval Reserve Armory

The Naval Reserve Armory is located at the foot of Terry Avenue North in the South Lake Union neighborhood of Seattle. The facility was built by the Works Progress Administration (WPA) in 1941 - 1942.

In the 1930s, Seattle Naval Reservists were training and reporting for reserve duty on the USS *Eagle*, a 1919 steel patrol ship. The ship was docked at the Canadian National Dock on Lake Union. The dock was adjacent to the Seattle City Light steam plant. As a result, the ship was routinely covered with soot from the coal fired plant. Reservists began to seek a new moorage facility and petitioned the City of Seattle to move to the cleaner, relatively unused facility located at the city dock on the south end of Lake Union. At that time, talk began of building a Naval Reserve Armory at the dock.

USS Eagle 2 *(sister ship and replica of USS Eagle 56)*, date unknown. U.S. Navy Photo

Serious discussions began in 1935 when the City of Seattle agreed to convey land to the Navy with the condition that an armory's construction would begin within two years. By 1937, local newspapers reported that the armory was imminent. It was intended to house units of the Naval Reserve, Fleet Marine Corps Reserve, and units of the Sea Scouts.

The cost of building construction was estimated to be $75,000. By utilizing building materials from Fort Flagler, which was in the process of being dismantled, and barging it to Seattle, thousands of dollars could be saved. In 1937, however, the Navy couldn't afford to finance the construction and Seattle leaders proposed that the WPA be utilized to fund and carry out the construction. The WPA initially rejected the project in 1938.

Local leaders continued to knock on the doors of Congress, the Navy, and the WPA to make the project a reality. Senator Warren Magnuson took the project on and by summer of 1940 a grant of nearly $100,000 to construct the facility was signed by President Roosevelt It now had the status of a National Defense Project and ground was broken on October 5, 1940. It was to become one of the War's busiest training and mobilization facilities in the area. By the conclusion of the project, the building cost approximately $500,000.

In a ceremony honoring local citizen Mrs. Peter Barber, who had lost three sons in the Japanese attack on Pearl Harbor, it was dedicated on July 4, 1942. Designed by architects William Grant and B. Marcus Priteca, maritime themes were integrated into the Art Deco design.

During World War II, the facility served as an Advanced Naval Training School and thousands of recruits trained there during that period. A significant feature the building was an interior drill hall measuring 133 x 100 feet. Special training areas also included an indoor rifle range, a complete chart room, radio transmitter and receiver training equipment, a complete ship's bridge, and a combat information center. The facility included a "wet trainer," a watertight room which could be filed with water. The room provided sailors with experience in sealing off and then evacuating from a flooded ship's compartment.

The facility was decommissioned after the war, but received funding for renovation in 1946. It was finally disestablished as a Navy facility in 1998. The Navy donated the property to the City of Seattle in 2000 for the purpose of establishing a public park, and it was added to the National Register of Historic Places in July 2009. The facility is located in what is now Lake Union Park at 860 Terry Avenue North. It remains an imposing sight at the end of the lake. At present, the facility is the site of Seattle's Museum of History and Industry. A visit to the facility can also be combined with a visit to the Center for Wooden Boats, located next door.

Naval Reserve Armory. Photo courtesy of Washington State Department of Archaeology and Historic Preservation

Seattle City Hall Park and the Seattle Air Defense Wing

In August 1942, the Army Air Corps' Seattle Air Defense Wing was established. The defense of Seattle and the many military assets in Western Washington was critical. Assigned to Fourth Air Force, the wing was re-designated as the Seattle Fighter Wing in July 1943. Its mission provided air defense for the northwest, and it also provided trained fighter groups.

The unit was shortlived, however, and disbanded on June 7, 1944. Little remains of the air defense history of the wing other than City Hall Park. The installation was originally designated "Fortson Park" for Captain George Fortson, who died in the Philippines during the Spanish-American War.

From 1942 through 1944, the park served as the drill ground and as an outdoor recreation field for the Seattle Air Defense Wing. Quarters for the wing were at the Frye Hotel on the southeast corner.

Frye Hotel, Seattle. Post Card, Author's collection

Naval Receiving Facility, Seattle
Pier 90 - 91

As World War II loomed on the horizon, military activity on Puget Sound increased. The Navy took over two piers, Numbers 40 and 41, on Seattle's Smith Cove in March 1941. Initially, the Navy sought to condemn the properties and acquire them without compensation, but public outcry resulted in Navy payments of $3,000,000 to the City of Seattle for the piers and their facilities. (Piers 40 and 41 became Piers 90 and 91 when the Port of Seattle renumbered all Seattle Piers in 1944). The Navy also purchased private lands to develop the area north of the piers for use as a supply depot and receiving station. During and after the war, the piers hosted warships, personnel transport vessels, and cargo vessels.

The resulting Naval Station consisted of 253 acres, 53 acres of covered storage and 22.5 acres of uncovered storage for the Naval Supply Depot operations. The Naval Receiving Station included 20 barracks for enlisted, two barracks for WAVES, separate mess halls, recreation halls, an indoor swimming pool, a recreation field, and a hospital.

Pier 91 in 1944. Photo courtesy Coast Guard

Following World War II, the depot continued to operate in various capacities in support of all military branches. During the Korea and Vietnam conflicts freight movement increased. Cargo shipment during the Vietnam conflict was as high as it was during World War II.

After the Naval Supply Center opened in Bremerton, most operations moved away from Seattle. In March 1970, the Navy announced that operations at Piers 90 and 91 would be discontinued. The Port of Seattle signed a lease to operate the piers, and negotiated terms for purchase over the next few years. The Coast Guard operated support functions for its sea-going facilities there until the mid-1970s. The Port of Seattle used Pier 36, which it had owned and operated throughout the war as a down payment, and the Coast guard moved its operations there.

Today, fish processing, cold storage warehouses and cruise ship terminals occupy the Smith Cove terminal areas.

Des Moines Memorial Way South

In 1921, the Seattle Garden Club offered the idea of planting trees as a way to honor war dead from World War I. Four-year-old elms, 8 to 12 feet high, were to be planted at intervals of 60 feet on either side of what was then called High Line Road to create "a living canopy." With support from veterans groups, high school graduating classes, and various veterans groups, approximately 1,100 elm trees were planted along an eight mile stretch of road winding through SeaTac, Burien and Des Moines.

Significant to this living memorial were eight trees which recognized women who had served but never came home. Prior to World War II, women were not eligible for any of the benefits that came with military service nor were they eligible for military commissions. The Seattle Ex-Service Women's Club moved ahead, however, and sought recognition for these women. *The Seattle Times* on February 22, 1922, printed the following announcement.

DEAD SEATTLE EX-SERVICE
WOMEN TO BE HONORED

Smiling faces and courageous hearts, tender
hands and soft voices which ministered to the

> sick and wounded, cheered the gloomy and homesick, suffered and died in the cause of freedom — women "soldiers" from Seattle — will be honored tomorrow afternoon by the Ex-Service Women's club, whose members will dedicate trees to their memory along Memorial Highway near Des Moines.

Four days later a feature article appeared in *The Seattle Times:*

> The supports of the eight saplings . . . carry small silk American flags to mark them from their fellows which have been dedicated under auspices of the Seattle Garden Club to men who died in the service of their country.

Through the 1920s, the Boy Scouts maintained the trees on behalf of the Garden Club. By 1933, this responsibility had been turned over to American Legion Posts: Seattle Post #1 and Glendale (later Burien) Post #134. An ongoing committee from these Posts took over custody of the trees from the Garden Club and the Scouts. While the effort was made to maintain the memorial, elm disease and traffic eroded the effort.

In the 1960s, Dutch Elm disease destroyed elm trees throughout the Pacific Northwest. Most of the trees in the joint memorial were destroyed. As traffic increased and the roads were widened, more of the trees were removed. The Seattle Garden Club worked to replace them with a granite monument at Sunnydale School, Des Moines Memorial Drive. The monument displays the engraved names of the individuals who had died, and also shows a relief carving of an American elm.

Historic groups have joined with veterans groups to preserve this living memorial. Bronze plaques have replaced some of the trees. Banners on power poles along the road mark and commemorate the original tribute. The Des Moines Memorial Drive is the earliest "living road of remembrance" in the country. It was the only living road of remembrance to use elm trees. At approximately ten miles, it is also the longest road of remembrance.

Third Seattle Armory Becomes Seattle Center House

The very first Armory in Seattle was built on Union Street between Third and Fourth Avenues. Following the Seattle Fire in 1889, this first Armory became the seat of city government.

A second Armory replaced it in 1909, and was utilized for several years in Seattle as a site for dances and all kinds of civic events. This second facility at Virginia Street and Western Avenues looked much like a fortress. During the Great Depression in the 1930s, the Armory served as a food distribution center for Seattle.

The third National Guard Armory's construction began in 1938 and was completed the following year. Visitors to Seattle Center House at Seattle Center today could very well overlook the history of the building. Center House was originally built to serve as the Armory Building. The 146th Field Artillery and tanks occupied the building and adjacent grounds. The Armory was also home to the 66th Field Artillery Brigade. According to newspaper clippings from the time, the Armory was constructed for approximately $1,250,000.

On dedication day, April 17, 1939, Major General John O'Ryan delivered the opening address. An unannounced "invocation" however, created a bit of controversy when Rev. Louis School stepped up to the microphone and delivered a prayer with an anti-war theme. The crowd in attendance was not pleased.

The basement of Seattle Center House still shows the signs of a firing range and the remnants of swimming pool for the troops. The swimming pool was never finished.

The 1962 Seattle World Fair provided an opportunity to convert "old into new." When the possibilities of a World Fair in Seattle started to become a reality, the second floor drill hall of the old Armory was converted into the Fair's Food Circus. It was described as the first vertical shopping mall. Today, the basement area is used as storage by Seattle City Center. After decades of being known as the Food Circus, the facility is now known officially as the Seattle Center Armory and houses the Seattle Children's Museum, food outlets, and shops at Seattle Center.

A modern Seattle Armory is located at 1601 W. Armory Way.

Aerial of National Guard Armory Seattle June 29, 1939. Courtesy of MOHAI, PEMCO Webster & Stevens Collection

White River Massacre Site

An Indian attack on settlers' homes along the White River, on what was then known as Brannon's Prairie, on October 28, 1855, was a critical incident during the uneasy years of 1855 and 1856. This incident spurred the development of various forts and blockhouses throughout the area. Today, this site and the place where Army Lieutenant William A. Slaughter was killed in December of that year are now part of the City of Auburn.

Auburn was once known as Slaughter, named in tribute to the slain lieutenant. Inhabitants of the town of Slaughter, however, realized that the town's name might be detrimental to business. The local hotel was called the "Slaughter House." Residents agreed that the town's name should be changed, and it was subsequently named Auburn.

Until 1906, the Green River flowed into the White River in downtown Auburn. In 1906, however, the White River changed course above Auburn after a major flood and afterwards emptied into the Puyallup River. The lower portion of the historic White River is now considered part of the Green River.

Two markers in a small park in the City of Auburn commemorate the Indian attack on the settlers' homes and also the location where Army Lieutenant Slaughter was killed.

The park is just to the north of downtown Auburn next to the Green River. It is located along the old Kent-Auburn Highway, at the junction of 30th Street NE and Auburn Way North.

Memorials

Numerous memorials to soldiers, sailors, marines, and airmen, have been erected throughout King County. Some are simple plaques, while others are more elaborate parks with historical military memorabilia. Two in particular are noted here.

Seattle Memorial Stadium at the northeast corner of the Seattle Center grounds was dedicated in 1947 as a tribute to Seattle youth who perished in World War II. A memorial wall is inscribed with over 700 names of fallen service members.

Another site of interest is Hamlin Park in Shoreline. The Southeast corner of the park was used as a marching and parade ground for the Fircrest Naval Hospital. It was also used for various military maneuvers and training in World War II.

Hamlin Park. Photo used by permission of Larry Neilson. Photo copyright © 2010 by Larry Neilson / Big BadBattleships.com

At the park, two 8"/35 caliber guns (254 mm) which were used at the Battle of Manila Bay, May 1, 1898, aboard the *Boston* are displayed. Hamlin Park is just off 15th Avenue NE in Shoreline.

Naval Training Center, University of Washington

In World War I, the University of Washington offered space for a military training camp. The Washington Naval Militia established a training center there in the summer of 1917. The Center trained young men and women in basic naval skills. Women were trained to be "Yeomen F" (F for female) and become ready to take on clerical positions and serve as telephone operators.

The camp consisted of tents and some temporary construction and was located on the present site of the University of Washington Health Sciences complex. On the main campus, Lewis Hall served as an officers' hospital and Clark Hall served as the camp's enlisted hospital. Both hospitals provided essential care during the 1918 flu epidemic.

The Naval Training Center trained approximately 5,000 personnel before it closed in 1919 at the conclusion of World War I. Both Lewis Hall and Clark Hall are used today as classrooms and offices.

Seattle Naval Hospital

Hospital beds were in short supply during World War II. As wounded returned from the Pacific theatre, large hospitals in such as Oak Knoll Naval Hospital in Oakland, California were not sufficient. The Puget Sound Naval Shipyard Hospital in Bremerton was not able to be expanded to meet expected needs. Seattle was selected as an alternative site for the receipt of patients due to its location on the coast, but also due to its ready access to transportation resources including sea lanes, rail, air fields and a good road system.

Construction began on the Seattle Naval Hospital in March 1942 and it opened in August of the same year. It was located on 165 acres in Shoreline, north of Seattle, at 15th Avenue NE and NE 159th Street.

The hospital had a 500-bed capacity in a series of 41 one-story wood-frame wards. It had two surgical wards, a surgery building with four operating rooms, and staff quarters for 780 personnel. The first wounded from the South Pacific arrived in January 1943. Special hospital trains from San Francisco brought large groups of patients to Seattle. As the war continued, patient loads soon exceed the hospital capacity. An expansion program, approved in May 1943, added another 500 beds to the facility. In July of 1943, Eleanor Roosevelt visited the hospital and made it a point to visit wounded in all of the hospital's seven wards.

Near the end of the war a five-wing building for military dependents' care opened. In 1945 hospital staff included 15 Seattle physicians and surgeons serving as navy doctors. The hospital ultimately reached a capacity of 1,500 beds, but had 2,000 patients at its peak. Overflowing with incoming and recovering patients, the wounded were often placed in hallways and other available space.

The hospital closed after World War II, and the facility was transferred to King County in 1947. The Firland Sanitarium, a tuberculosis hospital, relocated 399 tuberculosis patients from its old facilities in the Richmond Highlands area to the former naval hospital on November 25, 1947. By 1948 the population had grown to 750 patients.

Firland occupied the facility until October 1973. In 1952 the Fircrest School for developmentally disabled patients moved into one section of the former naval facility. The two facilities were separated by a fence.

In 1961, eighty-five acres were transferred to Shorecrest School District to become the site of Shorecrest High School.

Robinson Point Lighthouse

The Robinson Point Lighthouse is located on Maury Island, approximately halfway between Seattle and Tacoma. The Point was named by the Wilkes Expedition in 1841 to honor John Robinson, who was part of the historic expedition which mapped and documented flora and fauna along the west coast.

In 1879, the Lighthouse Board recommended that a steam fog whistle help mark the island. The Board requested $7,000 for the new station. In 1883, $8,000 was appropriated for the new signal. The landowner of the 26 acres wanted $2,000 for the property. The Lighthouse Board considered that to be an exorbitant price so the process of condemnation was initiated. During the lengthy legal proceedings of condemnation, however, the landowner died, and the heirs subsequently agreed to lower the price to $1,000.

Construction began during early summer of 1884, was put on hold through the winter months and began again in March 1885. Water was brought to the station from pits dug at the base of the bluff and a 350-foot trough moved the water out to the point. Cisterns stored water for the fog signal which had once served Point Adams Lighthouse on the Oregon Coast. The first building was a 36 x 16-foot structure to house the boiler and fog signal machinery.

The keeper's residence was a one-and-a-half story house erected approximately 630 feet south of the fog signal. A cistern also stored water for the residence. The first residence measured 20 x 3 feet. Construction on the station was completed in June 1885, and fog signal operation began on July 1 of that year. Franklin Tucker, the keeper at Cape Flattery on the Olympic Peninsula, was transferred to Point Robinson to become the head keeper.

Robinson Point Lighthouse with fog signal. Photo courtesy of the U.S. Coast Guard

The light shone fixed red and was originally attached to a 25-foot post. It began operating in December 1887. Its placement, however, raised complaints from mariners because the light was obscured by the keeper's house for ships moving from Tacoma north to Seattle. In 1894 the height of the light was increased by 5 ½ feet. A frame tower was constructed for the light in 1897.

The Robinson Point station was an extremely popular post for keepers and their families. Originally, the station was maintained by a single keeper. In 1897, Keeper Charles Davis reported that the steam whistle had blown for 528 hours during the previous year. Thirty-five tons of coal per year was required for the boilers. Keepers were required to shovel the coal, and Keeper Davis requested an assistant to help shovel that amount of coal in coming years. The Lighthouse Board requested a Congressional appropriation of $3,000 for a second dwelling. Congress did not provide funding until 1906, but by then the cost had risen to $5,000.

Construction bids were solicited, but came in much higher than the appropriated amount. A working party was formed and construction began on the new home. The second dwelling was not completed until 1907.

The current lighthouse, completed in 1915, has a 38-foot tower and a fifth-order Fresnel lens. A third-class reed horn, which was powered by compressed air, replaced the original steam whistle. The first light was produced by an incandescent oil vapor lamp. Both the light and the fog signal were converted to electric power in 1918. The Robinson Point Lighthouse is a twin of the structure built two years earlier on Alki Point.

Robinson Point Light was automated in 1978. The original fifth-order Fresnel lens was kept in place and was active in the lantern room until 2008. After more than ninety years of active service, the lens was replaced with a plastic beacon which was mounted outside the lantern room. The light now shines two white flashes every twelve seconds: on for three seconds, off for one second, on for another three seconds, and off for five seconds.

Modern radar and radio signal towers are now located at Point Robinson to assist Puget Sound Vessel Traffic Service in monitoring ship traffic in the south Sound.

In the 1990s, discussions indicated that the site might be available for leasing for a seafood-processing plant. Local citizens joined together to form Keepers of Robinson Point and partnered with the Vashon Parks Department to lease the property from the Coast Guard to help conserve the site. The dwellings are now available for weekly rentals.

Aerial view Robinson Point Light, 1950.
U.S. Coast Guard photo

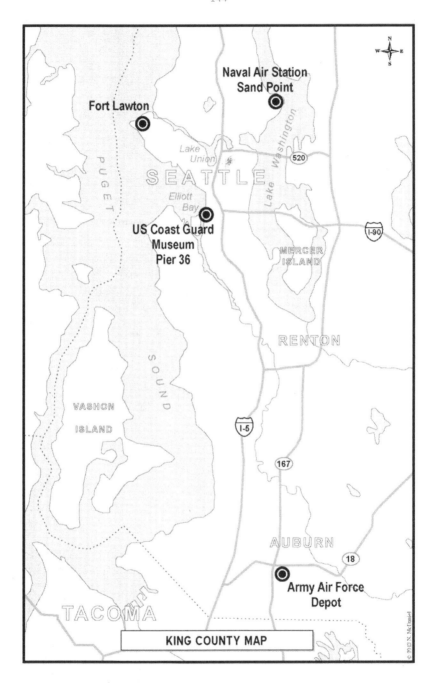

Chapter 7
Pierce County

Fort Lewis

In 1916, citizens of Tacoma and south Puget Sound were becoming concerned about the war that was taking place in Europe. A civilian business and professional men's military-like training camp was held at American Lake to provide training to patriotic citizens. The camp had been organized by private civilians and encouraged awareness and a high degree of personal readiness for all citizens. Stephen Appleby, a Tacoma bank cashier was a member of this cadet corps, and vice-president of the Northwest Business Men's Preparedness League.

Appleby had been a captain in the Minnesota National Guard and was familiar with the process the Army used to establish new posts. He also was aware that an Army survey team was looking for potential sites in the area, but the camp site near American Lake was not on their list of places to visit. Appleby took the initiative and contacted the survey leader, Captain Richard Parks, and convinced him that the survey team should visit the American Lake camp.

The team did, indeed, visit and was favorably impressed with the potential site as well as its adjoining properties. Tacoma business leaders supported building an army camp. These same business leaders formed a committee to travel to Washington, D.C. to meet directly with the Secretary of War. The committee proposed that 70,000 acres would be donated to the federal government with the proviso that it become a permanent military installation. The concept of this proposed gift was presented to President Wilson and soon the offer of this gift to the nation was approved.

Back in Pierce County, a ballot to allow the issuance of bonds to pay the $2 million purchase price was submitted to the people. Eighty-six percent of Pierce County voters voted to purchase and subsequently donate the land to the federal government for the purpose of a military camp. Pierce County then purchased 62,433 acres and donated them to the United States.

Construction began in May 1917. The first two buildings were ready by June 1917. One of them was the headquarters building and the other was the administrative office for the construction company, Hurley-Mason. At the peak of construction activities, ten thousand workers were employed to put in water lines, sewer lines, and 1,757 buildings. When completed, the capacity of the camp was estimated at 44,685 soldiers within a 2,500 acre compound. Camp Lewis had been built at the lowest cost per capita of any U.S. Army base to date--$142 per assigned soldier. The most expensive, Battle Creek, Michigan, cost $182.

Wood frame construction was used throughout the camp. Dormitories were two-story buildings with a mess hall/kitchen on the first floor. Heat came from coal stoves in the barracks. Steam from boilers in each building provided heat in the officers' quarters. Latrines and showers were placed between the barracks in separate buildings.

On July 18, 1917, the new camp was named Camp Lewis per War Department General Order No. 95. Named after Captain Meriwether Lewis, the commander of the Lewis and Clark expedition, this new camp was the second largest of the then 16 National Army camps.

Hurley-Mason Construction workers were rightly proud of their accomplishments and donated funds to build a gate which would span the road leading to the headquarters building. Named "Liberty Gate," it stood at its original location for 40 years until it was moved during the construction of Interstate 5.

The Ninety-first Division was the first unit to occupy the new camp. By December 1917, the population of the camp totaled 37,000 officers and enlisted. Major General Henry Greene began to train citizen-soldiers into a viable fighting force. Troops coming from Washington and Alaska wore uniforms which had a green fir-tree insignia. Training in anticipation of deployment to Europe, the recruits learned close order drill and hand-to-hand combat, and attempted to become proficient marksmen. They engaged in mock trench warfare and practiced for gas attacks in specially constructed rooms.

Main Gate at Fort Lewis, Photo by Ellis, Real Photo Post Card, Author's collection. Note: This gate is also known as Liberty Gate

Back in Washington, D.C., President Wilson was becoming concerned about the morale of his fighting forces. He created a Commission on Training Camp Activities (CTCA) to help provide a more wholesome atmosphere. The Commission brought in community recreation activities including sports, libraries, and entertainment. The Ninety-first Division also had football and baseball teams which included professional players who had been drafted or had joined to help the war effort. In 1919, the Camp team played a Marine team in the Rose Bowl. (The Marines won 19 to 7.)

The CTCA was also concerned with "diverse and open dens of vice" in Seattle where troops often went on off-duty weekends. As a result, General Greene made Seattle off-limits from the fall of 1917 until 1918. To make the camp more appealing, Greene proposed the design and construction of recreation centers, theatres, restaurants, ice cream parlors, banks, etc. Located across the main road from the camp (Pacific Highway), the new recreation oriented section was named Greene Park.

A hotel, which came to be known as Red Shield Inn opened on December 7, 1919. Today it is the only surviving facility of Greene Park and serves as the Fort Lewis Museum.

Fort Lewis Museum, ca. 2009. Photo by Author

As World War I continued, the Ninety-first trained and eventually shipped out in June 1918. Its first combat came with the Meuse-Argonne battle in September under the leadership of Major General William Johnston. In October, the unit fought in Belgium in the Battle of Flanders, which was to become one of the final battles of the war.

With the end of World War I, the population of Camp Lewis declined as well as the state of facility repair. General Pershing visited in January 1920 and noted that the buildings were in need of maintenance. Some barracks and hospital buildings had been converted to homes. Some buildings had been destroyed by fire. As a result the physical appearance of the camp fell far short of the original idea for a military installation. Later that year, approximately 500 horses arrived from Camp Dodge, Iowa. By 1921, Camp Lewis had become the home for eight polo teams, and effectively introduced polo to Western Washington. In 1921, the Fort also became the headquarters for the 3d Infantry Division. Most of the Division was, however, scattered throughout several western states. Only 850 to 1,000 troops from the Division were stationed at Camp Lewis.

Tacoma citizens were becoming extremely disillusioned with the new Army post. Soldiers assigned were fewer in number than had been planned. Buildings were in disrepair. Community leaders from the Tacoma Rotary Club and the *Tacoma News Tribune* asked the government either to station more troops there, or to return the land to Pierce County. They noted that not only had county citizens had to pay $187,000 per year to pay off the bond, they were also losing approximately $100,000 in property taxes.

By 1925, the state of military posts across the nation was receiving attention in Congress. Hearings were held regarding the deterioration and the future of these properties. Testimony indicated that barracks and family housing were essentially unsafe. Hearings resulted in some facilities being sold, and the proceeds of these properties being used to fund renovation of remaining facilities. Camp Lewis did well. It received the largest share of appropriations, and funding was made available for housing and a hospital, to begin the construction of red brick barracks and other buildings. In 1927, Camp Lewis was renamed Fort Lewis, and it was designated to become a permanent post.

In the 1920s a steel balloon hangar which had been disassembled at Fort Casey was reassembled at Camp Lewis. In 1938, balloons gave way to a greater use of fixed wing aircraft and construction began on Gray Airfield, named after Captain Lawrence C. Gray, an Army balloonist who had been killed in an air crash. By June 1939, McChord Field, adjacent to Fort Lewis, was also under construction by Works Progress Administration personnel. McChord Field was named after Colonel William Caldwell McChord, a military training aviator who had been killed in an air crash in Virginia. Aircraft exhibitions captured the imagination and secured the pride of Tacoma citizens. Later that same year Japanese bombers began to venture into China and Korea. Airpower was becoming a more important force than ever before. The two airfields, Gray and McChord, were becoming integral to the preparation for the national defense.

Units at Fort Lewis

3rd Infantry Division

2nd Infantry Division

4th Infantry Division

The 3d Infantry Division and other Fort Lewis personnel numbered approximately 5,000 in 1938. By July 1940, the post garrison numbered 7,000 with the arrival of IX Army Corps who moved to Lewis from the Presidio in San Francisco. When the Selective Service Act was passed in September 1940, troops assigned to Fort Lewis numbered approximately 26,000 guardsmen and regulars. Room in barracks became scarce and construction began again.

Maintaining its designation as a training base throughout World War II, Fort Lewis was responsible for training some of the war's most notable fighting units including the 2nd, 3rd, 33rd, 40th, 41st, 44th, and 96th Infantry Divisions. In addition several brigades and smaller units also received training at Fort Lewis. In 1943, an addition to the hospital made it one of the largest in the nation. Dedicated to Colonel Frank Madigan, the sprawling hospital had eight miles of corridors and hundreds of wards.

By July 1944, the post was designated as an Army Service Forces Training Center, the largest facility in the nation training medics and engineers exclusively. The 2nd Infantry Division went to England in September 1943 and subsequently deployed to Normandy on June 7, 1944, D-Day Plus One. After Normandy, the Division went on to help capture Brest, was deeply involved in the Battle of the Bulge, went on into Germany, and was in

Czechoslovakia at the end of the war. The 2nd returned to Fort Lewis in 1955, but was moved to Alaska in 1956. That same year the 4th Infantry Division arrived but was quickly reorganized as a Combat Division.

32nd
*Infantry
Division*

During the Berlin Crisis of 1961, the 32nd Infantry Division was called to active duty and resided at Fort Lewis until 1962. By July 1966, elements of the 4th Division were leaving for Vietnam and by September, the Division had entirely departed.

Fort Lewis was also beginning to expand its sphere of responsibility south to the Columbia River. Vancouver Barracks on the Columbia River became a sub-post in 1958. Camp Bonneville, a training area near Vancouver, Washington, was also used as a training area by Fort Lewis troops. Fort Lawton became a sub-post in 1965.

As the U.S Army Personnel Center, Oakland became overloaded due to the Vietnam conflict, the U.S. Army Personnel Center, Fort Lewis was established. This center consisted of an Overseas Replacement Station, a Returnee-Reassignment Station, and a Transfer Station.

Training once again became a focus for Fort Lewis. The U.S. Army Training Center, Infantry, Fort Lewis was activated in May 1966. A Drill Sergeants' School was established in August of the same year to produce qualified drill sergeants to train in the Training Center. By January 1968, Fort Lewis was officially the United States Army Training Center, Infantry, Fort Lewis.

In June 1968, the 62nd Medical Group was transferred out of Germany to Fort Lewis. With an effective, distinguished history throughout World War II, it has continued to serve in Southwest Asia in both Operations Desert Storm and Desert Shield, in Operation Restore Hope in Somalia, and numerous humanitarian relief efforts.

In 1972, Fort Lewis was designated Headquarters, 9th Infantry Division. Then Army Chief of Staff General William Westmoreland passed the colors to Major General Fulton on May 26, thereby signaling the reactivation of the "Old Reliables."

Fort Lewis' relevance to Pacific operations was enhanced with the activation of I Corps in October 1981. I Corps and Fort Lewis were extremely substantial contributors to Desert Shield and Desert Storm in 1990-1991.

Following September 11, 2001, I Corps and Fort Lewis assumed a leading role in the War on Terrorism. The Brigades, equipped with Stryker armored vehicles (named for Medal of Honor recipients Private First Class Stuart Stryker (1924 -1945) and Specialist Four Robert Stryker (1944-1967) have deployed to Iraq and Afghanistan. It became the first all-volunteer division in the U.S. Army.

62nd Medical Brigade

I Corps

9th Infantry Division

Fort Lewis Leaders and Legends

Many notable officers spent time at Fort Lewis. One of them went on to become President of the United States. Then Lieutenant Colonel Dwight Eisenhower reported for duty in February 1940. He joined the 15th Infantry Regiment as 1st Battalion commander and as regimental executive officer. The Eisenhower

House is today located at 2310 Clark Road and is identified with a plaque.

His wife, Mamie, was fond of the Officers' Club china which had at its center a drawing of Liberty Gate. She ordered a set of her own from the manufacturer and today this set of china is on exhibit at the Eisenhower Museum in Abilene, Kansas. Their son, John, attended and graduated from Stadium High School in Tacoma and then went on to West Point and later to receive the rank of Brigadier General. In 1941, Colonel Eisenhower was selected as the 3rd Infantry Division Chief of Staff, and then subsequently assumed the Chief of Staff position in IX Corps.

Life at Fort Lewis in World War II

After the attack on Pearl Harbor on December 7, 1941, Fort Lewis assumed battle conditions. The 115th Cavalry Regiment established defenses along Puget Sound beaches.

The 3rd Infantry Division set up defenses on post and the 41st Infantry Division also set up positions around Fort Lewis, Camp Murray, and McChord Field. (They later deployed to New Guinea and experienced more jungle combat than any other Army Division.)

Fort Lewis remained segregated until after President Truman's Executive Order in 1948 to desegregate. Until the Korean Conflict, there were separate facilities throughout the Fort. In 1945, however, a significant step towards integration occurred when Marie Lindsey, a 21-year-old black woman, was appointed as a librarian. Her selection to this position was unheard of at the time. By 1951, she was promoted to Chief Librarian and was instrumental in the design of new library facilities.

In 1943, Fort Lewis became the site for German and Italian Prisoner of War compounds. The prisoners worked around the post and at the Mount Rainier Ordnance Depot, the vehicle repair center. The main German POW compound was located at Gray Field in temporary barracks originally built for soldiers in training.

1943 Barracks, Fort Lewis. Real Photo Post Card, photographer unknown. Author's collection

Post Chapel, ca. 1945. Photo by Ellis, Real Photo Post Card, Author's collection

Airships at Fort Lewis, ca.1943. Ellis Post Card, Author's collection.

Today, Fort Lewis' wooden barracks have been replaced with brick and mortar construction. Modern facilities replace temporary buildings. A state of the art Madigan Army Medical Center replaces the rambling wooden buildings which comprised the base hospital.

Fort Lewis Became Part of Joint Base Lewis McChord

In February 2010, Fort Lewis became part of Joint Base Lewis McChord (JBLM). The principal Army maneuver units stationed at JBLM are US I Corps, 2nd Brigade, 3rd Brigade and 4th Brigade 2nd Infantry Division; all of which are constituted as Stryker Brigades. JBLM is also home to the 17th Fires Brigade, the 62nd Medical Brigade, the 593rd Sustainment Brigade, the 555th Engineer Brigade, the 42nd Military Police Brigade, the 201st Battlefield Surveillance Brigade, the 11th Signal Brigade, the I Corps NCO Academy Headquarters, the Western Region Cadet Command, the 1st Personnel Support Group, the 1st Special Forces Group (Airborne), 2d Ranger Battalion, the 75th Ranger Regiment, and Headquarters 5th Army (West).

Mount Rainier Ordnance Depot

The Fort Lewis vehicle repair facility, Fort Lewis Motor Base, was constructed in 1941 to rebuild Army trucks. Just two months later, after the Japanese attack on Pearl Harbor, the nation moved headlong into war mobilization. More buildings were added in 1942 and the facility expanded to become the Fort Lewis Quartermaster Motor Base.

In August 1942 the U.S. Quartermaster Corps turned over vehicle repair to the Ordnance Corps, and the facility came to be known as the Fort Lewis Ordnance Base. The facility continued to grow with more warehouses and storage areas, and by December of 1942, the facility was renamed as the Mount Rainier Ordnance Depot. (MROD)

MROD served Washington, Oregon, Idaho, Montana and Alaska. As the war continued, the depot also picked up the responsibility of the Pacific Theater of Operations as a major part of its mission. Located near railway lines, State Highway 99, and next door to McChord Field, the depot was in a perfect position to move finished products back to the field. The Port of Tacoma and shipping facilities in Seattle also served MROD.

By early 1943, MROD was working on nearly 1,000 vehicles each month. Vehicles were moved down assembly lines where skilled workers replaced parts, cleaned engines, replaced belts, and reassembled them for deployment. Small arms repair was also part of the mission. As small arms were repaired and restored, they moved into a box and crate shop where they were packed and prepared to go back to the front.

Local high schools, most notably Clover Park School District in Lakewood, began to train high school students to work in the depots. Students could take classes in machine drawing and blueprint reading as well as pre-aviation courses. In September 1942, Secretary of War Henry L. Stinson asked the nation to double the number of women working in support of defense industries. Clover Park High School established a women's mechanic-training program and with federal funding, became one of the first school in the country to train women in this field. The school's eight-week courses culminated in students taking a basket filled with vehicle parts and assembling an engine. After the engine was assembled, the instructor handed the student a key to start it. If it started and ran, she had a job on the assembly line at $1.50 per

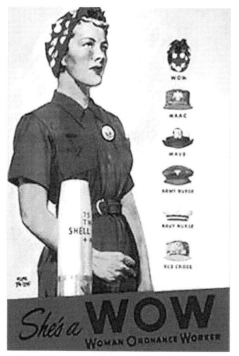

U.S. Army Poster She's a WOW Woman Ordnance Worker

hour. The experiment was a success. Only 1 percent of the students failed to graduate.

The women in the critically important ordnance depots were called the WOWs--Women Ordnance Workers. Approximately 85,000 WOWs worked in depots across the country. As a badge of their unique status, the women wore a red bandana for wear at work.

Women represented 44% of the entire MROD work force. Affordable housing was quickly constructed for them at American Lake Gardens.

The wartime workload was greater than the capacity of the depot even though the depot operated 11 hours each day, 7 days a week.

In June 1944, an Italian Service Unit (ISU) arrived. These men wore U.S. uniforms with the U.S. crest buttons removed but with a shoulder patch that read "Italy." Two companies served at MROD, living in barracks in the MROD camp. German POWs from the Fort Lewis prisoner-of-war camps also served at the depot. Many worked in the wood salvage yard.

By 1944, MROD was operating at its highest capacity and was overhauling 1,000 vehicles each month. Over 2,300 people were employed by 1945. At war's end, many of the WOW workers left. Most did not find comparable jobs in the civilian world; bias against women in an automobile shop made employment extremely difficult.

MROD workers were proud of their contributions and wanted a structure resembling the main gate of Fort Lewis. The MROD gate would be a monument to their contribution to the war and the United States' victory. Construction started in January of 1945, with the top cross timber reading Mount

Rainier Ordnance Depot. The structure is still there and can be seen just off of Interstate 5, although the sign now reads Fort Lewis Logistics Center.

Fort Lewis Logistics Center Gateway. U.S. Army photo

United States efforts in Korea brought increased work and once again the depot went to expanded shifts, employing nearly 2,000 people. By 1961, however, the Department of Defense announced its plan to close the depot and move its functions to Utah. Despite lobbying by the Washington Congressional delegation, the decisions to close remained firm and the center began to reduce functions.

In 1962, the depot was renamed the Mount Rainier Army Depot and functions changed to repair of communications systems. In August 1963, the Mount Rainier Army Depot became part of Fort Lewis and subsequently renamed the Fort Lewis Logistics Center. Its functions now include warehousing, and limited repair services. Offices of the Army and Air Force Exchange Service (AAFES) are now located there and so is the Defense Reutilization and Marketing Office (DRMO). The Fort Lewis Logistics Center continues to repair and salvage equipment and support deployments.

Most of the original World War II wooden buildings were demolished after MROD became the Fort Lewis Logistics Center. Of the nearly 200, there are now approximately 30 left.

The contributions of this vital organization extended far beyond the war effort. Training programs for women and their successful employment at the depot helped develop a firm foundation for women's employment outside of traditional jobs. Training programs in local high schools helped set the stage for one of the state's prime vocational training high schools.

Prisoners of War, Fort Lewis

Only a few records show that Fort Lewis was a Prisoner of War (POW) facility during World War II. The first POWs arrived in early 1942--four Japanese, two Italians, and one German. The Japanese and Italians were moved to other POW camps, and soon the camp was filled with only German prisoners. Approximately 4,000 German prisoners of war were held at Fort Lewis during World War II from 1942 to 1946. The Fort Lewis Military Museum has a roster that lists the names of those prisoners.

Five camps are known to have been located on Fort Lewis. Many of the prisoners were from the Afrika Corps. Others had been captured in Italy and France. Some were captured in June 1944 at Normandy. Maps which show the locations of the various camps are not available. Speculation is that they were classified to help prevent escape if they were ever to fall into the hands of the prisoners or German sympathizers.

Photos are not available. Photographing prisoners was a violation of the Geneva Convention. International Red Cross reports found the prison conditions to be fair and acceptable. Wayne Shoemaker, who had been a clerk at the camp, wrote an article about the POW camp experience for a 1993 *Fort Lewis Military Museum Association Newsletter.*

Shoemaker noted that he had been assigned as guard and as the company clerk between 1944 and 1945 because he was the only one in his unit who could type. Shoemaker's description of the five camps noted that one of the camps was located just inside the Fort Lewis main gate, north of Gray Army Airfield. Another was on the east side of the field and seemed to house the more disruptive POWs and Nazi Party members. An additional camp was near the current Logistics Center, adjacent to what is now Interstate 5.

Barbed wire and guard towers marked the camp

perimeters. Weapons were not allowed, so if some degree of force was required to keep order, guards had to call on soldiers outside of the compound. Each camp had its own mess hall, barracks, barbershop, libraries, and beer hall. Camps also had their own newspapers.

POWs were employed at maintaining the camp, clearing brush, mending uniforms, or in crop harvests in the area. Paid 80 cents per day, they could spend their wages on beer or supplied recreational equipment in the camps.

Escapes were not common, because there was no escape network once outside. For the most part, the prisoners received better food and had better living conditions than they had had in the German Army. Shoemaker noted that even if they could escape back to Germany, it would mean a return to the war.

Shoemaker also noted that he often shared morning cake and coffee with the prisoners. They would always shake his hand and rise in a Nazi salute when he entered or left a room. Friendships developed over the cake and coffee and he noted in this article that they even surprised him with a birthday cake for his May 1945 birthday. He wrote that the cake was a six-layer sponge cake with cherry and pineapple filling.

One escape did occur, however, when Kurt Zimmerman escaped by hanging under a truck as it left the camp. Zimmerman found the way to Seattle and lived with a woman there for about two weeks. She kicked him out after an argument. He subsequently turned himself in and asked that he be returned to Fort Lewis.

Shoemaker also wrote about a "wedding" he had attended. A German prisoner had the glove of his fiancée with him. His fiancée back in Germany allegedly had his helmet. Ceremonies took place both in Fort Lewis and in Germany, and the couple regarded themselves as married. He commented that all of the POWs celebrated with home-made liquor that they had distilled from raisins and cherries.

Shoemaker was eventually transferred to Arizona. The POWs wrote him a letter to take with him to show to any German POWs in Arizona at his new station. The letter wrote that Shoemaker was honest and strict, but fair. The letter was signed by all the POWs in the camp. They also petitioned Fort Lewis commanders to keep him at Fort Lewis. Shoemaker declined offers to allow him to stay and decided to accept his original orders.

The camps remained in operation until 1946 until German POWs were repatriated. A handful of graves of POWs who had died of war wounds or disease are still to be seen in the Fort Lewis cemetery.

Camp Harmony
(Puyallup Assembly Center)

Camp Harmony was not a military installation. It was not a stockade to keep hostile natives out. It was site where people were detained. It was a temporary facility located at the Western Washington Fairgrounds in Puyallup, where Japanese Americans were forced to gather due to heightened war tensions and distrust of Japanese citizens in the months following the attack on Pearl Harbor. Japanese-Americans, known as Nikkei, were detained there per President Roosevelt's Executive Order 9066. This order set into motion 110,000 Japanese Americans from their West Coast homes. Camp Harmony served as one of several temporary stops until the families could be transferred to more permanent "relocation centers." The name Camp Harmony was first used by an Army public relations officer as the center was being constructed. Approximately 7,500 people were housed there during the process of "relocation."

When the Executive Order was signed, local Nikkei farmers from the Kent, White River, and Puyallup River Valleys quickly had to negotiate long-term leases to transfer farm machinery to other farmers in the area. The government indicated that the farmers should plant for the 1942 growing season and took planting as a sign of national loyalty. Neglected crops and damaged crops were interpreted as acts of sabotage.

"Civil control stations," such as Camp Harmony, were set up by the Wartime Civil Control Administration to register families and provide pre-induction medical screening. The centers also helped arrange for storage and sale of properties. Each family was given a five digit identification number and a day to arrive at departure sites with their personal belongings.

At Camp Harmony, families used mess halls, communal latrines and shower rooms, and lived in barracks. Leaking roofs on hastily constructed buildings made the 1942 wet spring even wetter. The residents used their cooking skills in the mess halls, as clerks in organizing activities, and as teachers for their children. Sports teams were organized and competed in an intramural system. Women had knitting, sewing and crochet groups.

As the nation's farm families sent their young men off to war, residents of Camp Harmony were recruited to help harvest crops throughout Oregon, Idaho, and Montana. Most of the transfers out of Camp Harmony were to the newly constructed relocation centers in California. Transfers began in June and continued through October of 1942. Camp Harmony was closed in November 1942.

Most of the resident areas of Camp Harmony are now parking lots for the Western Washington State Fairgrounds. Nothing remains to remind fairgoers what took place there during 1942.

Fort Steilacoom

Fort Steilacoom, south of what is now Tacoma, was founded by the U.S. Army in 1849 as a result of the increasing tensions that began with the massacre at the Whitman mission in 1847. Dr. Marcus Whitman, his wife, and eleven others were killed by local Cayuse and Umatilla natives. The killings are usually ascribed in part to a clash of cultures and in part to the inability of Dr. Whitman, a physician, halt the spread of measles among the Native Americans, who then held Whitman responsible for subsequent deaths. The incident remains controversial to this day: the Whitmans are regarded by some as pioneer heroes; others see them as white settlers who attempted to impose their religion on the Native Americans living near their Walla Walla mission.

The Whitman massacre was only the beginning of a troubled time as the West coast became more settled due to the influx of settlers heading to the California Gold Rush; Fort Steilacoom became another element in the Pacific Defense System, and helped establish an American power symbol in the region.

On the west side of the Cascades, local natives were not happy with the treaties which had been imposed on them. Most of the treaties, including the Treaty of Point No Point, the Point Elliott Treaty, and the Medicine Creek Treaty had the unfortunate result of curtailing traditional fishing rights by restricting natives to reservation lands. As a consequence, tribes began to feel that they had been misled, and in addition were in danger of being eradicated by starvation. The Nisqually tribe attacked white settlers along the White River on October 29, 1855, as a result of their unhappiness with the Treaty of Medicine Creek.

In 1855, Chief Leschi of the Nisqually Tribe, traveled to the territorial capital at Olympia to protest the terms of the treaty. That October, Acting Governor Mason ordered that Leschi and his brother Quiemuth be taken into "protective custody," and sent the militia after them. The Puget Sound War of 1855-1856 had begun. Leschi became war chief, in command of around 300 men. He led a small number of raids which spread panic among the white population. Earlier, Territorial militiamen Abram Moses and Joseph Miles had been killed and Territorial authorities blamed the killings on Leschi. Despite the Acting Governor's order, the chief managed to remain at large for well over a year.

In November 1855, the first Regular Army forces arrived at Fort Steilacoom under the command of Captain Erasmus Darwin Keyes of the 3rd Artillery Regiment. Shortly thereafter, a new post commander, Lieutenant Colonel Silas Casey, 9th Infantry Regiment arrived.

Following a series of murders along the White River, Fort Steilacoom became a refuge for settlers fleeing from the perceived threat of local native tribal insurgents. The fort was, however, seriously undermanned for the tasks for which it was responsible. Regular Army and Volunteer forces were busy responding to local skirmishes and maintaining a patrol in the area. In December 1855, one of Fort Steilacoom's most notable officers, Lieutenant. William Slaughter, was killed in an ambush along the Green River. He and the two soldiers killed with him were brought back to the Fort for burial.

Captain Erasmus Keyes. Library of Congress photo

Not all settlers were sure that Chief Leschi was the problem. Many settlers recognized the situation for what it was and blamed the Government for the resulting problems.

Governor Stevens was convinced that settlers were providing cover and helping Leschi hide, and as a result, he declared martial law over Pierce County in April 1856.

Leschi was taken into custody in November 1856, and his brother Quiemuth turned himself in shortly thereafter. Quiemuth was murdered on November 18, 1856, by an unknown assailant in Governor Stevens's office in Olympia, where he was being held for the night on his way to the jail at Fort Steilacoom. Leschi was put on trial in 1858 for the murder of Colonel Moses, which he denied having committed, and was sentenced to hang.

Notable citizens and federal officers were opposed to his hanging. James Bachelder, who had once served as the post sutler and subsequently held the appointment of U.S. Commissioner and Justice of the Peace, Third Judicial District, Washington Territory, also stood on the side of Chief Leschi. Bachelder joined the officers of Fort Steilacoom in objecting to the execution of Leschi in 1858. He used his power as Justice of the Peace to delay the execution by arresting the Pierce County Sheriff on the day of the execution on January 22, 1858. Bachelder was hung in effigy by the citizens of Olympia and was later removed from office.

Lieutenant Colonel Silas Casey. Library of Congress photo

Leschi's first trial had resulted in a hung jury because of the judge's instruction that killing of combatants during wartime did not constitute murder. In a second trial, he was convicted and sentenced to death. Lieutenant Colonel Casey demanded that his execution not be on the fort and further demanded that if he must be executed it was to happen at least 300 yards off post and that his soldiers not be in any way involved in the hanging. Chief Leschi was hanged in what is now the city of Lakewood on February 19, 1858. He was exonerated 146 years later in 2004.

By 1857, Lieutenant Colonel Casey was successful in gaining federal funds to modernize the fort and potentially make it a more appropriate headquarters for the 9th Infantry.

With a diminished native threat, the mission of the Fort shifted more to the functions road-building and providing a law enforcement presence in the area. Stick-frame and brick structures replace log structures. Foundation bricks were fired on site and lumber was obtained from local mills.

Road building efforts were spurred by the concern over supply routes between Vancouver Barracks on the Columbia River and Fort Steilacoom and then north to Fort Bellingham. Survey work was completed by soldiers from the 9th Infantry at Fort Steilacoom, and plans were completed for a military road between Vancouver and Fort Steilacoom. Federal funds were not forthcoming, but the seed had been planted to someday complete a north-south road from the Columbia to Bellingham.

When the Civil War broke out, troops of the 4th Regiment from Fort Steilacoom left for California and subsequent transport to the east. President Lincoln made the decision to keep the 9th Infantry on the west coast for the duration of the War and volunteer troops were recruited. During the War, companies G and K of the 1st Washington Infantry Regiment, soldiers from the 1st Oregon Infantry Regiment, and Company E of the 4th California Infantry Regiment manned Fort Steilacoom.

At the end of the Civil War, many of the posts which had been established during the 1850s were closed, including Fort Steilacoom. The fort's 640 acres were turned over to Washington Territory.

In 1871, Washington Territory established the "Insane Asylum of Washington Territory" on the site. Later, the name was changed to Western State Hospital.

The Historic Fort Steilacoom Association (HFSA) was established to ensure that original buildings remained and to provide an interpretive service for visitors to the properties. The HFSA is a non-profit organization, run by volunteers, who meet regularly to help develop programs to keep the history of Fort Steilacoom alive.

Four of the original buildings remain. An on-site museum and gift store is open to the public on weekends throughout the year.

Civil War Enactments are routinely held at Fort Steilacoom. Living History weekends and lectures are popular attractions for re-enactors, local residents, and tourists. Information on activities at Historic Fort Steilacoom is available at: www.historicfortsteilacoom.org

Fort Steilacoom Quarters 4 and Cannon Shed, ca. 1993. Photographer Orville H. Stout, courtesy of the Historic Fort Steilacoom Association

Fort Steilacoom Quarters 2, ca. 1993. Photographer Orville H. Stout, courtesy of the Historic Fort Steilacoom Association

Browns Point Lighthouse

Located near Tacoma, the current Browns Point Lighthouse was built in 1933 to mark the entrance to Commencement Bay. The 1933 structure was preceded by a post lantern in 1887, and a wooden tower, built on the property in 1903.

The shoal which it marks was recognized as an important turning point by the Lighthouse Board in 1873, and the Board recommended that it be marked with a light. Post lanterns were regarded as temporary lights. They were mounted on scaffolds and had a drum-type lens. A tank which encircled the lens could hold enough fuel for eight days. The first light, however, could not be seen through the fogs of Puget Sound.

In 1895, the Lighthouse Board recommended that the location be marked with a lighthouse, but it took until 1900 for Congress to appropriate the $6,000 for the purchase of land, and construction of the lighthouse and a keeper's dwelling. The landowner held out for a higher price than offered, so in 1901, the Government condemned several acres of land on Point Brown and eventually gave the landowners $3,000.

The first facility was erected in 1903 along with a keeper's house. A fog bell was suspended near the top of the tower. The bell, which weighed nearly 1,200 pounds, had also seen duty at the Dungeness Spit Lighthouse and at the Point No Point Light Station. The clapper was activated by a Gamewell Fog Bell Striking Apparatus, which used a system of descending weights which rang the bell every 20 seconds. It had to be rewound every 45 minutes. The system was often out of order and the light keeper had to strike the bell manually for hours, and even days, during foggy periods.

In October 1903, the new station keeper, Oscar Brown, and his wife Annie, arrived on the tender *Heather*. He brought a horse and a cow, and all of his household furnishings which included a piano. The piano reportedly sat outside under a tarp for several days until Tacoma residents could help him move it into the house.

Brown tended the bell for the next 30 years, and also gave piano lessons to local youth. The Browns became treasured members of the community and instead of being called Point Brown, the area was soon called Brown's Point.

In 1922, electricity reached the lighthouse and the light

was subsequently replaced with an electric floodlight. The fog bell striking apparatus was modified to be used with an electric motor.

In 1933, the wooden tower was replaced with an Art Deco concrete tower which stood 38 feet high. The new optic, a non-rotating 375-mm drum lens used an electric light bulb which could be seen for 12 miles with a signature of three white flashes every 15 seconds.

The beacon was later upgraded to 11,000 candle power. The fog bell was retired and replaced with a new foghorn. In 1934, the 1,200 pound fog bell was sold for $50 to the College of Puget Sound (now the University of Puget Sound) where it was used to announce the changing of class periods. It was donated in 1984 to the Fox Island Alliance Church.

Oscar Brown retired from the Lighthouse Service in 1939 after the responsibility for navigation aids was transferred to the Coast Guard.

The lighthouse was automated in 1963 and the Browns Point Light Station was closed. Tacoma Metro Parks obtained the land from the U.S. Coast Guard in 1964 and worked with historical societies to help restore and renovate the light station's buildings.

1903 Browns Point Light. U.S. Coast Guard photo

Browns Point Lighthouse ca. 1950. Photo courtesy U.S. Coast Guard

The Browns Point Light Station was officially designated as an Historic Place and listed on the Washington Heritage Register in 1989. It was also added to the National Register of Historic Places in the same year.

Fort Nisqually, DuPont and Point Defiance

Fort Nisqually was not a military site, but it served as a source of protection for traders and settlers. It was the first European trading post on Puget Sound. As a result, it will be included in this book because it played an important role in the history of Puget Sound.

Fort Nisqually was a trading and farming post of the Hudson's Bay Company in the area of what is now DuPont. The 1833 location of DuPont is now on the The Home Golf

Course. Logs mark the location of living-space walls but there are no buildings remaining.

The Hudson's Bay Company established the original post at Nisqually because of its anchorage, convenience to several fur-trading Native American tribes, and the surrounding grazing land and potential croplands. It was located at the mouth of Sequalitechew Creek on the flat plains lying north of the Nisqually River Delta. The fort's first building was a storehouse located on the beach near the Sequalitchew Indian Village. Nisqually House was built in 1832 and was staffed by three men.

A year later, in May 1833, Chief Trader Archibald MacDonald, Dr. William Fraser Tolmie, and seven Company men arrived to begin construction on a more permanent fort. By 1833, growth of trade and staffing resulted in the fort being too small. It was relocated in 1834, about a mile from the original fort. The new site was closer to a fresh water source as well as a larger stand of timber.

Fort Nisqually was operated and served by Scottish men, Native Americans, Hawaiians, French-Canadians, Metis, West Indians, Englishmen, and in the final years before the end of British claims to Puget Sound, a few American settlers. The main export was beaver pelts. Hudson's Bay Company had also established the Puget Sound Agricultural Company as a subsidiary, and subsequently began to export livestock and crops to Russia, Alaska, Hawaii, Mexican California, Europe, and Asia.

Dr. Tolmie was the Chief Factor of the fort as well as the manager of the agricultural company from 1843 to 1857. He had earned the respect of settlers, natives, and the British, and was instrumental in recording some of the first observations of native history.

Only one small military engagement was recorded in the fort's history. American and British forces, however, regularly visited the fort. With the 1846 treaty between the United States and Great Britain, the fort was left on American property. As the fur trade began to decline, and tax collectors began knocking on the Hudson Bay Company doors, Fort Nisqually closed in 1869. The Company was paid $460,000 for the land by the United States.

The fort was rebuilt at Point Defiance in the 1930s as part of President Roosevelt's New Deal program. The restoration project provided jobs for Tacoma area citizens. Two original buildings were moved to the new location: the granary and the factor's house. The addition of a trade store, working blacksmith shop, a kitchen and gardens has made the site a Living History museum. Today, the "new" fort is a U.S. National Historic Landmark

The reconstructed Fort Nisqually Blockhouse which is located at Point Defiance Park, Tacoma. Photo by Author

McChord Field — McChord Air Force Base

In the late 1800s, Mr. John Rigney, an Irish immigrant influential in the establishment of Fort Steilacoom, acquired a large tract of land. Part of this property was destined to become McChord Field. In 1917, Pierce County citizens approved a bond measure to buy 70,000 acres which would eventually be known as Camp Lewis and then later Fort Lewis. Ten years later another bond measure was passed to establish an airfield just north of Camp Lewis. The land was purchased from the Rigney family with the agreement that the new airfield would be named Rigney Field. Heated discussions ensued and the Pierce County Commissioners prevailed and named the new airport "Tacoma Field." The facility opened on March 14, 1930.

Tacoma Field was soon operating in the red, however. Business was not active enough to meet the $40,000 in operating costs, principal on the bonds, and expenses. At the same time, the Secretary of War had instructed the Army to develop six strategically placed air fields throughout the country. One of the fields was to be placed in the Pacific Northwest. Tacoma Field was chosen as the preferred location in the area. On February 28, 1938, the facility was transferred to the U.S. Government and subsequently renamed McChord Field in honor of Colonel William Caldwell McChord on July 3, 1940. McChord, then Chief of the Army Air Corps' Training and Operations Division, died in an attempt to land his Northrop A-17 in Virginia in 1937.

Only one hangar and two air strips comprised the facility. The Works Progress Administration was brought in to begin clearing land for more hangars and landing strips. Hangars 1, 2, 3, and 4 were constructed, along with housing, warehouses, maintenance facilities, a hospital, and a heating plant. By 1939, a radio transmitter building, a water tower, sewer system, fire station, and two runways were completed. By June 1940, the base was ready for the arrival of the 17th Bombardment Group (Medium). The base was formally dedicated on July 3, 1940.

At the beginning of World War II, McChord Field was the headquarters of the Air Force Northwest Air District which had the mission of defense of the Pacific Northwest and the Upper Great Plains. The 17th Bombardment Wing was relocated from March Field in California and was outfitted with the Douglas B-18 medium bomber.

Anti-submarine patrols along the coast were flown by the

17th Bombardment Wing with a new bomber, the North American B-25, following the attack on Pearl Harbor. The 17th was the first unit in the Army Air Corps to operate the B-25. It also achieved another "first" distinction on Christmas Eve of 1941 when it dropped four 300-pound bombs on a Japanese submarine which had approached the mouth of the Columbia River.

In early 1941, the 12th Bombardment Group (Medium) and the 47th Bombardment Group (Medium) activated at McChord, flying the B-18, the B-18A and B-23 bombers.

In 1942, the 17th Bomb Group was reassigned to Columbia Army Air Base in South Carolina. Later in April of that year, these crews were selected to carry out the Doolittle Raid on Japan, the first air raid by the United States to strike the Japanese home islands.

McChord Field then took on a training mission under the auspices of the Army Air Forces Training Command. It became the site for training B-17 Flying Fortress and B-24 Liberator crews. McChord also trained several graduates out of flight and technical schools of AAF Training Command, who were then sent on to further training prior to being deployed to combat units overseas.

In 1943, replacement crews for the B-17 and B-24 were being phased out. Second Air Force was beginning to train crews for the B-29 Superfortress units who were heading to Twentieth Air Force. New combat groups were organized and trained primarily in Kansas and Nebraska.

McChord's aircraft maintenance facilities provided modifications for P-39 lend-lease aircraft being sent to Russia via Alaska from April 1944 through May 1945. As the war ended in Europe, McChord was instrumental in redeployment of troops arriving from Europe and heading to the Pacific.

During the war years, McChord operated numerous kinds of aircraft including the B-17, Curtiss P-40, Douglas A-20 and A-26 in addition to the B-18 and B-23. In 1945, McChord was assigned to the Continental Air Forces and was the headquarters for the 1st and 2nd Bomb Wings following their return from Europe. Just a year later, in 1946, McChord was assigned to the Air Defense Command (ADC) with the mission of air defense of the United States.

WW II Hangar at McChord Field, 1942. Real Photo Postcard, Author's collection

McChord AFB Main Gate, late 1940s or early 1950s. U.S. Air Force photo

McChord Field became independent of Fort Lewis with passage of the National Security Act of 1947 and the creation of the United States Air Force. The field was subsequently renamed McChord Air Force Base in 1948.

In the late 1940s, McChord was also the home for an air rescue detachment which flew the Canadian-built SA-10A. The SA-16 Albatross was also used for search and rescue, along with Air Force Reserve operated AT-6s, A-26s and Beech C-45s.

The 325th Fighter Group (All Weather) operated two F-82F Twin Mustangs out of McChord between 1948 and 1950. This was the first fighter configured for air defense interceptor missions. It had been designed for long range bomber escort missions during WW II, but arrived into service too late for this mission. As a result, it was adapted to the air defense mission.

During the Cold War, several fighter interceptor squadrons were stationed at McChord. In addition, several Radar and Command and Control organizations were headquartered at there. The 25th Air Division was headquartered at McChord from 1951 until 1990. Interceptor squadrons stationed at McChord included:

- 64th Fighter-Interceptor Squadron
- 317th Fighter-Interceptor Squadron
- 318th Fighter-Interceptor Squadron
- 465th Fighter-Interceptor Squadron
- 498th Fighter-Interceptor Squadron

McChord was the first of 28 stations built by ADC as part of the new air defense radar network. The 505th Aircraft Control and Warning Group was activated at McChord in May 1947 and was the first postwar general surveillance radar organization. Defensive radars also became operational in June 1950 utilizing World War II era radar units (AN/CPS-4 and AN/CPS-5). These units were operated by the 635th Aircraft Control and Warning Squadron.

In February 1951, two AN/CPS-6B medium-range search and height-finding radars were installed. Performance of the new radar units, however, was inferior to the older World War II vintage radars. Calibration issues delayed readiness at this and other sites.

The Air Defense Control site (P-1) was deactivated and

moved to Fort Lawton in April 1960 where it became part of the Seattle Defense Area Army Air Defense Command Post for Nike missile operations protecting the Seattle area.

McChord's role in strategic airlift history is equally notable. In 1947 Tactical Air Command (TAC) moved the 62d Troop Carrier Group from Bergstrom Field in Texas to McChord Field. Its location and assets made the field the primary gateway to Alaska and to the Orient.

The 62nd Troop Carrier Wing was activated at McChord Field on August 15, 1947. Assigned to 12th Air Force, the unit was instrumental in the 1948 Berlin Airlift.

The Douglas C-54 Skymaster arrived at McChord in October 1949. With the arrival of the C-54, the designation of the Wing was changed from the 62nd Troop Carrier Wing (TCW) (Medium) to "Heavy." Budget reductions in 1950 resulted in deactivation of the wing, but activities with the Korean conflict resulted in the Wing being activated again in 1951. In 1952, the 62nd took command of Larson AFB (formerly Moses Lake AFB), and the 1705th Air Transport Group was the primary transport unit at McChord.

Throughout national and international defense missions, McChord-based units consistently played important roles. Airlift capabilities made it an increasingly important base for moving troops and equipment in support of the nation's most important missions.

In 1954, the McChord units transported a French garrison to Dien Bien Phu, in what was then known as French Indochina. By 1955, the term Cold War was part of the mission of the Wing. By a 1957 treaty with Canada, the US and Canada agreed that an air attack against the North American continent would be opposed by both countries. Both countries would contribute forces, equipment, bases and leadership to form the North American Air Defense Command (NORAD). The 25th NORAD Region became one of nine regions under NORAD command.

The North American Air Defense Command (NORAD) began to build the Distant Early Warning Line (DEW Line) to detect Soviet missiles. McChord units began flying what was to turn out to be approximately 13

25th Air Division

million pounds of supplies to the Alaskan arctic regions to build the DEW Line. McChord missions included these operations until 1969 when the system was completed.

By 1958, the Semi-Automated Ground Environment (SAGE) Data Center and Combat Center was established at McChord. Operational in 1960, SAGE became part of a network that linked Air Force and other radar stations into a centralized center for Air Defense. Its main purpose was to provide early warning for a Soviet nuclear attack. SAGE headquarters were realigned under the 25th Air Division in 1966. The Data Center remained under the 25th Air Division until 1983 when technology advances made the SAGE system obsolete.

Today, the Western Defense Sector is at McChord and continues to provide security for continental United States air space.

McChord's heritage also includes a fighter mission. In the early 1950s the 325th Fighter All-Weather Group was assigned to McChord. They were the first jet units and the first Continental Air Command units to fly all-weather jet interceptors. New fighter facilities and the air defense tracking system were built during the early 1950s. The runway was lengthened to 8,100 feet and temporary wooden, facilities built during World War II were upgraded or replaced. In 1952, the 325th was deactivated and replaced with the 4704th Air Defense Wing and the 567th Air Defense Group. The 325th Fighter Wing reactivated in 1956 and the 325th Fighter Group (Air Defense) continued to serve under the wing through March 1960.

The Wing also supported efforts involving the International Geophysical Year 1957-1958, and then again in 1962 by airlanding and airdropping supplies to scientific stations in the Arctic Ocean. In 1960, the 62nd Troop Carrier Wing (TCW) supported United Nations efforts in the Congo. Worldwide airlift of nuclear weapons and equipment also became a mission for the Wing up through 1971. In 1964, McChord units were instrumental in responding to the Alaskan earthquake and tsunami victims.

Strategic Air Command (SAC) placed a squadron of KC-135 tankers at McChord in June 1960. With the arrival of the tankers, night lighting was installed on what was soon to be called the "SAC ramp," and a SAC alert facility was constructed to house the KC-135 crews. The tanker unit, the 22nd Air Refueling Squadron, was deactivated in 1962.

Reassigned to Military Airlift Command (MAC) in 1968, McChord became one of only three bases in the western

United States to fly the C-141 Starlifter. Tactical Air Command (TAC) continued to keep a fighter alert detachment at McChord with the F-106 Delta Dart and later the F-15 Eagle.

In 1965, the 62nd Troop Carrier Wing was redesignated as the 62nd Air Transport Wing. With the redesignation came more flying hours, missions and people. As a result, the 62nd Air Transport Wing became one of the largest wings in the United States Air Force. In 1966, the Wing was designated as the 62nd Military Airlift Wing (MAW).

In 1975, the tactical C-130 Hercules fleet which had been part of TAC was transferred to MAC. As a result of the reorganization, the 36th Tactical Airlift Squadron (36 TAS) transferred to McChord from Langley AFB, VA.

When Mount St. Helens erupted in May 1980, the 36th TAS C-130s provided support during the search and rescue missions which followed. As the ash from the eruption began to drift toward Tacoma, the aircraft were evacuated to other bases throughout the west. When fires in Yellowstone National Park began to devastate the area, it was the 36 TAS that carried Army troops from Fort Lewis to fire-fighting missions in and around the Park.

Again, in 1991, when Clark Air Base personnel were evacuated following the eruption of Mount Pinatubo, it was McChord crews who carried the bulk of the evacuees. In 1992, the Air Force experienced a significant reorganization and the Military Airlift Command was disestablished. McChord AFB became an Air Mobility Command Base (AMC).

Aircraft at McChord changed again when the C-141 was phased out and the C-17 Globemaster III was phased in. The 437th Airlift Wing (437 AW) located at Charleston AFB in South Carolina received the first C-17s. McChord was the second base in the Air Force to receive the new aircraft.

A C-17 Globemaster III taxis on the McChord runway upon arriving at Joint Base Lewis-McChord. U.S. Air Force photo/Abner Guzman

Joint Base Lewis-McChord

In 2010, reorganization with the implementation of Base Realignment and Closure (BRAC) 2005 once again changed the sign at the front gate. McChord took on a joint service flavor when McChord joined with its neighbor Fort Lewis to become Joint Base Lewis-McChord.

McChord Air Museum

The McChord Air Museum has a significant collection of military aircraft, art, aircraft simulators, and a restoration hangar where aircraft are being restored for future display. The Museum occupies three separate areas of the base to accommodate an air park, the main building, and a restoration hangar. Aircraft include an SA-10A Catalina, the C-124 and a C-141. An F-106 simulator provides visitors with an orientation to aircrew training.

The collection also includes a gallery and a gift shop which is housed in the first control tower at McChord. The control tower, built in 1952, was deactivated in 1995. Museum staff and volunteers restored the cab. The gift shop has an extensive collection of photos, books, t-shirts, and Air Force memorabilia. While access to the base is limited, access to the museum can be attained by presenting appropriate vehicle registration, insurance, and driver's license.

Camp Murray

National Guard Minuteman outside of Camp Murray Headquarters. Photo by Author

In the historical process of "ownership" of property, what is now Camp Murray, adjacent to Fort Lewis, passed from native hands to lands occupied by the Hudson's Bay Company. When more and more settlers arrived in the area, the land occupied by the Company was encircled by private holdings, and Congress questioned the Company's title to their claims, especially to those properties which were not fenced.

Much of the property in what is now southwest Pierce County and northern Thurston County was originally Hudson's Bay Company holdings. When Congress questioned these claims, the Legislative Assembly of the Territory questioned them as well. As a result, action was taken with Great Britain to extinguish these claims and compensate the Company. As expected, the Hudson's Bay Company filed an exorbitant claim for the property it described as its Nisqually and Cowlitz farms. After several years of litigation, discussion, and negotiation, the Company agreed to accept $650,000 for improvements and the properties were released and made available for American settlers in 1867. Homesteaders who were already on the property received patents for their claims. Some of this land would eventually become Camp Murray.

The Territorial Legislative Assembly of 1854-1855 passed the Militia Law, which allowed the formation of militia companies for protection against neighboring hostile natives. During the Civil War, Governor Pickering attempted to form the Washington Territorial Militia into a Volunteer Regiment based on President Lincoln's proclamations. This effort was only marginally successful due to the ongoing issues with local Native American concerns. Many men felt it much more important to stay home and provide protection against a perceived threat from the local native population. As treaties were being signed with local tribes, an increasing level of dissatisfaction and unrest was developing. As a result, many of Washington's already-organized militia soldiers went to California to join the war effort.

In 1885, the Washington Territory Militia "officially" formed and was recognized as the Washington National Guard in the Legislative Assembly of Washington Territory.

In the Biennial Report of the Washington State Adjutant General, 1888-1889, Rossell O'Brien noted that the development of armories in counties which had militias was a critical need. Other counties had set aside property and drill facilities for their militias, but there was no such facility available in Pierce County. He noted that National Guard officers in Seattle had been successful in forming a stock company, the First Regiment Armory Association, and had built a large armory to house its National Guard personnel.

In 1903, the Washington State Legislature voted to appropriate funds to purchase properties to establish armories. From 1903 through 1932, several adjoining properties were purchased or procured through donation and/or condemnation to form a nucleus of 231 acres which comprised Camp Murray. The name Murray came from its proximity to Murray Creek, which itself had been named for one of the prominent settlers in the area. The name was reinforced by being the name of the adjacent Northern Pacific Railroad Station, also named for Murray Creek.

Congress in 1903 passed "An Act to Promote the Efficiency of the Militia." The Militia Act, as it was commonly called, authorized the National Guard of the United States and individualized the states' militias to achieve training comparable to that of the regular army. As a result, state militias could acquire a regular army officer on the retired list to become an Inspector-Instructor.

The act also provided for maneuvers between organized militias and the Regular Army. The American Lake area was scheduled for the first of these maneuvers involving the Washington National Guard from July 8 to July 17, 1904. The details, preparations, and numbers of personnel involved made maneuvers an elaborate operation.

The Blue Camp was located at Camp Steilacoom. The Brown Force was located at Camp Nisqually near the old Hudson's Bay trading post. The Maneuver Division was located at Murray Station, on the Northern Pacific Railroad line. General Arthur MacArthur, Commander of the Division of the Pacific, arrived to observe. A submarine cable was laid across American Lake to the general's residence on the north shore of the lake.

The troops assembled on the morning of July 8 to review the first tactical issue which they would address on the following day. The Regular Army had 102 officers and 1,585 soldiers. The militia had 170 officers and 2,154 enlisted ready for the challenges. The combined total force of both the Regular Army and the militia was the largest military contingent every assembled in Washington up to that time.

Six different "tactical problems" were presented at the maneuvers. Attacks and defense of camps, confronting convoys, and amphibious invasions were part of the training. Infantry, artillery and cavalry action, along with Signal Corps and Hospital Corps challenges were integral to the exercises. The success of the 1904 maneuvers led to additional training in 1906, 1908, 1910 and 1912. In addition, the training in the area helped support the establishment of Camp Lewis in 1917.

In 1914, members of the militia made the recommendation that a fireproof warehouse be constructed at Camp Murray to store tentage, wagons, etc. The first building, "The Arsenal," provided storage, office space, and was recognized as the beginning of Camp Murray. Following that, residences, mess halls, barracks, and many other buildings were constructed.

The Washington National Guard Museum at "The Arsenal," Camp Murray. Photo by Author, 2010

Camp Murray's Washington National Guard troops answered President Wilson's call to provide an increased presence along the Mexican Border in 1916. In 1917, intensive recruiting to meet the country's call for World War I resulted in a field artillery battalion joining the 146th Field Artillery Regiment in France at campaigns including Aise-Marne, St. Mihiel and in the Meuse-Argonne.

Washington National Guard troops continued to provide service in local disasters, at prison uprisings, and World War II, Korea, Vietnam, Operation Desert Storm, Operation Desert Shield and Operation Enduring Freedom. The Guard has always been there for Washington State residents' relief following floods or severe winter storms. In 1980, Washington National Guard members supported recovery activities following the eruption of Mt. St. Helens. Guard members have been instrumental in responding to fires, and other emergencies declared by the Governor. Washington Guard personnel have also assisted at national emergencies such as Hurricanes Rita and Katrina.

Camp Murray has continued to expand and modernize its facilities. At present, Camp Murray is the site for the Washington State Emergency Management Division, which operates as a division of the Washington Military Department.

Static M-47 Tank Display adjacent to "The Arsenal" Museum. Photo by Author, 2011

Inside Washington National Guard Museum at "The Arsenal," Camp Murray. Photo by Author, 2011

Static displays of aircraft and an M-47 Tank are located at Camp Murray's front gate. Major General George Haskett Plaza provides a display area for the AH-1 Cobra helicopter on static display. The Museum, housed in "The Arsenal," features the history of the Washington National Guard from pre-statehood through present operations in the Gulf Wars and Afghanistan. On display are original Model 1890 Colt 45 Gatling Guns, a Model 1902 3-inch field piece, and uniforms and memorabilia of Guard members.

Camp Murray is located just off Interstate-5, south of Tacoma.

Tacoma Narrows Bridge

The highlight of the history of the Tacoma Narrows Bridge is generally the story of the collapse of the first bridge, known by all as "Galloping Gertie." The more important fact, that it was constructed as a military necessity, is generally overlooked but it was a major topic of discussion for Tacoma residents in 1940.

The people of Western Washington had discussed constructing a bridge across the Narrows for many years. In the first half of the 20th century the Olympic Peninsula was generally undeveloped. Forward-thinking developers realized that construction of a bridge could provide opportunities for development and investment. In 1923 the Federation of Improvement Club Committee in Tacoma looked at the feasibility of such a project. Another investigation in 1927 by the Tacoma Chamber of Commerce Roads and Bridges Committee resulted in the formation of a fundraising committee for a preliminary study.

When McChord Field was finally transferred to the Federal Government in 1938, construction began there on a large scale. Aircraft hangars runways, barracks, hospitals, and warehouses were immediately built. In June 1940, the first bombers began to arrive at the field. Two weeks after the transfer and renaming of Tacoma Field to McChord Field, the Washington State Toll Bridge Authority submitted a plan to build a suspension bridge across Puget Sound at the Tacoma Narrows. The prime reason at that time was to provide a direct link from McChord Field to the Puget Sound Navy Shipyard in Bremerton. Transfer of munitions, equipment, and personnel was becoming a priority as the country found itself on the eve of World War II.

In June 1938, the Public Works Administration (PWA) granted funds for the first Tacoma Narrows Bridge, the reward for over 14 years of community efforts to have a bridge constructed.

Construction began in November 1938. Tacoma residents would often come out on weekends, bringing a picnic lunch to watch the construction process. Surprisingly, considering the speed with which the bridge was built, only one worker died in its construction; Fred Wilde, a carpenter, stumbled and fell 12 feet, sustaining injuries which contributed to his death.

On July 1, 1940, approximately 7,000 people came to the beautiful new bridge to witness its official dedication and its grand opening. Edward R. Murrow, celebrated CBS correspondent, attended the ceremonies; he was also the brother of State Highway Department Director, Lacey Murrow.

Tolls were imposed on the bridge traffic in order to repay loans from the Federal Public Works Administration and the Reconstruction Finance Corporation. Traffic exceeded original predictions by a factor of 300%. As a result, the toll was reduced from 75 cents to 70 cents within a few months.

On November 7, 1940, however, the bridge collapsed. It had often been an exciting ride across when the wind blew. The bridge would frequently "gallop" or "bounce." It had not been realized that a combination of wind and traffic could cause the span to vibrate so violently that it tore itself apart. After its collapse, the engineering issues were addressed, but World War II was imminent, and a replacement bridge was not completed until 1950. Today, that span, the replacement for the Galloping Gertie, still stands. It was joined in 2007 by a parallel span to accommodate vastly increased traffic.

Program cover, official opening of Tacoma Narrows Bridge and McChord Field 1940. Photo courtesy of Washington State Department of Transportation Library

Tacoma Narrows Bridge Toll Booth, 1940. Photo by Simmer, Real Photo Post Card, Author's collection

Tacoma Narrows Bridge. New span (2007) on left. Old span (1950) on right. Photo courtesy Washington Department of Transportation

Fort Hays and the Battle of Connell's Prairie

Fort Hays was located at Connell's Prairie, approximately 18 miles southeast of Tacoma. The fort was one of the two blockhouses made out of cedar which were built by Washington Territorial Volunteer troops. Built in 1855-1856, during the Indian War at Connell's Prairie, the area is near what is now known as the town of Bonney Lake.

The Battle of Connell's Prairie took place on March 10, 1856, when Major Gilmore Hays and approximately 100 men approached the White River from the south to begin construction on a blockhouse and a ferry across the river. As an advance unit of approximately eleven men got to the river, they encountered a force of approximately 150 native warriors who were led by Chief Leschi. The warriors attacked. By the time Major Hays and the rest of the troops arrived, the warriors had flanked the volunteers. Even though they were outnumbered, only four volunteers were wounded. The natives suffered approximately 30 casualties.

The news of the battle spread quickly and Puget Sound bands were discouraged by the news. This was the last comparatively large-scale battle west of the Cascades.

The blockhouse was completed and named for Major Hays, 2nd Regiment, Washington Territory Volunteers.

The site of the battle is marked by an historical marker which was placed by the Washington State Historical Society in 1924 on the roadside near Buckley.

Fort White

Fort White was located near Fort Maloney at a crossing of the Puyallup River. It is thought that the fort was named for Captain Joseph A. White, who commanded the Pioneer Company of the Washington Territorial Volunteers at the battle of Connell's Prairie. Captain White resigned his command after the Battle of Connell's Prairie and was replaced by Captain Urban Hicks. Another school of thought suggests that the fort may have been named for its location at the confluence of the White River and the Puyallup River. Today, this location is near a shopping center on Meridian Street in Puyallup. No markers indicate its presence.

Fort Hicks

Information on Fort Hicks is sketchy. Historical documents and accounts indicate that this Washington Territorial Volunteers blockhouse was built in 1855-1856 on the Military Road between Fort Steilacoom and Puyallup. Urban Hicks was the captain in the Pioneer Company of the Washington Territorial Volunteers who assumed command of the unit following Captain White.

Fort Maloney

Fort Maloney was a blockhouse at the Puyallup River Crossing near present-day Meridian Avenue in Puyallup. It was built on the north bank of the Puyallup River, and was named for Maurice Maloney, who had been the commander at Fort Steilacoom during the Indian Wars of 1855-1856. Fort Maloney was a typical blockhouse built to provide protection and a base of operations during those wars.

Fort McAllister

Monument to Lieutenant McAllister and Michael Connell located near Buckley. Photo by Author, 2010

Fort McAllister was a blockhouse on South Prairie and was an additional fort built by the Washington Territorial Volunteers. Fort McAllister is located to the south of Connell Prairie. It was named for James McAllister who was one of the first persons killed at the beginning of the Indian Wars in 1855-1856. McAllister was from Thurston County and was an officer of Eaton's Rangers, the unit which was in pursuit of Chief Leschi when both he and Michael Connell were killed.

Camp Montgomery

Camp Montgomery was located on property which is now in the city of Spanaway, on the old Military Road which ran from Fort Steilacoom to Fort Walla Walla. The road is also known as the Naches Pass Branch of the Oregon Trail.

John Montgomery was born in Scotland in 1817, came to the West Coast, and was employed by the Hudson's Bay Company at Fort Nisqually. He declared his intention to become a citizen of the United States just prior to the end of his contract with the Company. He filed for 320 acres under the Donation Land Claim Act, and built a log cabin and a large barn. When the Indian Wars broke out in the fall of 1855, he offered the barn to be used as a storehouse for soldiers in the field. Governor Isaac Stevens accepted his offer and Camp Montgomery became an important supply center.

During the Indian Wars, Camp Montgomery, in addition to being an important military post, played prominently into what would be Washington's first civil rights crisis. Governor Isaac Stevens became aware that settlers in the Nisqually Valley, many of whom had family connections with neighboring tribes, were supporting the "enemy." Stevens ordered these men, many of whom had native wives, to evacuate their farms and go to Fort Steilacoom. They refused and Stevens imposed martial law and ordered their arrest. The farmers appealed to the Chief Justice of the Territorial Supreme Court for writs of *habeus corpus.*

Governor Isaac Stevens

Judge Edward Lander, who

was in the militia, resigned his commission so that he could convene a court at Steilacoom. He opened the court but was quickly interrupted by army officers. He closed the court at the order of the Governor and he and his records were taken into custody.

Stevens announced that his decree of martial law applied only to Pierce County and he ordered that Lander be released. Lander opened the court again, issued decrees that the farmers should be released, and cited the Governor for contempt. Stevens summoned a company of Territorial Volunteers to arrest Judge Lander. The Governor told the Judge that he could go free if he got permission from him, the Governor, to hold the court. Lander refused and Governor Stevens ordered him imprisoned with the farmers at Camp Montgomery.

Judge Edward Lander

The Chief Justice of the Territory, Judge Francis Chenoweth, got out of his sickbed on Whidbey Island and went to Steilacoom via canoe. He ordered the Pierce County Sheriff to organize a posse of 50 men. Stevens responded by sending a company of Volunteers. When the Volunteers came face to face with the posse, the Volunteers backed down.

Judge Chenoweth issued new writs which released Lander and the settlers. Stevens formed a court martial in which to try the settlers, but his militia legal advisors informed him that he did not have military jurisdiction over the settlers. Stevens canceled the court martial proceedings and the settlers were released. Judge Lander eventually fined Governor Stevens $50. Stevens' supporters paid the fine. Both the Territorial Legislature and the U.S. Senate censured Governor Stevens. The Secretary of State wrote to Stevens: "Your conduct, in that respect, does not therefore meet with favorable regard of the President."

In 1931, the Monday Civic Club of Tacoma erected a marker at "Old Camp Montgomery."

Fort Lander, a blockhouse in King County was named for Captain Edward Lander.

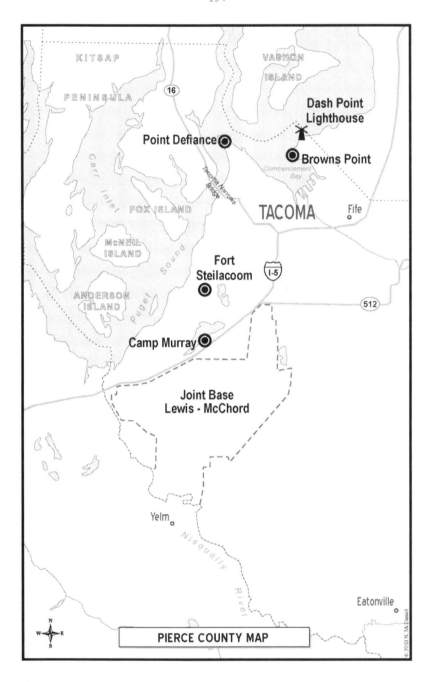

Chapter 8
Thurston County

Puget Sound Mounted Volunteers, Blockhouses and Stockades

In the fall of 1855, settlers of South Puget Sound grew increasingly concerned about their safety in the face of the Indian Wars. On October 14, 1855, Acting Governor Mason issued a proclamation that called for forming two companies of volunteer soldiers that could be utilized in securing the peace. Olympia was designated as one of the places were the volunteers could enroll.

The Company that enrolled at Olympia was called the Puget Sound Mounted Volunteers. Surveyor General Tilton traveled to Seattle to procure arms from the *Decatur* and the *Jefferson Davis* which were on station in Elliott Bay to provide security for Seattle. Georgiana Mitchell Blankenship in her *Early History of Thurston County* provides the details of his trip. Traveling both in canoes and overland, Tilton came back with 30 muskets, 40 carbines, 50 holster pistols, 50 sabers and belts, and 3,500 ball cartridges.

Settler Nathan Eaton was also authorized by Acting Governor Mason to organize a company of Rangers. Both Companies proceeded to the White River Valley in October 1855. Volunteers from Mound Prairie and local citizenry built a blockhouse there for protection.

Thurston County citizens also constructed stockades and blockhouses in what is now Tumwater and Chambers Prairie. Business throughout the area ground to a stop while male proprietors prepared to go to war or were engaged in building stockades and blockhouses.

Stockades were also built in Olympia along what is now Fourth Street. Volunteers and settlers built a blockhouse at the corner of Main Street for protection; this blockhouse housed a cannon. Blockhouses and stockades were also built at Skookumchuck (which later became Centralia), Grand Mound Prairie, Chambers Prairie, Bush Prairie, Tumwater, Tenalquot Prairie, Yelm Prairie, and Doffelmeyer's Point. No stockades were built by Federal troops in Thurston County.

These preparations turned out to be precautionary more than any real or needed protection. Actual fighting in the Indian Wars took place in the White and Puyallup Valleys and not as far south as Thurston County. By December 1856, the militias were disbanded.

It should be noted that not all residents moved into these stockades and blockhouses. Some residents said clearly that they thought the blockhouses were unnecessary and may have been harmful to relationships with local natives, specifically the Chehalis tribes who were their neighbors.

Fort Henness

Near the center of Grand Mound Prairie, at Skookumchuck, (now known as Centralia) a blockhouse provided shelter to approximately 227 men, women and children. Families set up their own shelters and moved their families within the walls of the new fort. Some families remained in the fort for nearly 16 months. The men in the fort formed Company F, the first Regiment of Washington Territorial Volunteers and subsequently elected Benjamin Henness as their captain. The unit became a supply unit and was involved in transport of supplies to northern units.

Built in 1855-1856, it had stockades, two blockhouses, and several cabins and outbuildings. Named for Benjamin and Lucretia Henness, it was used by the Washington Volunteer militia as well as by local citizens.

The fort had two bastions at opposite corners. Gates were located at each end and a well was located within the walls of the stockade.

Today, nothing remains of the fort's structures. There are historical markers, however, that commemorate the site.

Fort Chambers

A Thurston County Historical Marker marks the site of the blockhouse which was built on the Andrew Chambers Donation Claim in 1855. The marker was placed at the site by the Sacajawea Chapter of the Daughters of the American Revolution in 1929.

The blockhouse, which was, in effect, Fort Chambers, is described in part in an important memoir of Mrs. George Blankenship. She wrote a vibrant history of Thurston County in 1914 entitled *Early History of Thurston County, Washington*. In this memoir and historic account, she describes a bit of what life was like at Fort Chambers:

> This block house on Chambers Prairie was standing until a few years ago. As I had a big Dutch oven I baked all the bread that was consumed by these fourteen people, and I can tell you I baked every, and all day, too. When the block house was finished we all moved in. The families who were there at that time and who had rooms in the block house were Thomas Chambers, the McMillans, Mrs. White with her children, the O'Neals, the Parsons and Mrs. Stewart.
>
> Mrs. Stewart gave birth to a baby the day after we moved in. Almost all our men had joined the volunteers to fight the Indians and we women, with the children, had to stay there all the time with one or two men left to guard us.
>
> We brought our water from the creek, the banks of which had been cleared of brush so the Indians couldn't ambush there. It, was very unhandy to do our work, for each family had only one room in the block house to live in, and everything cooking, washing, sleeping had to be done in this one room.
>
> I got so tired of that way of living that we

were the first family to return to our home, but we were not molested and soon took up our regular way of living ..... .

Blankenship, Georgiana Mitchell, *Early History of Thurston County, Washington: Together With Biographies and Reminiscences of Those Identified with Pioneer Days*. Nabu Press, 2010, page 128—131.

A plaque at 6909 Rainier Road, Olympia, marks the site.

Fort Eaton

Fort Eaton was located near the intersection of Yelm Highway and Meridian Road. A monument erected in 1932 by local Thurston County residents marks the spot where a stockade was built in 1855-1856. Records indicate the stockade was built in a square with approximately 16 log buildings inside of its walls. It was built on what was Nathan Eaton's property.

Civil War Memorial
Masonic Cemetery, Olympia

The Masonic Cemetery in Olympia is the site for Washington's memorialization of the Civil War. The memorial was erected in memory of Union soldiers and sailors of the Civil War.

Major General Robert Milroy, commander of Union forces supporting the Battles at Gettysburg from his position in Winchester, Virginia, is also buried at the Masonic Cemetery in Tumwater. After the war, Milroy became the superintendent of Indian Affairs in the Washington Territory. He was active in ensuring that the Yakima chief, Kamiakin would be allowed to remain on his ancestral lands and not be evicted by area ranchers. He died in Olympia and was buried in Tumwater.

Civil War Memorial at the Masonic Cemetery, Olympia. Photo by Author 2010

WWI Memorial, Capitol grounds. Photo by Author, 2010

World War I Memorial

The World War I memorial is a bronze statue of three fighting men and a Red Cross nurse. The four individuals are standing under the winged symbol of Victory. Designed by Victor Alonzo Lewis, it pays tribute to the sons and daughters of Washington who fought in World War I or who were in direct battlefield support of the fighting. It is located on the Capital Grounds.

World War II Memorial

The World War II Memorial is located on the northeast lawn of the west campus of the Capitol Grounds. Designed by artist Simon Kogan, it was dedicated in 1999. Kogan was a Russian immigrant who made his home in Olympia. The memorial was one of the first in the country to honor those who served in World War II. Its particular focus is the 6,000 Washington residents who died in World War II battles.

The symbolism and artistry of bronze blades representing military units and individuals is unique and a haunting remembrance of a generation of Washington sons and daughters lost to war. Bronze "wheat stalks" graphically represent the magnitude of casualties. The wheat stalks were formed from melted torpedo railings used on old U.S. warships and were donated by the Puget Sound Naval Shipyard.

Large rocks, engraved with battle names and events of World War I surround the wheat field. The memorial is significant in that it also pays tribute to Washington State citizens who contributed on the home front, such as doctors, nurses, and factory workers.

Nearly 3,000 tiles are permanently placed on the walkway engraved with a unique message of remembrance on behalf of a veteran, family member, or friend. A bronze plaque describes the historical aspects of the war.

World War II Memorial, Capital grounds. Photo courtesy of the State of Washington

Korean War Memorial

Korean War Memorial on Capital grounds. Photo courtesy of the State of Washington

Dedicated in 1993, this memorial was designed by Deborah Copenhaver Fellows. The artist's father was a Korean War veteran. Veterans groups raised more than $320,000 of the $400,000 needed for the project. A major impetus in the fundraising efforts was the veterans group Chosin Few, which is made up of survivors of the bloody battle at the Chosin Reservoir in November 1950.

The two-ton bronze statue represents GIs of different ethnic backgrounds huddling around a pile of sticks in the rain. One soldier is attempting to start a fire. Behind the figures the flags of the 22 nations which joined the war effort. Stone tablets in front of the statue have the names of Washington residents who were killed in battle. Plaques on each side of the memorial tell the story and provide a chronology of the conflict. The memorial is on the east campus of the State Capitol.

Vietnam Veterans Memorial

The names of Washington State sons and daughters lost in the Vietnam conflict are engraved on green granite. Next to each name is a small hole so that mementos may be left in remembrance. All items are collected and placed in the state archives. Names are listed chronologically.

The inscriptions on the memorial were compiled from the words of Vietnam veterans throughout the state. Veterans were asked what they wanted the memorial to say. These words were utilized to provide the meaningful words on the memorial:

Washington State Vietnam Veterans Memorial

To all my brothers and sisters who made it back, but never made it home. In memory of those who have died from physical and emotional wounds received while serving in the Vietnam War. We honor and recognize their pain and suffering, but above all we respect the courage of these Washington State residents. When our country called, you were there. We have not forgotten, you are not alone.

You Now Rest in Glory.

The names of 1,116 Washington State residents killed or missing are engraved on the wall. Since its dedication, the Vietnam Veterans Memorial has been the site of many private reflections and tributes. Items such as flags, flowers, letters and personal effects have been left to honor the memory of those who did not return. All items are collected and placed in the state archives. The memorial is located east of the legislative building on Sid Snyder Drive SW on the Capital grounds.

Vietnam Veterans Memorial on Capital Grounds, Photo courtesy of the State of Washington

Olympia Airport

The Olympia Airport is one of the oldest public airports in the United States. Aircraft operated from the field as early as 1911. Originally named Bush Prairie Airfield Site, it was purchased by the City of Olympia in 1928, and soon began to pave runways and construct facilities to support the airport.

During World War II, the airport came under military control and the facility served as a satellite field to McChord Field. Used primarily for practice take-offs and landings, the field was also available as a potential landing site in the case of an Army Air Corps aircraft emergency.

When the war was over, the airport was transferred back to the City of Olympia with the provision that the airport would be operated as a public airport. In 1963, the Port of Olympia purchased the airport from the city of Olympia along with adjoining acreage which serves as an industrial business park for the Olympia area.

Today, the airport serves as an operating base for the

aviation assets of the Washington State Patrol, a base for aeromedical evacuation, and a site for fixed wing and helicopter flight instruction.

The Olympic Flight Museum, a non-profit organization, is located at the airport. Military aircraft including a P-51D, an AGM2 "Tora" Zero, an AT-6 Texan, and a Czechoslovakian L-39 Albatross are part of the collection. The museum was established in 1998.

The Olympia Airport is home to the Olympic Air Show which is held annually during the summer months.

AT-6 Texan

AH-1S Cobra

Photos courtesy Olympic Flight Museum

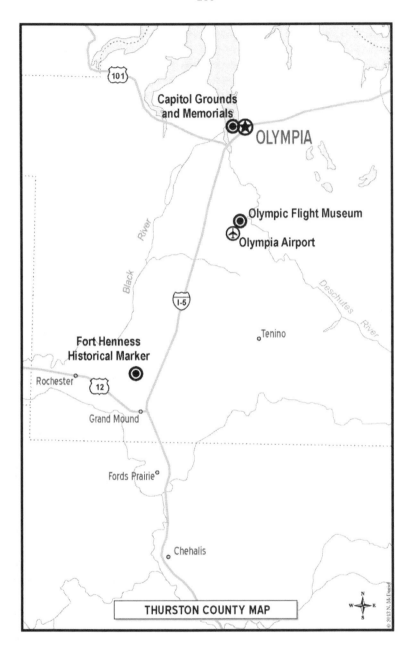

Chapter 9
Mason County

Naval Air Auxiliary Station Shelton

The City of Shelton saw the beginning of its new airport in 1927 and named it the Mason County Airport.

In 1942, the United States' need for expanded military infrastructure was impacting the nation. The U.S. Army originally purchased the Mason County Airport for its own development, and later sold it to the U.S. Navy. It was renamed Naval Auxiliary Air Station Shelton.

The Navy built two 5,000 x 150 foot asphalt runways. Barracks to house over 1,300 personnel were constructed. Originally, the air field was intended to have a mission of providing a base for interceptor aircraft. As World War II developed, the mission shifted towards a Navy Utility Squadron, or "VJs."

The main focus for the base was providing target towing, maintenance service for aircraft, and as the home for an anti-aircraft gunnery school.

Airships, part of the Lighter Than Air (LTA) squadron ZP-33 at Tillamook, Oregon, were also assigned in a detachment status to the Shelton field. The K-Class aircraft were approximately 252 feet long with a lift capacity of 7,700 pounds. In comparison, today's average Goodyear blimp is 190 feet long. Patrolling shipping lines, searching for submarines, and providing observation for the unique threat of Japanese incendiary balloons were the missions of the LTA assets. Airship Squadron ZP-33 operated in part, out of Shelton from December 1942 to September 1945.

One of the fixed wing units which trained at Naval Air Station Shelton was Composite Squadron Sixty-Six (VC-66). The squadron had both the single-seat F4F Wildcat fighter

U.S. Navy Grumman TBF-1 Avenger. U.S. Navy photo

U.S. Navy Grumman F4F Wildcat. U.S. Navy photo

JM-1. U.S. Navy photo

and the three-man TBF Avenger torpedo bomber. The unit received its initial training at NAS Seattle and then received several months of squadron training at bases up and down the west coast.

The unit arrived at Shelton in August 1943, where some of the flying squadron members found that the hunting skills they brought from home came in handy to keep deer and even a bear off of the runway. Aviators in Shelton were involved with training activities which included gunnery work, formation flying, and tactics. VC-66 detached from Shelton in late October and continued its training activities in California.

Utility Squadron Thirteen (VJ-13) was commissioned at Naval Auxiliary Air Station Shelton in January 1944. High- speed tow planes, including the JM-1, were assigned to the unit. Personal and historical accounts of the unit indicate that weather was a major factor in cancellation of missions. The unit had two detachments, one at Ault Field on Whidbey

Island and another at NAS Astoria.

When the war ended, the Navy moved out of the Shelton airfield. By 1947, all operations had ended. The Civil Air Patrol maintained the airport and it regained the name of Mason County Airport. The facilities were basically idle. The Air Force considered turning it into a guided missile site, but the plan was abandoned.

By 1955, the federal government agreed to give the airfield back to Mason County with the agreement that the county would subsequently deed the facilities to the Port of Shelton. In May 1957, the 1,080 acres were handed over to the Port of Shelton for further development.

In May 1966, the airport was renamed Sanderson Field in honor of United States Marine Corps Major General Lawson Sanderson. A Shelton native, he was a noted early aviator who contributed the new technique of dive-bombing to military flying. A noted aviator, he held the world air high-speed record from 1923 to 1930. He was a distinguished Marine commander in the Guadalcanal Campaign, World War II. When the Japanese relinquished Wake Island on September 7, 1945, the then Brigadier General Sanderson was the official to whom they surrendered.

The Marine Corps sought to recognize Major General Lawson for his innovations in air attack and for his exemplary service. As a result, the Marines established the Lawson H. M. Sanderson Award which is awarded annually to the most outstanding Marine attack squadron.

Sanderson Field continues to serve as an alternate facility for military aircraft for Navy, Army and Air Force units. Several World War II buildings remain at the field.

*Sanderson Field, Shelton, 2009.
Courtesy Washington State Department of
Transportation*

Vietnam Veterans Memorial Mason County

A memorial to Mason County residents killed or determined MIA during the Vietnam War is located at a small park near the post office in downtown Shelton. Seven names are listed on the memorial.

Vietnam Veterans Memorial in Mason County, 2010. Photo by Author

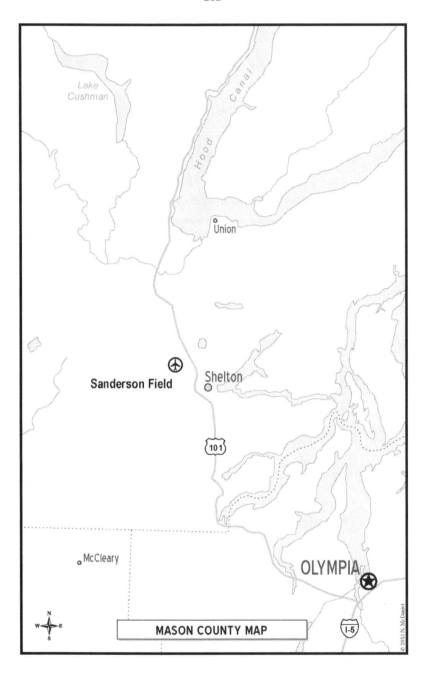

Chapter 10

Kitsap County

Fort Ward

Fort Ward's place in military history is closely tied to the other coastal artillery installations on Puget Sound such as Fort Casey, Fort Worden, and Fort Flagler.

Harbor defense budget appropriations had not fared well since they had been cut out of the federal budget in 1875. When President Cleveland came into office in 1885 he noted that seacoast defenses were becoming less capable of defending the country. Advancements in steam powered ships and armaments had been rapid. Fixed coastal defense installations had not kept up at the same rate of change. He appointed a special board to make a complete study of coastal defenses. The Endicott Board, which was convened by Secretary of War, William Endicott, made observations that coastal defense installations and their accompanying weapon systems should be upgraded. Fort Ward was established in 1890, as part of this coastal defense weapon system. It was built on a cape called Beans Point at the southern tip of Bainbridge Island. It overlooked Rich Passage, the narrow seaway leading to Bremerton. Its primary objective was the projection of Bremerton Naval Shipyard.

Coast Artillery had existed as a distinct branch within the Army since 1901 when Congress became convinced that coast artillery defenses should exist as a tasked organization. Its stated mission was to protect fleet bases, defeat naval and air attacks against cities and harbors, undertake beach defense while acting as Army or theater reserve artillery, and provide a mine-planter service.

The Beans Point installation was renamed in 1903 in honor of Colonel George H. Ward, the commander of the 15th Massachusetts, which fought at the Battle of Gettysburg on Cemetery Ridge. Ward, wounded during the battle, died the following day from his injuries.

Work began on the new installation. As the buildings were finished, troops began to arrive. Coastal batteries located at Fort Ward were:

- Battery Nash: 3 8" Disappearing Carriage (DC) (On the bluff, however now on private property)
- Battery Warner: 2 5" Pedestal Mount (Now on private property)
- Battery Thornburgh: 4 3" Masking Pedestal Mount
- Battery Vinton: 2 3" Masking Pedestal Mount and 2 additional 3" guns to guard an underwater mine field placed across Rich Passage

Fort Ward, ca. 1913. NARA photo

The guns were removed in July 1920, never having been fired in anger, and were ultimately shipped to France. Later in the 1920s, Fort Ward was placed on the inactive status list. A few solders were still stationed there primarily as a caretaking force. In 1928, the fort was essentially abandoned until 1935 when it became for a few years a fresh air camp for inner city children from Seattle.

In 1938, the Navy took over the Fort Ward property from the Army and proceeded to confiscate properties from several adjacent owners. The location was ideal to intercept and eavesdrop on radio communications coming out of Japan. By

1939, an intercept site had been relocated from Astoria, Oregon to Fort Ward. As a result, the fort became a top-secret military listening post. By 1940, Fort Ward was one of the five sites in the country which was linked directly to Washington D.C. It was known as *Station S*.

The building and its mission were so top secret that personnel on base were instructed not to even look at the building as they walked by it. *Station S*, a 24-hour operation which listened in on Japanese Morse Code was located in the old Post Exchange building.

RDF (Radio Direction Finding) capabilities allowed the Bainbridge station to help track ships. Rhombic antennae on the parade ground provided resources for both the secret station and the ongoing outward mission of the fort. Using triangulation, the accuracy of the operation was increased. Bainbridge operated what was known as the West Coast High Frequency Direction Net as the Net Control and Plotting Center. It used its own findings as well as other stations' RDF data to keep a log of Japanese ship locations. The Chief of Naval Operations, as well as other west coast Navy commanders, were in direct receipt of this information.

To the public, the Navy described the only mission at the location as the Naval Radio Station Bainbridge Island and said that it was one of a very few Naval Reserve Radio Schools in the nation. Forty students at a time would arrive for training in Morse Code, typewriting, basic seamanship, and radio operations. Upon graduation, graduates would be assigned throughout the Navy either afleet or ashore. Top graduates were often asked to stay on at *Station S*.

The facility was particularly busy in the first few days of December 1941. The volume of messages between December 4 and December 6 was at an all-time high. Shipping activity had also increased. On December 7, *Station S* intercepted a message regarding Japan breaking off negotiations with the United States. That message was immediately forwarded to Washington D.C., but delivery was delayed. U.S. intelligence officials had not anticipated that the Japanese would attack. By then, Japan had secretly moved its naval forces to support the attack on Pearl Harbor.

Station S took over the Canadian radio intelligence work in November 1942. In that same year, a Navy radio transmitter station was built at Battle Point, just north of *Station S,* which relayed messages to 13th Naval Command in Seattle. WAVES (Women Accepted for Volunteer Emergency Service) arrived in 1944. Many of them worked at *Station S*.

After World War II and entry into the Cold War, the school began to teach Russian code and began to listen to Soviet messages. By 1950, messages from North Korea were being monitored.

The Naval Radio School was renamed the U.S. Naval School Communications-Technicians until it was closed in 1953. Naval Security Group activities ceased and Fort Ward was returned to caretaker status. In 1960, 137 acres of the installation were turned into Fort Ward State Park. The Battle Point station closed in 1971 and that property was turned over to the Bainbridge Park District. Towers came down in 1972. The area is now known as Battle Point Park.

Fort Ward State Park has 4,300 feet of shoreline. Many of the historic military structures remain. An underwater park provides recreation for scuba divers, and a boat ramp provides access to the scenic Rich Passage.

Fort Ward, ca. 1932. U.S Army photo

Puget Sound Naval Shipyard

In 1877, the United States had no ship repair facilities north of San Francisco which could accommodate large military and commercial steamers, or sailing ships. Repair either had to be done in San Francisco or at the British Columbia Dry Dock at Esquimalt. Under the circumstances, paying Great Britain for any services was not a Congressional priority.

Navy Lieutenant Ambrose Wyckoff was sailing through Puget Sound waters on a hydrographic survey. He marveled at the good harbors, timber, iron ore, and the mild climate. When he returned to Washington D.C., he began the lobby to create a Naval shipyard on Puget Sound. Congress appointed three Naval officers to look for a site and this Commission recommended Port Turner (now Port Orchard Bay). After a second commission reviewed the first commission's recommendation and agreed this was the best site, Wyckoff was sent back to the area to begin negotiations. However, when $10,000 was appropriated to purchase the property, it was $15,000 less than what the Navy had requested. Settlers were also aware of the Navy's intentions to purchase land and saw the opportunity to make some serious profits by inflating the prices of their land.

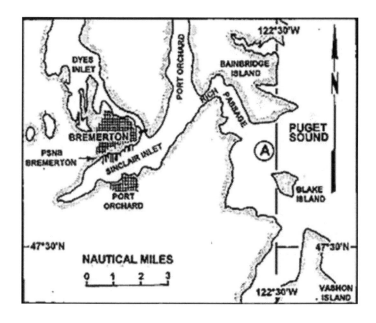

Two local businessmen, William Bremer and Henry Paul Hensel, saw the situation develop and became instrumental in helping Wyckoff consummate the deal. They purchased property at the inflated price and then sold some of it to the Navy at $50 an acre and convinced two other property owners to do the same. There were profits to be made by investing in the future of "Bremerton."

Lieutenant Wyckoff assumed command of the new 145-acre site which had been designated as Puget Sound Naval Station on September 16, 1891. Additional acreage was purchased to total a little more than 190 acres. The total cost of the acquisition was $9,587.25.

The first dry dock, 650 feet long by 130 feet wide and 39 feet deep, was completed in 1896. In the same year, the administration building and five officers' quarters were also completed. U.S. Marines were attached to the new facility to provide security.

Although there were aggressive plans for a larger installation, there was no immediate development. Lt. Wyckoff left to recuperate in Arkansas from an illness. The new Chief of the Bureau of Docks and Yards felt that Puget Sound was a poor choice for a shipyard, and the county slipped into economic depression.

Building 50, Puget Sound Naval Station, ca. 1900.
Photo courtesy Naval Sea Systems Command,
www.navsea.navy.mil/shipyards/puget/Page/Historic
al Photos

Wyckoff returned in 1899 and applied renewed new energy to the project, and the shipyard started to grow. By 1903, the renamed Navy Yard Puget Sound had more than 1,000 workers and was the largest employer in the area.

Soldiers Barracks, Puget Sound Naval Station, Washington, ca. 1905. Real Photo Post Card, Author's collection

Wireless radio was installed in 1906, and in 1911 a hospital was built. In 1909, ground was broken for a second dry dock. Completed in 1913, it was the Navy's largest dry-dock and the only one on the West Coast capable of handling the largest navy ships. A third dry dock was completed in 1918.

During World War I, Navy Yard Puget Sound built ships for battle. It constructed 25 subchasers, seven submarines, two minesweepers, seven sea-going tugs, and two ammunition ships, in addition to 1,700 small boats.

Following the war, many of these ships were due for overhaul and much of the work was done at Navy Yard Puget Sound, but by the early 1920s, little work was heading to Puget Sound. During the 1920s, only two ships were built. During the Great Depression, however, the shipyard actually grew as it received Federal money from various agencies. New orders were received for five destroyers as well as other smaller ships.

By 1939, the shipyard was once again busy and was employing approximately 6,000 people. The Works Progress Administration (WPA) was put to work on the Shipyard and constructed several buildings as well as being instrumental in the repair of roads and railroad tracks. In the same year, construction began on Dry-dock No. 4. Dry-dock No. 5 was started in 1940.

Navy Yard Puget Sound, 1904. Postcard, Author's collection

Launching submarine H4 at the Naval Station on October 9, 1918. Photo courtesy Naval Sea Systems Command

As World War II loomed, the emphasis on shipbuilding was reduced in favor of facilities for repair and overhaul. During World War II, the prime mission of the yard was the repair of battle-damaged Pacific Fleet warships. After Pearl Harbor, five of the Navy's surviving battleships were sent to Bremerton for repair. They included the USS *Tennessee,* USS *Maryland,* USS *Nevada,* USS *California* and the USS *West Virginia.* During the war, the shipyard had repaired 26 battleships, (some multiple times), 18 aircraft carriers, 13 cruisers, and 79 destroyers, and had employed 30,000 workers. Shipbuilding did not completely stop; 5 aircraft carriers, 13 destroyers, and 8 destroyer escorts were built at Bremerton in that period.

Navy Yard, Bremerton, Washington, ca. 1942. Real Photo Post Card, Author's collection

With the Navy Yard operating at maximum capacity 24 hours a day, housing was scarce in Kitsap County. Many employees lived in Seattle and commuted by ferry. The famous *Kalakala* ferry and six Black Ball Line ferries made more than 35 trips a day to and from Seattle.

As World War II came to end, the nature of the work began to change. Navy Yard Puget Sound became Puget Sound Naval Shipyard in 1945. Repair work was replaced with deactivation of the Pacific Fleet vessels. Many ships came to Bremerton to be stripped of guns, equipment, and supplies and then sold for scrap metal. Others were put into a "mothball" status where they were sealed, equipped with dehumidification equipment and rafted together. By the end of 1946, the workforce dipped to fewer than 9,000 workers.

U.S.S. *Arizona, 1937.* Photo courtesy Naval Sea Systems Command,
www.navsea.navy.mil/shipyards/puget/Page/Historical Photos

The Korean conflict brought the workforce back to approximately 15,300 to bring some of the reserve fleet back to service. But by 1954, the shipyard took on the deactivation mission once again. The U.S.S. *Missouri*, which provided the stage for Japan's surrender to the Allied Powers on September 2, 1945, came to Bremerton and was opened to visiting tours. School students from surrounding counties visited the ship as part of field trips for many years.

Construction once again became a focus for the Shipyard in 1955. The USS *Coontz*, and the USS *King*, guided missile frigates, were constructed. Nine aircraft carriers were converted to the more modern angled flight deck which could handle larger and faster jets. (The USS *Essex*, USS *Kearsarge*, USS *Yorktown*, USS *Hancock*, USS *Lexington*, USS *Shangri-La*, USS *Franklin D. Roosevelt*, and the USS *Coral Sea*).

In 1961, the mission included repair of submarines. By 1965, the shipyard was established as a nuclear-capable repair facility. The largest ship ever to be built on the West Coast up to that time, the U.S.S. *Sacramento*, was built at Puget Sound Naval Shipyard. By the mid-1970s, the emphases were on submarines and nuclear-powered ships as well as the overhaul of conventional aircraft carriers.

Construction of USS King *(DLG 10) and USS* Coontz *(DLG 9) guided missile frigates in Dry-Dock 3 in January 1958. Photo courtesy Naval Sea Systems Command, www.navsea.navy.mil/shipyards/puget/Page/Historical Photos*

During the 1980s, the heaviest workload consisted of nuclear submarine overhauls. From 1987 to 1997, the Shipyard served as the homeport for the nuclear aircraft carrier, USS *Nimitz*, and when she left port, the USS *Carl Vinson*. The deactivation and recycling of nuclear powered ships was a focus during the 1990s. Puget Sound Naval Shipyard was the only Naval facility which could provide that service.

Currently, approximately twenty-five percent of the workforce is dedicated to reactor compartment disposal and inactivation. As a result, the recycling process makes the U.S. Navy the only organization in the world to design, construct, operate and recycle nuclear powered ships.

In 2003, Puget Sound Naval Shipyard and the Naval Intermediate Maintenance Facility, Pacific Northwest (facilities located at Bangor, Everett, and Bremerton) consolidated into one centrally-managed maintenance activity. This consolidation allowed prioritization of activities with an opportunity to provide critical maintenance at the lowest cost to the tax payer.

The Shipyard is an active, security-controlled facility and not open to the public for tours. Limited access is provided to tour parts of the facility by appointment.

Puget Sound Naval Shipyard was placed on the National Register of Historic Places as a Landmark District in August 1992.

Puget Sound Navy Museum

Located in Building 50, one of the first buildings to be erected at what was then Puget Sound Naval Station, is the Puget Sound Navy Museum. Its location is in the heart of downtown Bremerton, next to the ferry terminal and the Puget Sound Naval Shipyard, at 251 First Street, Bremerton. Visitors traveling from Seattle may take the scenic Seattle-Bremerton ferry departing from Pier 52 in downtown Seattle. From the Bremerton Ferry Terminal, exit to the left and follow the sidewalk. The Museum is the large, white building located within Harborside Fountain Park.

The museum is one of the twelve museums which are funded and administered by the U.S. Navy. Together with the Naval Undersea Museum in Keyport, the two museums form Navy Museums Northwest (NMNW). The museum is a unit of the Naval History and Heritage Command, headquartered in Washington D.C.

The current collection numbers more than 18,000 pieces. Collections range from 1840 to the present. One of the most popular permanent exhibits is one that shows and documents a sailor's life aboard the USS *John C. Stennis*. Another popular permanent exhibit is about special operations submarines, and their capabilities to run silent and run deep. Another permanent exhibit also describes the history of the Puget Sound Naval Shipyard and the earliest days of the facility.

A research library, photograph collections, and exhibits describing the various shops' contributions to Naval history round out the museum's collections.

The Museum is open from Monday through Saturday with the exception of federal holidays. Admission is free.

Naval Undersea Warfare Engineering Station, Keyport

"Keyport" has had many official names. It has been called Torpedo Station, Puget Sound; it has been called Keyport Torpedo Station; it has been called Pacific Coast Torpedo Station; for two years it was known as U.S. Naval Ordnance Depot Puget Sound. It is currently known as Naval Undersea Warfare Engineering Station... or, as most locals regard it, Keyport.

In 1908, a team of Naval officers came to the West Coast in search of a site with fairly specific qualifications. It needed to have clear water, not over 10 fathoms deep and not less than five. It should have a sandy bottom and little to no current. It should have little variation in tide and the water should not be extremely cold. The officers looked up and down the coast and while some properties were offered as donations, the team settled on Keyport. Details were sketchy as to the purpose of the site, but in June 1910, Congress appropriated $145,000 to purchase necessary land for a torpedo station. By September, landowners were aware that the Navy was intending to purchase property near the little village of Keyport.

Many landowners had homesteaded the property and were not willing to sell it for any price. Condemnation procedures began, but in 1911, the Navy decided to drop the proceedings, and opted instead to establish the station at the Puget Sound Navy Yard in Bremerton for the short term. The ideal conditions of depth and current were at Keyport, and locating a torpedo station there remained as a long term goal. Arguing back and forth for approximately three years, landowners were finally convinced. By 1914, the battle was completed. Landowners were compensated from a total appropriation of $60,850.

The property was officially turned over to the Navy in July 1914. Rear Admiral Cottman, then Commandant of Puget Sound Navy Yard, allowed the farmers to stay on their property until after the crops had been harvested but all of the residents had to vacate the property no later than November 1, 1914.

Building 1 was built in 1915. It housed almost the entire operation, including torpedo overhaul, administrative functions, carpenter shop, machine shop, and even had space left over for the power plant. Marines joined the force at Pacific Coast Torpedo Station in 1916 to provide guard service. There were no barracks, so the Marines lived in tents and Navy personnel occupied what was once the community's store and Grange hall.

Radio towers, 400 feet high, were erected to send overseas messages to U.S. interests in Guam and Hawaii in 1917. By 1919, Marine barracks were constructed to provide housing for the security and guard capability for the new station.

Recreation facilities were also constructed for the troops. The torpedo station had a winning baseball team in 1926. Out of forty games, the team lost only five of them. The first parking lot was built in the 1920s; as more and more employees drove their cars to work, cars were parked at odd angles throughout the installation. Station leadership approved the concept of each employee who had a car donating a day's work to clear a designated spot for the new lot.

In 1921, Assistant Secretary of the Navy Franklin D. Roosevelt visited the station. Approximately 100 workers were there to greet him.

As torpedo technology developed, so did the station at Keyport. Sixty-one additional acres were purchased in 1929. Expansion of facilities and the addition of a fence line were required. The fence was built partly to enhance security, but mostly to keep neighboring cows and other livestock from wandering throughout the base. The property needed to be logged, so to save time one of the men filled two inner tubes

Marine Barracks, Keyport, 1920s. Photo courtesy Naval Undersea Museum

with dynamite and wrapped them around the tops of two trees. The tree tops indeed came down, however one tree fell across the only ingress and egress road and started a rapidly spreading forest fire. The practice was soon prohibited and logging proceeded in the tried and true fashion that was being exercised in every other place around the area.

The challenge of finding lost test torpedoes was solved in an interesting way. Torpedoes which were about to be tested had smoke pots placed in them. If the torpedo sank, the smoke pot would send up a stream of bubbles to the surface of the water, enabling the torpedo to be more quickly located.

In the 1920s, the Pacific Coast Torpedo Station became a center for instruction and had developed a full-fledged torpedo school. Students came to Keyport from throughout the Navy for a three month course in torpedo fundamentals and the basics of ranging. Mark 8 and 9-1 torpedoes were the focus of instruction and deployment.

Throughout World War I, the pace of operations continued at an even rate. It wasn't until World War II that the pace quickened. With a new awareness for the need for security, the first Army unit was set up at the Station in August 1942 to provide security. They were also trained as backups in torpedo maintenance. During the war the town of Keyport was flooded with new residents as the station continued to hire more and more workers. Accommodations were not easy to find, and stories circulated that employees were even renting large closets as rooms from Keyport residents. The "Silent Service" of Naval submariners was becoming more prominent and the ability to enter deep into Japanese territory via submarine made the service increasing popular. As a result, work at the Keyport facility was also increasing. Work schedules were seven days on with the eighth day off.

During the war it was not uncommon for as many as 100 torpedoes to be produced and tested in a single day. In 1944, approximately 17,000 torpedoes were produced.

An aerial view of the budding Pacific Coast Torpedo Station, ca. 1923. Photo from the Naval Undersea Museum Collections

As technology continued to advance, more refined methods of testing were required. Studies indicated that an acoustic range in Hood Canal was needed. Beginning in 1944, the Applied Physics Laboratory (APL) of the University of Washington became closely tied to Keyport. This relationship resulted in the eventual requirement for and development of a 3D Tracking Range.

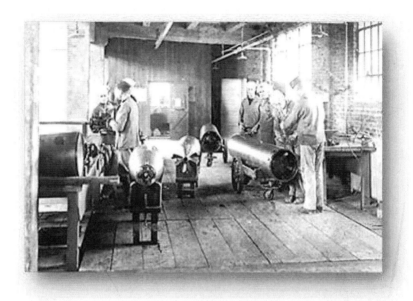

A class of students works on torpedoes in the Torpedo Storehouse of the Pacific Coast Torpedo Station, February 1918. Photo courtesy of the Naval Undersea Museum Collections

Acoustic-based tracking systems were installed during the last year of World War II. The Navy began to shift the emphasis from torpedoes being used only on surface ships to use on deep diving submarines. New tracking methodologies would have to be developed in order to seek out these targets.

By 1948-49, the torpedo ranges in Port Orchard Inlet and in Hood Canal were found to be too shallow to test the newer deep running antisubmarine weapons which were being developed. The only protected body of salt water that could provide a testing facility was at Zelatched Point on Dabob Bay in Jefferson County. The deep water in Dabob Bay provided a range where tracking could be accomplished in all three dimensions. The new range was the first tracking range capable of 3-D tracking and is still considered to be one of the quietest and most secure underwater ranges in the world.

In the early 1950s, activity was lagging at Keyport. Production of weapons after World War II was put on hold throughout what was to be known as the military-industrial complex. Only 221 civilians and 100 military were assigned to the site and the Torpedo Station was directed to consolidate its mission with the Naval Ammunition Depot at Bangor on the other side of the peninsula. The new, combined mission was called Naval Ordnance Depot. The name lasted for two years.

The Marines had been a part of the Keyport history since its inception. The Department of Defense began to undertake outsourcing of many of its traditional functions in the 1950s. In 1958, the Marine security force was replaced with civilians. The real estate footprint grew, as well, as adjacent land was acquired. With the advent of technology and electronics, the new Dabob Bay Range began to be used full time.

Keyport diving school students, September 1918. Photo courtesy of the Naval Undersea Museum

One of the most interesting facets of the Keyport facilities was the diving program. The Torpedo Station had been a source of Navy divers since its first class in 1919. In those days, the technology of diving was not refined, nor was it particularly safe. It was a common practice for the diver to work at a depth of forty feet and when he was done, shoot to the surface. In 1926 a diver experienced "the bends" (decompression sickness) and this practice stopped. Since the nearest decompression chamber was in Victoria, British

Columbia, there was not enough time to get a diver to Canada. It became common practice to suit up the diver and lower him into a deep area near Seattle where the depth was approximately 200 feet, and bring him slowly back to surface.

By the 1940s the diving school was fully equipped to train and qualify second class divers. The program was highly regarded for its instruction and for its mission in recovering torpedoes which had gone off course. The Diving Locker (hyperbaric chamber) was acquired to treat the bends in a somewhat more efficient and effective manner.

The 1960s found the Station at the pinnacle of excellence in underwater ordnance test and research. In 1968, the Station began using the Cable Controlled Underwater Vehicle (CURV II). This submersible was controlled through a cable attached to a ship. Through a television camera the CURV could be manipulated and controlled to pick up sunken torpedoes. The Polaris Missile was also one of the premier programs of the 1960s at Keyport.

During the 1970s, the organization chart at Keyport changed as did its programs and functions. Realignment of missions at other Navy units resulted in expanded missions at Keyport. Detachments in Hawaii and Southern California reported to Keyport. In 1976, Indian Island operations received detachment status and also reported to Keyport. With the new responsibilities and expanded missions, the name was changed again from Naval Torpedo Station to Naval Undersea Warfare Engineering (NUWES). In addition a new test range off of the Washington Coast near Quinault was added.

Robots became a focus for NUWES in the early 1980s, when they became instrumental in fueling, painting, and welding on torpedoes. Utilization of the Tethered Remotely Operated Vehicle Navy (TROV) began to be used extensively in the 1980s to recover lost objects from the ocean bottom. Its technology continues to be developed and used today.

Today Keyport is one of two divisions of the Naval Undersea Warfare Center (NUWC). It provides Fleet readiness support for submarines, surface ships, torpedoes, mines, land attack systems, and Fleet training systems.

Support services also include in-service engineering, test and evaluation, custom engineered solutions, and cutting-edge technologies that sustain and maintain the United States' Undersea Warfare Systems.

Naval Undersea Museum

In 1979, the Foundation that would eventually support and manage the Naval Undersea Museum was established. Groundbreaking for the museum occurred in 1985. A visit to the museum is a must. The Museum has exceptional exhibits, both inside and out. It also has an extensive research library, and programs throughout the year on special-interest subjects. Located outside of the secure gates, the Museum has full public access. It is an exceptional museum for anyone interested in undersea technologies, the oceans as part of our planet, diving technologies over the years, and, of course, torpedoes.

Naval Undersea Museum. Photo by Author, 2012

The Naval Undersea Museum's mission is to "preserve, collect, and interpret Naval undersea history, science and operations for the benefit of the U.S. Navy and the people of the United States." Located near the front gate of Keyport, the museum has permanent exhibits which address the ocean environment, torpedo technology, diving, mine warfare, and submarine technology.

Artifacts on display include major torpedoes dating from the early Whitehead and Howell torpedoes to current weapons. A simulation of a control room from the fast-attack submarine *Greenling* (SSN 614) provides a hands-on display which is fascinating for both submariners and military history enthusiasts. Periscopes, ship control panels, and the ballast control panel help explain the day-to-day life and the mission of the submariner.

The Ocean Environment exhibit provides a series of hands-on activities where properties of the ocean are explained. Visitors ranging from experienced sailors to school students have the opportunity to learn about the ocean. Pressure, density, buoyancy, light, sound, and salinity are discussed in understandable detail. One of the most interesting aspects of the Ocean Environment exhibit is a video which describes the "black smokers" (hydrothermal vents) and tube worms just 300 miles off of the coast of Washington State on the seabed of what is known as the Juan de Fuca Ridge.

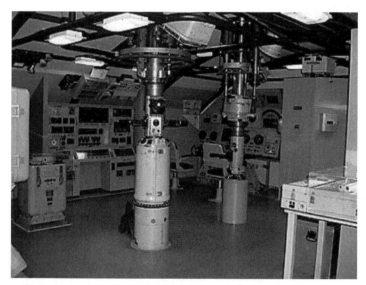

Simulation of the Control Room of the Greenling *(SSN 614). Photo courtesy Naval Undersea Museum*

Outdoor exhibits, adjacent to the parking area also provide an insight into Naval research and operations.

On 1 September 1969, Trieste II *was placed in service, with the hull number X-1. Reclassified as a deep submergence vehicle (DSV) she continued her active service in the Pacific Fleet into 1980. On display at Naval Undersea Museum. Photo by Author*

Naval Submarine Base Bangor

Naval Submarine Base Bangor's history began in 1942 as the Navy searched for a site from which to ship ammunition to the Pacific area during World War II. The Navy purchased 7,676 acres near the small community of Bangor on Hood Canal for approximately $18.7 million.

The ammunition magazine was officially established on June 5, 1944, one day before the Normandy invasion in France. Construction began six months later in January 1945.

Initially, the station had a two-berth marginal wharf, the focal point of its activity, 41 five-car barricaded sidings, a 250-car classification yard, 39 magazines, 9 storehouses, a group of transfer and segregation buildings, four permanent and one temporary barracks, and administration and shop buildings. Later construction added 68 more magazines.

One of the most notable features of the Bangor construction took place outside the gates. The point nearest to the depot on the continental railroad system was at Shelton, Washington, 45 miles to the south. It was therefore necessary to build a new rail line from that point to serve the station. This entailed construction of an additional 45 miles of track. Another spur, 4.6 miles long, was built to serve the Navy Yard at Bremerton. Ammunition shipped by train from ammunition depots throughout the country could now arrive at Bangor for loading on the various ships heading to the Pacific area of operations.

First established as an ammunition depot, the base continued to operate as a depot through both the Korean and the Vietnam wars. Its primary focus was to ship conventional weapons to theaters abroad.

In 1955, the National Security Council recommended that the Navy begin development of a submarine-launched ballistic missile system. Four years later the Polaris missile system was a reality. The first Fleet Ballistic Missile (FBM) submarines operated out of the Polaris Missile Facility Atlantic (POMFLANT) in Charleston, South Carolina. When the Navy looked at the development of a Pacific facility, it chose Bangor Naval Ammunition Depot to be the Polaris Missile Assembly Facility. Commissioned as Polaris Missile Facility, Pacific (POMFPAC) the facility at Bangor outloaded its first Polaris A3 missiles to the USS *Stonewall Jackson* (SSBN-634) on 26 March 1965.

The facility was re-commissioned Strategic Weapons Facility Pacific (SWFPAC) in July 1974. Along with the command name change, came a new mission: SWFPAC would become the missile production facility for the new generation Fleet Ballistic Missile (FMB) deterrent weapons—the Trident I (C4) missile.

SWFPAC would provide maintenance, spare parts, and nuclear warhead storage for Pacific nuclear submarines. As the Cold War weapons of the 1970s came on line, it was imperative to find a home port for the new class of Trident submarines. The Bangor base was selected in 1973 to be the home port for the first squadron of the *Ohio*-class Trident Fleet Ballistic Missile submarines.

The Trident submarine base was officially activated on February 1, 1977. By August 1980, SWFPAC was approved as a Trident-capable facility and production of the new missile began. Its first C4 missile was airlifted from SWFPAC to the Eastern Space and Missile Center (Eastern Test Range) in December 1981 for eventual outload to the USS *Ohio*.

During the same time period, the Polaris A3 missiles were beginning to be phased out of the Pacific. The last A3 tactical offload from the USS *Robert E. Lee* (SSBN 601) was completed by SWFPAC in February 1982. Bangor played a significant role in both the Polaris and the Trident technologies. As a home port it was to become an even more important facility for submarine operations throughout the Pacific.

The first of eight TRIDENT submarines in the Pacific, USS *Ohio*, arrived in August 1982, becoming the first member of the Pacific TRIDENT Submarine Fleet. The USS *Ohio* deployed on Patrol in the Pacific in October 1982.

The first eight boats were homeported at Bangor. They included:

Submarine	Commissioned
SSBN 726 USS *Ohio*	11 Nov 1981
SSBN 727 USS *Michigan*	11 Sep 1982
SSBN 728 USS *Florida*	18 Jun 1983
SSBN 729 USS *Georgia*	11 Feb 1984
SSBN 730 USS *Henry M Jackson*	6 Oct 1984
SSBN 731 USS *Alabama*	25 May 1985
SSBN 732 USS *Alaska*	25 Jan 1986
SSBN 734 USS *Nevada*	16 Aug 1986

In June 2004, SUBASE Bangor merged with Naval Station Bremerton, and the new command was named Naval Base Kitsap.

Senator Henry M. Jackson and Admiral Hyman Rickover visit the Naval Ammunition Depot at Bangor, Washington on 11 September 1964 for the commissioning of the Polaris Missile Facility, Pacific (POMFPAC). Photo courtesy of the Naval Undersea Museum Collection

USS Henry M Jackson *(SSBN-730). U.S. Navy photo*

The Navy still owns the railroad tracks from Shelton to Bangor and Bremerton, 48 miles overall. Puget Sound & Pacific Railroad runs trains on them and maintains the tracks. The Navy rarely uses the Bangor tracks, except for an occasional exercise. It hauls scrap on the Bremerton spur from Puget Sound Naval Shipyard and Intermediate Maintenance Facility.

The Navy facility at Bangor has been a significant source of employment for both Kitsap and Jefferson counties since World War II.

Deterrent Park, located on the Bangor installation, is the site of several tributes to submarine operations, and to the men who served on the boats.

Because of security considerations, access to the Bangor installation is restricted to military pass holders. Access to submarine operations areas is further restricted to only authorized individuals.

Sail of the USS Woodrow Wilson *SSBN-624 at Deterrent Park, Bangor Submarine Base. Dedicated in April 2000, the* Woodrow Wilson *was the last of the "41 For Freedom" boats to be decommissioned. The "41 for Freedom" refers to United States Navy Fleet Ballistic Missile (FBM) submarines that comprise the following classes: the* Washington, *the* Ethan Allen, *the* James Madison, *the* Lafayette *and the* Benjamin Franklin. *These five classes of missile submarines are limited by the 1972 ISLBMs to 656 missiles, (thus totaling forty-one subs), hence the nickname "41 for Freedom." Photo by author*

SSBN 726 USS Ohio *maneuvers through Hood Canal Bridge, 1980s. U.S. Navy photo*

Nike Missile Sites

Kitsap County was the home for four Nike Missile Control/Launch facilities during the early 1960s.

Poulsbo: The control facility was located about 1.5 miles southeast of downtown Poulsbo on Caldart Avenue. It is currently the site of North Kitsap School District Offices and the Frank Raab Municipal Park. The launch facility was located on Finn Hill Road and is now private property. This site was one of five Nike Ajax sites built on the west side of Puget Sound. (S-81)

Kingston: Kingston's Nike control site was north of Kingston on Ohio Avenue. The launch facility was located at what is now 8998 Kingston Road. There are a few Army structures remaining at the launch site, but the area has been developed with other civilian buildings as well. (S-92)

Winslow: The control site was south of the town of Winslow at 4900 Rose Avenue. The current use of the property is for Eagledale Park, part of the Bainbridge Parks District. The launch facility is west of Winslow on High School Road. It is now Strawberry Hill Park. The launcher area was leveled, and replaced with playing fields. (S-82).

Olalla: South of Bremerton, and across the water from Vashon Island, was the Olalla site. The launch facility is at what is now 7450 Nelson Road, under private ownership and not accessible. The control site was north of the town of Olalla and is the current site of a substance-abuse recovery center, and not accessible. (S-62).

Middle Point Military Reservation

Middle Point Military Reservation, in use from 1899 through 1958, was part of the Harbor Defense of Puget Sound. In 1899, the military reservation was acquired by condemnation and at the beginning included approximately 716 acres. Part of the Endicott Period military reservation, its location made it a sub-post of Fort Ward on Bainbridge Island.

Construction was started immediately in 1900 on a mine storage facility, a mine casemate, a mine cable tank, and, most notably, Battery Mitchell. The battery was named after First Lieutenant Robert Mitchell, a young officer in the U.S. Artillery from Wewoka, Indian Territory, who died in 1904 following surgery to address injuries sustained playing football.

Battery Mitchell. Photo by Author, 2013

The mine facilities were completed and ready for service in 1905 at a total cost of $20,800. Battery Mitchell was built to provide protection for the mine facilities; however it was never armed because it was felt that Fort Ward provided adequate protection. Ready to receive 3-inch guns on a pedestal mount, it was constructed at a cost of approximately $9,500.

Middle Point Mine Storage Building. Photo by Author, 2013

The battery was a two story structure with both guns designed to be placed on the upper level. A separate magazine for each gun was located on the lower level. Its construction was a bit unusual since it was enclosed on all four sides by concrete, and the upper level was level with the ground

Never having been used for its intended purpose, the military reservation was transferred from the Army to the Navy in 1925. Middle Point Military Reservation was converted into the Manchester Naval Supply Depot. One hundred and eleven acres of the original site were purchased by Washington State Parks in the 1960s. The Navy retains the rest of the reservation.

Visitors to Manchester State Park can still see some of the buildings erected in the early 1900s. The mine storage building and the mine casemate are now part of the Park's infrastructure.

Manchester Navy Fuel Depot

The prime mission of the Manchester Fuel Depot is to supply bulk fuel and lubricants to Navy afloat and shore activities. It is located adjacent to what is now Manchester State Park, six miles east of Port Orchard, Washington on Puget Sound. It was once part of the Middle Point Military Reservation. Built to defend the Bremerton Navy Yard, it was also known as the Old Navy Dump and the Manchester Annex. The property, acquired in 1899, was part of the plan which has come to be known as the Harbor Defense of Puget Sound.

During World War I, the depot was used as a torpedo testing station and also as a storage area for coal and oil. During World War II, the Navy established a fuel depot and also a fire training school on the property. From 1940 to the early 1950s, the Manchester Net Depot constructed, repaired, and stored submarine nets. These nets were made out of steel cable, and were then suspended from gate vessels positioned at strategic points. The Coast Guard also oversaw the implementation and maintenance of submarine nets at the Manchester Annex.

A Navy Fire Fighting School was also established at the site during World War II. Formally established in 1942, the initial purpose of the Fire Fighting School was to train World War II Navy personnel to extinguish ship fires.

The Fuel Depot received the first petroleum shipments in December 1941 and became an important support facility for both fleet and shore units throughout the war.

An antiaircraft artillery (AAA) battery was established during the 1950s on the northeastern end of the property. The fuel depot function continued to expand during the 1950s and became the largest underground west coast Navy fuel storage area. During the 1980s, and continued expansion, the facility could store 1.8 million barrels of fuel.

In the 1960s some of the property which had originally been part of the Middle Point Military Reservation and the Old Navy Dump / Manchester Annex was declared excess and was purchased by the Washington State Parks system. The National Oceanic and Atmospheric Administration (NOAA) and the Environmental Protection Agency (EPA) also acquired part of the property. The Navy still owns most of the site, however, and is now designated as a Naval Supply Center.

Currently, the yearly throughput averages 2.3 million

barrels of fuel to the depot's various customers, which include United States Air Force, United States Army, Department of Homeland Security, and United States Coast Guard. Docks at the Depot can accommodate ships as large as AOE-class oilers.

Point No Point Lighthouse

Point No Point Lighthouse, 2013. Photo by Author

Native Americans, including the Skokomish, Chimacum, and S'Klallam tribes, called the area where the Point No Point Lighthouse is located *Hahd-skus,* which means "long nose." Charles Wilkes, a member of the U.S Exploring Expedition, first saw the area, which marks the junction of Admiralty Inlet and Puget Sound, in 1841. His first impression was that it was a large point of land. When he further explored the area, he discovered it to be much smaller, and thus he named it Point No Point.

By 1872, marine traffic in Puget Sound was increasing, and a request was made to the Lighthouse Board to establish a light at Point No Point. Funds were made available, but the owner of the property was reluctant to sell. Frances James, the owner, had previously proved to have a difficult nature. This was evidenced by his involvement in a gunfight with another lighthouse keeper at Cape Flattery where he had once been based. By 1879, however, James agreed to sell forty acres on the point for $1,000.

Work was begun and by the end of the year, the structure was essentially complete with the exception of the lens and the glass. The Lighthouse Service was adamant that the light needed to be functional by the end of the year. They charged the keeper, John Maggs, who was also a dentist in Seattle, with hanging a kerosene lantern from the tower on New Years' Eve. Ten days later, a fifth-order Fresnel lens arrived. The glass panes arrived on February 1, and the lighthouse became functional shortly after that.

Mrs. Maggs was expecting a baby; it would be a little girl, and the first child born at the station. Because extra milk would be needed for the new baby girl, a schooner arrived with a cow. The cow was lowered over the side of the schooner into shallow water, where she then swam ashore.

Life was not without difficulty at the station. When an assistant keeper by the name of Manning and lighthouse keeper Maggs became involved in a dispute over ringing the bell perhaps unnecessarily, Manning pulled a pistol on Maggs and proceeded to take control of the tower. Maggs called for help in the form of the Inspector of the Lighthouse Service, and Manning and his family was asked to leave the station immediately.

In 1900 the fog bell was replaced by a Daboll trumpet in a new fog signal building. The light source was soon after upgraded to a fourth-order Fresnel lens. The lens is still mounted in the building today, although one of the prisms was cracked by lightning in 1931.

Automated in 1977, the keeper's house continued to provide housing for Coast Guard personnel. The property was declared surplus by the Coast Guard in 1998 and a long term lease was granted to Kitsap County.

In 2006, the light was extinguished and three years later, the property was offered at no cost to eligible entities under the provisions of the National Historic Lighthouse Preservation Act. Kitsap County submitted its application for the property in the spring of 2010. During that year as well, a grant was received from American Express to help preserve the facility. The facility is open for tourists during the summer season.

Port Gamble

A small blockhouse was built in 1853 at Port Gamble to protect the community from attacks. While most blockhouses did not see much in the way of military action, the little blockhouse at Port Gamble provided protection for both settlers and military personnel.

In November 1856, shortly after the threats from local Native Americans had dissipated, seven Haida canoes came into Puget Sound. The Haida had often raided their neighbors to the south. This time the raiders paddled to Steilacoom where Army Lieutenant Colonel Casey called for help from the Navy. The steam sloop *Massachusetts* was in the Sound, and could provide some assistance.

By the time the *Massachusetts* could begin to engage, the canoes paddled back to Port Gamble and arrived at the sawmill there on November 19. The mill superintendent sounded the alarm whistle and the mill hands and their families moved to a wooden blockhouse (called a Malakoff blockhouse because of its building style). They took with them about 30 rifles, muskets, and plenty of ammunition. The next morning the *Massachusetts* steamed into Port Gamble. Two days of gunfire and some discussion ensued.

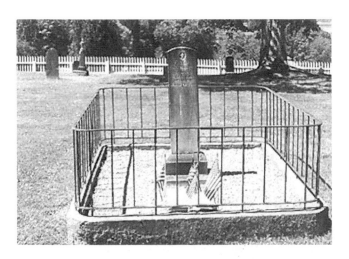

Grave of Gustave Englebrecht at the Buena Vista Cemetery, Port Gamble. Photo courtesy of Findagrave.com

During one of the exchanges, Coxswain Gustave Englebrecht fired his weapon and struck one of the Haida warriors. When he raised his head to observe what he had done, the Haida force returned the favor and fatally shot him in the head. The Haidas surrendered and were escorted back to what is now Canada by the *Massachusetts*. They returned, however in the summer of 1857. They surprised Isaac Ebey on his farm on Whidbey Island and proceeded to behead him.

Englebrecht, the first Navy man to die in battle on the Pacific, was buried at what is now known as Buena Vista Cemetery in Port Gamble.

Veterans Memorials, Monuments, and Other Sites in Kitsap County

Kitsap County has over twenty sites dedicated to veterans. Monuments and memorials span the nation's history to include conflicts in the Middle East. These monuments include:

- **Bainbridge Memorial Field**, located at Bainbridge High School
- **Bainbridge Island Japanese American Memorial**, located at the former Eagledale ferry dock
- **Bataan Park,** Bremerton, located at the corner of Sylvan and Olympus
- **Evergreen Rotary Park**, a World War I Memorial located at 1400 Park Avenue in Bremerton
- **Tomb of the Unknown Soldier and USS *Saratoga* MIA Memorial**, Ivy Green Cemetery, 1401 Naval Avenue, Bremerton
- **Puget Sound Navy Museum**, at Harborside Fountain Park, Bremerton
- **NAD/Soroptimist Park**, featuring an F8 Crusader, 6002 Kitsap Way, Bremerton
- **USS *Turner Joy* Museum Ship and the Statue of the Lone Sailor,** Bremerton Boardwalk, Bremerton
- **Hal's Corner**, featuring a battery and anchor from heavy cruiser USS *Bremerton*, Sheridan and Warren Avenue, Bremerton

- **Miller Woodlawn Cemetery,** Mast from heavy cruiser USS *Bremerton*. Memorabilia left at the roving Vietnam Wall is buried at the foot of the mast, 5505 Kitsap Way, Bremerton
- **Bremerton Memorial Stadium**, Ohio and 15 Street, Bremerton
- **Path of Freedom Memorial**, chronicles Kitsap County citizens who lost their lives in combat during WW I through the present, Ohio and 15 Street, Bremerton
- **Navy Undersea Museum**, 610 Dowell Street, Keyport
- **Kitsap County Fairgrounds,** dedicated to Korean War Veterans, 1190 Fairgrounds Road, Silverdale
- **Blue Star Memorial Highway**, sign at 7601 Tracyton Boulevard, Bremerton
- **Manchester Veterans Memorial**, Colchester and E Main, Manchester
- **Grave of Coxswain Englebrecht**, Buena Vista (Port Gamble) Cemetery, Port Gamble
- **World War II Memorial, Kitsap County Courthouse**, 614 Division Street, Port Orchard
- **Traffic Triangle** located at Cline, Kitsap and Bay Street, Port Orchard
- **Memorial Armory**, World War I and World War II Washington National Guard, 19133 Jensen Way, Poulsbo
- **Liberty Bay Park,** downtown Poulsbo
- **Veterans Memorial Park**, 985 Retsil Road SE, Retsil
- **Washington Veterans Home Cemetery**, 900 Olney Avenue SE, Retsil
- **Civil War Memorial erected by Women's Relief Corps in 1912 and a Spanish American War Memorial**, Washington Veterans Home Cemetery, Retsil
- **Kitsap County Veterans Memorial**, built by the Silverdale Sunrise Club and the Home Builders Association of Kitsap County, Waterfront Park, 3337 NW Byron, Silverdale
- **Henry R. Johnson World War I Memorial**, dedicated to Silverdale citizen Henry Johnson who lost his life in the Meuse-Argonne Offensive, Waterfront Park, Silverdale

USS *Turner Joy*, DD 951
U.S. Navy Destroyer Museum Ship

Tied up along the Bremerton boardwalk, near downtown and the Puget Sound Naval Museum, is the U.S.S. *Turner Joy*. Now a Museum Ship, the destroyer is a wonderful opportunity for sailors, families, history buffs, and children to experience a bit of nostalgia and have an educational experience at the same time. The Bremerton Historic Ships Association was created in 1988 as a non-profit organization with the mission of acquiring and preserving vessels for historic and educational purposes. The *Turner Joy* arrived in 1991.

The ship was named for Admiral Charles Turner Joy. Admiral Joy's long Navy career included tours in World War II where he was instrumental in planning and executing combat operations against Japan. As Captain Joy, he commanded the cruiser USS *Louisville,* which saw duty in the Aleutians and South Pacific during World War II. He was a commander of an amphibious group when Japan surrendered in 1945, and was then assigned to duty in China. Following his tour in China he became Commander Naval Forces Far East and then was appointed as the senior United Nations delegate to the Korean Armistice talks. When he retired, in 1954, he was the Superintendent of the U.S. Naval Academy. Admiral Joy died in 1956.

The *Turner Joy* was built by the Puget Sound Bridge and Dredging Company of Seattle, and was commissioned in 1959. At a length of over 418 feet, with a beam of over 45 feet, the ship was powered by four 1200-pound boilers, two steam turbines, and had two shafts. The ship could cruise at 32+ knots and was armed with three 5-inch, 54 caliber guns and two Mark 32 torpedo launchers that carried six Mark 46 torpedoes. The crew consisted of 275 enlisted and 17 officers.

The ship was the last built in the Forrest Sherman Class. She had several tours in the Pacific and is part of the historic Gulf of Tonkin incident in 1964. As a part of the task group supporting the *Ticonderoga,* she reported that torpedo wakes had been sighted heading towards the American warships from the west and the south. Radar indicated that the ships may have been under attack, and planes from the *Ticonderoga* were scrambled to fire in the direction indicated by radar. Historians note now that it could have been bad weather, and strange radar conditions which appeared on the radar screens

USS Turner Joy *off the coast of Vietnam 1968. Photo courtesy U.S. Navy*

   No matter the cause, it was the Gulf of Tonkin incident that prompted retaliation by U.S. forces. The *Constellation* joined the *Ticonderoga* and launched 64 sorties towards the bases from where the attacks may have been launched. Oil storage depots were also attacked.
   The *Turner Joy* participated in several operations off the coast of Vietnam. She was instrumental in providing gunfire support for American and South Vietnamese troops while at the same time providing interdiction of enemy logistics traffic. For her support, she received a total of nine battle stars. Damaged in Operation "Sea Dragon" off the coast of North Vietnam, she sustained direct hits on the fantail and other damage from shrapnel. She returned to Bremerton for repairs and reported to Long Beach for operations along the California coast. In 1968, she returned to Vietnam where her tours of duty took her into the I, II and IV Corps areas of South Vietnam. She completed her last tour of duty in September of 1968 and was involved in peacetime deployments out of Long Beach. In 1982, the Forrest Sherman Class destroyers were retired.
   In 1988, she was selected as a Naval Memorial and came to Bremerton's downtown waterfront. She retains most of the

1959 configuration, and has been faithfully restored to her appearance during the years between 1960 and 1982.

She was donated to the Bremerton Historic Ships Association in April 1991, and is a museum open to the public. A trip to Bremerton should definitely include a visit to the USS *Turner Joy*. The museum is open every day with the exception of Christmas, Thanksgiving, Easter Sunday, and some federal holidays.

USS Turner Joy *tied up at Bremerton Waterfront, ca. 2005. Photo courtesy of Bremerton Historic Ships Association*

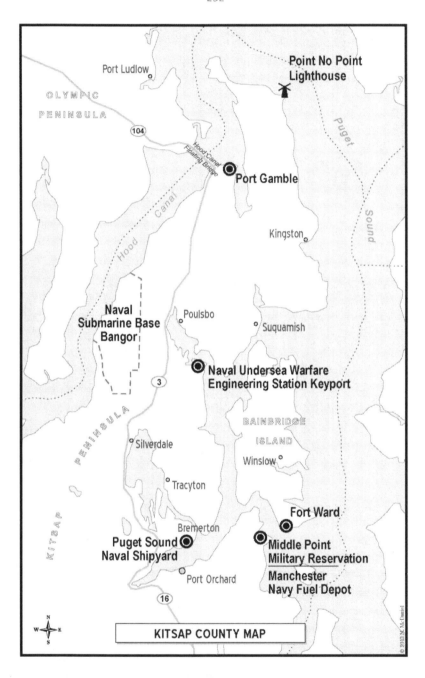

Chapter 11

Jefferson County

While one of the smallest counties in terms of population, some of the most important military historic sites in the area are in Jefferson County. State Parks now occupy military installations which were keys to the defense of the nation.

Fort Townsend

As more and more settlers came to the Puget Sound area and as treaties with Native Americans were perceived as "faulty" at best by tribal leaders, relationships deteriorated.

In 1852, legislative leaders petitioned Congress for troops to be sent to the Puget Sound area. In 1854, General Harney, Commander of the Division of the Pacific, asked that troops be assigned to help protect the settlers. By August 1856, Fort Bellingham was established and Fort Townsend, two miles south of Port Townsend, the Port of Entry for the entire Puget Sound area, was established in October of the same year.

The site of Fort Townsend was picked partially because it had a fresh supply of water from a small stream running through it. The garrison consisted of 82 officers and men, including a company of the Fourth Infantry and a detachment of artillery commanded by Captain G. O. Haller. Construction, at a cost of a little over $35,000, was completed by 1858. The first buildings were built of logs and covered with shake/shingle siding. The new post was logged and after the logging was completed, the creek which supplied water began to go dry. Wells, cisterns, and steam powered pumps were installed which served the fort throughout the rest of its existence.

The boundary dispute with England over the San Juan Islands resulted in troops from Fort Bellingham and Fort Townsend being ordered to the San Juan Islands in July 1859. By 1861, the regular troops which had been assigned to Fort Townsend were withdrawn and volunteers garrisoned the post. During the Civil War, the post was reportedly used as a marine hospital although records are not clear as to whether the concept was developed into a reality.

Various generals, including General Halleck and General Babcock of the Department of Columbia, recommended that the fort be abandoned and the buildings be torn down. They recommended that troops and assets be moved to other locations which might have a greater strategic value to the defense of Puget Sound.

Old Fort Townsend: Interior of enlisted mens' barracks. These barracks at Fort Townsend burned to the ground on January 2, 1885, when one of the kerosene lamps exploded, and ultimately sealed the fort's demise as a military institution. Photo used by permission of the Jefferson County Historical Society

As the years went by, various units occupied the fort but for only short periods of time. By 1870, Fort Townsend was the only post in Puget Sound. Fort Bellingham had been closed and Fort Steilacoom was sold in 1870. As soon as the boundary dispute in the San Juan Islands was settled there would not be any further use for posts on the islands.

The fort was reactivated to some extent in 1874. Soon troops from Camp San Juan were sent to Fort Townsend. By 1876, the buildings which had started to fall into disrepair had been repaired and the post was once again housing troops and appeared to be more than a facility in caretaker status.

By 1877, lingering Indian wars found all remaining troops heading back to the field and the fort was garrisoned by detachments of the Twenty-first Infantry and the Fourth Artillery. Unit strength was four commissioned officers and eleven enlisted men.

General of the Army William Tecumseh Sherman visited the post in 1880, and noted about Port Townsend and Fort Townsend that it appeared the town was protecting the fort instead of the fort protecting the town.

Units moved in and out of the fort. In 1880 a new guardhouse was built and a new storehouse was completed. Barracks began to develop some signs of disrepair and were regarded as too small for the number of men assigned. From 1882 on, however, annual reports to the Secretary of the Army indicated that the installation was of little to no value for the defense of Puget Sound. If new buildings were to be built, they should be built at other locations which might be strategically more important.

Special projects became part of the mission of the troops assigned to the fort. Soldiers were often used to provide law enforcement activities and were noted in historical documents as having been used to track down and arrest local Native Americans who had made some incursions upon local settlers.

Records also show that soldiers were used to help provide "reconnaissance" for a telegraph line which would eventually run between Port Angeles and Cape Flattery.

The first exploration of the Olympic Mountains was done by the Army. Fort Townsend troops, with Lieutenant Willis Wittich as their leader, explored a route into the mountains from the Dungeness River. On later expeditions, Fort Townsend supplied pack animals and supplies for the expeditions.

In 1885, President Grover Cleveland appointed a civilian board, headed by Secretary of War William Endicott to evaluate seacoast defenses. This Board of Fortification (now usually referred to as the Endicott Board) presented a grim picture of neglect. They reported that America's seacoast defenses were not capable of protecting the country from a sea attack. The Board recommended a massive $127 million construction program for a series of forts, batteries, mines, and mortars on the coasts of the United States. Coast Artillery fortifications built between 1885 and 1905 are often referred to as Endicott Period fortifications.

Dance hall in the foreground and officers' quarters in the background. Fort Townsend, 1916. From Frances Carter Album. Photo used by permission of the Jefferson County Historical Society

The Fortification Board met but left out any plans to further defend the Puget Sound area. Again, annual reports from Army leaders of the Department of the Columbia indicated that Fort Townsend's fortifications had little value except to provide shelter for assigned soldiers. The Fortification Board met again in 1894 and selected eleven points on Puget Sound which would be suitable for constructing coastal defense fortifications.

Fort Townsend was not part of this list. In the same year, the barracks at Fort Townsend were destroyed by a fire which started from an exploding kerosene lamp. Troops finally abandoned the post and relocated to Vancouver Barracks.

The property was transferred to the Department of the Interior for approximately a year, and then reverted back to the Army. In 1936, the commander at Fort Worden determined that the buildings at Fort Townsend were a liability. He dispatched troops to tear the remaining buildings down and burn them. It was kept on the Army rolls until World War II, when it was used as a munitions defusing station.

Fort Townsend became the home for the Ordnance Investigative Laboratory (OIL), also known as the Explosive Investigative Laboratory during WW II. OIL provided bomb disposal and defusing services throughout Puget Sound and on deployments to Attu Island Alaska. A sister unit at Stump Neck, Maryland, provided similar services for the east coast. The unit utilized a powerful x-ray unit which was used to determine the structure of bombs, mines, etc.

Building for VanderGraft X-ray machine. U.S. Navy photo

The VanderGraft X-ray machine contained huge vacuum tubes to provide vacuum for the X-ray tubes. The OIL also X-rayed the bores of the first new 3"-50" caliber anti-aircraft guns mounted aboard cruisers at the Puget Sound Naval Shipyard after their proof firings. Medics at Fort Worden were interested in the utilization of the x-ray equipment. Navy officials, however, denied permission to use the machine on humans because it was a very dangerous unit given the slightest miscalculation. The ordnance unit deployed throughout the Pacific theatre to provide bomb and mine disposal services.

Diving operations were also an important part of the laboratory's activities. Inspection of the seaplane ramp at Port Angeles and recovery of sunken munitions off of Whidbey

Island were a frequent part of the unit's regular mission. At the close of WW II, personnel were relocated and the equipment was removed.

In 1953, Washington State Parks acquired the Fort Townsend property and it became a state park. It remains now as a quiet park with a picnic area and buildings for small parties and receptions. Little remains of the military installation, although the old parade ground still remains as a centerpiece of the park.

Fort Townsend Parade Grounds 2011. Photo by Author

Fort Worden

Fort Worden's earliest history began as a fairly basic and remote primitive guardhouse at Point Wilson, just outside of Port Townsend, to help provide settlers some protection from Native American Tribes and the First Peoples from what is now Canada. Port Townsend, Washington Territory's second incorporated city, was located on a strategic point of land where natives from the north and from the south often converged.

Rear Admiral John L. Worden. Photo Courtesy of U.S. Naval Historical Center

The military facility was named for Rear Admiral John L Worden, a noted Navy hero who had been in command of the *Monitor* during Civil War. He later served as the Superintendent of the U.S. Naval Academy. His accomplishments were headline news during the time that the new fort was being developed.

Fort Townsend, just two miles away from the new town, had been established in 1856 to help provide some deterrent factor to raiding and to show the flag to the tribes and also to the British military in Canada and in the San Juan Islands. Fort Townsend had unfortunately not been located at a strategic point where it could provide much protection from warships entering Puget Sound. As a result, it was abandoned in 1895. Following the Civil War, the focus on defense and the emphasis on military technology resulted in Government activities to develop coast and port defense installations.

General Totten, the Army's chief engineer since 1838, looked at sites with a view that the relationship between the United States and Great Britain was extremely tenuous. He was concerned with the strategy and the logistics involved in protecting the waterways into Puget Sound. He noted that closing the opening to Puget Sound at Admiralty Inlet could be accomplished by constructing a line of defense from Point Wilson across to Admiralty Head on Whidbey Island. He also noted that a third fort should be constructed. He also took into consideration possible forts at Foulweather Bluff, Double Bluff, Tala Point and in the mid-channel of Admiralty Inlet. He also favored Port Discovery as a potential site. He made these recommendations at the beginning of the Civil War.

President Andrew Johnson concurred and by 1866, more than 20 potential sites had been identified throughout the Puget Sound area, but no projects had been approved. Totten, who died in 1864, did not live to see any of his work come to fruition.

More studies examined locations up and down Puget Sound as potential sites for military installations. Examination of an idea of building a fort in the mid-channel resulted in that concept being scrapped. Constructing a fort in an area where the average depth is 200 feet was deemed as "impractical," and most likely, impossible.

As the United States was completing its westward expansion, the government was providing more emphasis on making the United States one of the great military powers of the world. The Navy expanded to become a more international force, and the Army began to assume more responsibility for the coasts and its ports. Settlers were coming to the Northwest in unprecedented numbers; lumber, fishing, and shipbuilding were bringing settlers to the Seattle area at the rate of 1,000 new residents per month in 1889. Despite the growth of settlers and expansion into the area, however, Puget Sound still did not make the list for the construction of military posts.

Fort Worden Parade Ground inspection. Alexander's Castle in background, ca. 1900s. Photo used by permission of the Jefferson County Historical Society

When the Puget Sound Navy Yard was established in 1891, the story changed. In 1895, The U.S. Army Corps of Engineers was tasked with building three forts designed to defend Admiralty Inlet through which ships moving into Puget Sound had to pass. These three posts were regarded as the coast defenses of Puget Sound. Coastal Artillery batteries were established at Fort Flagler on Marrowstone Island, Fort Casey on Whidbey Island, and at Fort Worden on Point Wilson. All three forts had similar features. All had a bluff above the beach and low-lying land on the beach, making them ideal sites.

108th company, Coast Artillery Corps, on parade, ca. 1900s. Photo used by permission of the Jefferson County Historical Society

Acquiring the land for Fort Worden took approximately 12 years. Property negotiations were complicated and extensive. Over 300 landowners in and around the fort negotiated with the government to sell and ultimately convey their land. Some property was acquired through condemnation. Logging began in 1897, and construction of the gun batteries started in 1898 on the bluff above the beach.

A narrow-gauge railroad and two dinky locomotives moved concrete and other materials around the fort. The rise from the beach to the upper bluff, however, required that even the locomotives needed to be winched uphill. Portland cement was used to build the gun batteries and other structures. A water pipeline was laid from Port Townsend to the fort to enable construction and water was pumped into large storage tanks inside the fort's boundary.

Main Barracks, Fort Worden, Port Townsend, Wash. Ellis Real Photo Post Card, Author's collection

The original 1895 recommendation for fortification on Fort Worden's bluff was for two 12-inch and five 10-inch guns mounted on non-disappearing carriages. In 1900, guns arrived via barge and by 1902, gun batteries were ready and the fort was officially activated.

Permanent buildings were designed and constructed from 1904 to 1915. In addition, sixteen 12-inch mortars would be installed. Underground storage magazines were built to be waterproof as well as bombproof.

In 1905, President Theodore Roosevelt noted that Puget Sound's growth and importance demanded more fortifications. William H. Taft, Secretary of War, and a board comprised of Army and Navy staff members, which became known as the Taft Board, recommended the addition of seven 14-inch guns, two 12-inch guns, changes in mounts and location of two 10-inch guns, seven 6-inch guns, four 4-inch guns, and eight 12-inch mortars. In addition, carriages, emplacements, mine defense, power plants, searchlights, and fire control were also recommended. The estimated cost was more than $ 5 million.

The first unit to be stationed at Fort Worden was the 126th Coast Artillery Company. Commanded by Captain Manus McCloskey, the unit consisted of 87 soldiers. They arrived aboard the SS *Majestic*, and were quartered in tents until the barracks could be completed.

At the same time Fort Worden was under construction, so were Fort Casey on Whidbey Island and Fort Flagler on Marrowstone Island. In 1904, the headquarters of the Harbor Defense Command of Puget Sound was transferred from Fort Flagler to Fort Worden. By the fall of 1905, four Coast Artillery companies occupied the fort. The Harbor Defense System of Puget Sound was complete and considered operational.

The large number of detached gun batteries built during the 1890s quickly made keeping track of them extremely difficult. The War Department assigned names to each battery, often selected to honor deceased military personnel, famous Indian chiefs, governors, or localities. In short, there was no systematic way of naming them.

The initial armaments at Fort Worden included six gun emplacements:

- **Battery Ash:** Located on Artillery Hill. Contained two barbette guns. Named for Brevet Lieutenant Colonel Ash, who died in the Civil War in Virginia
- **Battery Brannan:** Located on Artillery Hill. It had two plotting rooms for eight 12-inch mortars. Named for Brevet Major General John Milton Brannan who served in the U.S-Mexican War and the Civil War. (Note: It was modified in 1906 to one plotting room, and in 1918 half the mortars were removed.)
- **Battery Powell**: Located next to Battery Brannan. Contained eight 12-inch mortars. Named after Major Powell who died at the Battle of Shiloh
- **Battery Quarles:** Located on Artillery Hill, contained three 10-inch barbette guns. Named for Captain Quarles who died at the Battle of Churubusco, Mexico
- **Battery Randol:** Located on Artillery Hill. Contained two 10-inch barbette guns. Named for Brevet Brigadier General Randol, a Civil War hero
- **Battery Vicars:** Located on Point Wilson. Contained two 5-inch guns. Named after after First Lieutenant Thomas Allen Vicars, 27th U.S. Infantry, who was killed in the Philippine campaign against the Moros in 1902.

Between 1905 and 1910 six additional gun emplacements were added:

- **Battery Tolles:** Located along the beach bluff below Artillery Hill. Named for Brevet Colonel Cornelius W. Tolles, U.S. Volunteers, who died from wounds received during the Civil War. Originally contained four 6-inch guns. Two guns were removed in 1918
- **Battery Stoddard:** Located on the bluff facing Admiralty Inlet. Contained four 6 inch guns. Named for Major Amos Stoddard, 1st U.S. Artillery, who died in 1813 from wounds received during the War of 1812
- **Battery Benson:** Located on Artillery Hill. Contained two 10-inch disappearing guns. Named after Captain Benson who died in 1862. Had a tunnel that ran to buildings on the hill, barracks, water reservoir, a switchboard and signal station
- **Battery Putnam:** Located on the bluff facing Admiralty Inlet. Contained two 3-inch guns. Named for Colonel Haldimand Putnam, New Hampshire Volunteers, who was killed during the Civil War
- **Battery Walker:** Located on the bluff facing the Strait of Juan de Fuca. Contained two 3-inch guns. Named for Lieutenant Colonel Samuel H. Walker, Mounted Rangers, of Walker-Colt revolver fame, who was killed in Huamantia, Mexico in October 1847
- **Battery Kinzie:** Located on Point Wilson. Contained two 12-inch M1895 disappearing guns. Named for Brigadier General David Hunter Kinzie, a U.S. Civil War veteran who died in 1904.

Washington National Guard troops came to Fort Worden in 1906. Their arrival was part of a national focus to see if reserve forces could be effective in manning coastal defense installations. Eventually, the Coast Artillery Corps became a mixture of both regulars and reserve forces. As the number of coastal defense installations increased, the Army became concerned that it would not have enough regulars to man the installations. The Guard troops came to Fort Worden for two weeks each summer and camped in tents on Artillery Hill. Marksmanship competitions between the regulars and the Guard provided entertainment for Port Townsend residents. Many would bring their picnic lunch to the hillside near Battery Benson to watch the firing competitions between batteries.

In 1911, there were 600 troops stationed at Fort Worden. By the summer of 1918 and World War I, there were several thousand soldiers who had received artillery training at the fort. Building began again to house the troops. As the troops came to Fort Worden, however, the guns left to be used in action in the war. Forty-five of Fort Worden, Fort Flagler, and Fort Casey's guns were dismounted and sent to the European front.

By the end of World War I, both Fort Casey and Fort Flagler were in caretaker status. The Fort Worden garrison consisted of 19 officers and 300 enlisted.

Army Coast Artillery units were considered among the elite organizations at the time. Their jobs required the utilization of more technology than most. Technological advances and changing techniques increasingly separated coastal defenses (heavy) from field artillery (light). Officers were rarely qualified in both due to the separation of field artillery and coastal artillery into separate branches.

Distinctive insignia were approved after the units had been originally organized in the 1920s. The 14th Coast Artillery unit, which called Fort Worden home, had a crest of bright metal and enamel. On the crest was the head of a northern lynx in silver and surrounded by a ribbon in red enamel which formed a half circle around and below the face. On the ribbon, the ends which terminated above and behind the ears of the lynx, was the motto in gold letters: *Semper Vigilans.*

After the war, military thinking evolved to include balloons. In May 1920, the 2nd Balloon Company arrived at Fort Worden. After a short period of testing, military observers concluded that balloon companies would strengthen the coast artillery mission. Two balloon hangars were built, one at Fort Worden, and one at Fort Casey. By the time the hangars and the hydrogen-generating facilities were ready in 1921, the balloon companies had been transferred. The hangar at Fort Casey was torn down, but the building at Fort Worden was retained for storage. It served as the backdrop for the famous fight scene in the movie "An Officer and A Gentleman." Much of the movie was filmed at Fort Worden and in local establishments in Port Townsend.

Balloon hangar. Photo courtesy Coast Artillery Museum

In 1939, Europe was back at war. Temporary buildings were under construction in 1941 to house soldiers assigned to Fort Worden for training. Harbor defenses became a shared responsibility of both the Army and the Navy. Fear that the Japanese could invade the Pacific Northwest resulted in expanded operations. By 1943, approximately 4,500 military personnel were assigned to Fort Worden.

As this war drew to a close, Fort Worden's military population once again diminished to less than 100. Even smaller caretaker forces were assigned to Fort Casey and Fort Flagler. The last guns were removed in 1946.

The Navy came to Fort Worden in the early 1940s. A casemate was built by the Navy in 1943 as the Harbor Entrance Control Post, Harbor Defense Command Post, and signaling station. As sonar and radar came into regular use, the Navy assumed the responsibility for utilizing what had been an Army Signal Corps experiment utilizing underwater magnetic loops, hydrophones and sonar. With the old Army system, the information on potential targets would have been relayed to a plotting room and subsequently to the mortars and shells, which would have been sent high out over the Strait to come down on the target from almost directly overhead. Now, with the use of radar and sonar, the Harbor Defense System became a primarily defensive mission. Using data gained from spotters, sonar, and radar, the information was coordinated and relayed to Navy vessels in the Straits. The Navy continued to use the bunker into the 1960s as a place for reserve units to meet and train, including learning how to lay land mines.

The mission changed again in 1949. An Army Amphibious Brigade arrived at Fort Worden. Landing craft were kept both at Fort Worden and in Port Townsend at Point Hudson. While Army plans were to base West Coast Amphibious units in Admiralty Inlet, those plans changed with the Korean conflict. As activities in Korea came to a close, the Army abandoned the amphibious mission in Port Townsend. Fort Worden was decommissioned on June 30, 1953.

Long Range Radar on Battery Benson. Photo by Ron Novak, provided by Dick Wiltse

In the late 1950s, the Army set up a long-range radar on top of Battery Benson, in support of the Seattle Nike Missile Defense System. The Navy had a Harbor Defense Unit at Fort Worden from the 1940s through 1958. The last vessel at the Fort was the USS *Elder*, a cable/mine layer which was also used for underwater salvage. A Naval Reserve Inshore Undersea War Unit also used the Harbor Entrance Control

Post and the wharf for training from 1960 to 1969. They were the last military personnel at Fort Worden.

A military cemetery is located at Fort Worden. It contains interments from the Spanish-American War through the Vietnam War.

Fort Worden Military Cemetery. Photo by Author

Battery Kinzie, June 2011. Photo by Author

When the fort property was decommissioned, it was taken over by the Washington State Department of Institutions in 1957. It served as the Fort Worden Juvenile Diagnostic and

Treatment Center from 1958 to 1971. The park was transferred to the Washington State Parks and Recreation Commission. In 1973, in partnership with the Washington State Arts Commission, it became Fort Worden State Park. Today, the park is one of the most popular in the State. It is also home to Centrum, a nonprofit arts organization that presents workshops and performances in a wide variety of artistic disciplines. Fort Worden is recognized as an important gathering place for artists, performers, and visitors from all over the world. Fort Worden holds a place on the State and National Register of Historic Places.

Puget Sound Coast Artillery Museum

Puget Sound Coast Artillery Museum at Fort Worden State Park, July 2011. Photo by Author

Fort Worden is also home to the Puget Sound Coast Artillery Museum. It is located on Fort Worden in a former barracks along the parade grounds. The bulk of its collection addresses the history of the Coast Artillery Corps, which became a separate branch of the Army in 1907. The Army was tasked with providing seacoast defense while the Navy's role was to provide off-shore interception of enemy vessels.

The Museum has myriad photos of Fort Worden, as well as Fort Flagler and Fort Casey. It houses a collection of weapons issued to soldiers for personal protection. The wide range of items in its collection also includes a World War II chaplain's field organ. Of particular interest is a well-organized and extensive collection of Civil Defense items which were in use from post-World War II years throughout much of the Cold War. In addition to serving as docents, museum volunteers also help maintain the gun emplacements, put up interpretive signs, and give guided tours.

The Museum Staff can also provide tours of Artillery Hill, the underground Harbor Entrance Control Post and the Mortar Battery Plotting Room. Alfred Chiswell, President of the Museum, summed up the experience at Fort Worden and the Museum with "It's a beautiful historical site. There's a mystique about it."

Dick Wiltse, Museum Volunteer, giving a tour of Fort Worden. Photo courtesy of Puget Sound Coast Artillery Museum

Point Wilson Lighthouse

Point Wilson lies at the turning point from the Strait of Juan de Fuca into Admiralty Inlet and on into Puget Sound. Fog, winds, and rain are no strangers to Point Wilson.

The first hazard marker for passing mariners was a church bell. Although not located on the point, a ship's bell was donated to St. Paul's Episcopal Church in 1865 with the condition that the bell be rung on foggy days. One story tells that one night when the fog was particularly thick, a steamer was passing by Port Townsend. Not knowing exactly where they were, the captain guided the ship to safety by the ringing bell. An evangelist by the name of John Yates was purported to be on board and was moved and inspired to write the hymn, "The Harbor Bell."

Point Wilson Lighthouse, ca. 1960. Photo courtesy U.S. Coast Guard

As shipping in and out of Port Townsend increased, the citizens of Port Townsend lobbied for a light and a fog signal. A signal light station was built at Point Wilson, about two miles northwest of downtown Port Townsend. The first light was mounted on a tower, approximately 48 feet high. It flashed its light for the first time in December 1879. A fog signal building nearby also housed a boiler and a steam-powered fog whistle.

Point Wilson's first lightkeeper was David Littlefield. He was paid $800 per year. A Civil War veteran, he arrived in Port Townsend in 1867 to be a farmer. He soon married Maria Hastings, the oldest daughter of Loren B. Hastings, who was one of Port Townsend's founding fathers. He served in the lighthouse for four years, and then served Jefferson County as the Sheriff, the mayor of Port Townsend, a City Councilman, and Collector of Customs.

In 1896, the first construction at Fort Worden began on the bluffs immediately behind the light. Wind and currents resulted in a serious erosion of the beach area around the tower forced the construction of a new lighthouse in 1914. It had an octagonal tower a foot higher than the first tower. The fourth-order Fresnel lens is still in the lighthouse and shines a white light for 15 seconds, then off for 5 seconds and one red flash.

In 1921, Point Wilson was the scene of a ship tragedy when the inbound passenger ship S.S. *Governor* collided with the freighter S.S. *West Hartland*, which was departing Port Townsend on its way to India. The Point Wilson lightkeeper telephoned authorities in Port Townsend and rescue activities were begun. The *Governor* sank within minutes in 240 feet of water off of Point Wilson. The *West Hartland* was escorted to Seattle with the survivors on board.

The station continued its mission of warning mariners with both lights and fog horns; however, during World War II, the light was out because of the blackouts imposed during the war.

During the 1960s, Coast Guard housing was constructed adjacent to the lighthouse. In the 1970s, the Coast Guard erected a 90-foot radar/radio signal tower just east of the lighthouse to monitor and guide ships in north Puget Sound and the Strait of Juan de Fuca. The lighthouse was automated in 1976 and a radio-beacon transmitter was installed for use in locating ship positions. During this period the personnel of the Coast Guard vessel *Point Bennett* were responsible for the general maintenance of the station.

Today, a computer located at the Coast Guard Station at Port Angeles maintains the operation of the light. During the winters of 2005 and 2006, erosion of the beach around the lighthouse once again threatened the lighthouse. The tides and currents off of Point Wilson are among the strongest in Puget Sound. Engineers have addressed the situation and agree that in the future the only solution to save the lighthouse may be to move it to higher ground. In the meantime, the rock walls are being filled in as the beach areas erode. Moving the facilities will likely cost upwards of $5 million dollars.

In March 1971, Point Wilson Lighthouse was designated as an Historic Place. It is not open to the public, but photos are easily taken from only a few feet outside of its gate.

Point Wilson. Photo Courtesy of the U.S. Coast Guard

Fort Flagler

Fort Flagler, just across Port Townsend Bay from Fort Worden, completed the "Triangle of Fire" as the third point. Established in 1895, it was also an Endicott Period fortification. The fort was named after Brigadier General Daniel Webster Flagler who was the Army Chief of Ordnance.

Fort Flagler is located on the northeastern tip of Marrowstone Island. Of the three forts, Fort Flagler was the first site to be developed. By executive order in 1866, 640 acres were reserved for military purposes. It was surveyed in 1896, and in 1897 the government began the process of purchasing more land from adjacent land owners.

The fort was originally constructed with three gun batteries: Battery Revere, Battery Wilhelm, and Battery

Rawlins which were completed in 1899. The batteries were not accepted for service until August of 1902. Two additional batteries were completed in 1900 and 1902: Battery Bankhead and Battery Lee. Both of these batteries were accepted in 1902. Construction of support buildings and barracks was complete in June 1899 and the post was activated a month later. When construction of the new mortar Battery Bankhead was started, a rail line from the quartermaster dock was constructed to handle the movement of materiel and equipment. A telegraph system was also installed to provide a means of communication between Forts Worden, Casey, Flagler and Lawton.

Battery at Fort Flagler under construction with Marrowstone Point Lighthouse in the distance, 1897. Photo used by permission of the Jefferson County Historical Society

Battery B, Third Coastal Artillery, occupied the fort prior to its completion. Fort Flagler was designated Headquarters of the Harbor Defense Command, but when Fort Worden facilities were complete, the command designation shifted to Fort Worden in 1904.

Buildings and improvements took up about 60 acres of the land which had been cleared for timber. Two wharves, and 50 frame buildings to house 600 military personnel were constructed. Building specifications called for brick foundations, framed walls, and slate roofs. In 1903, water shortages became a problem. The question of whether to move the troops from Fort Flagler to Port Townsend was on the table. Water was hauled from Seattle and also from Port Townsend. A six-inch pipeline which brought in "city water" through a connection near Hadlock was constructed in the early 1900s to solve the problem.

Between 1905 and 1906 four additional batteries were completed, and accepted for service in 1907.

Batteries of Fort Flagler

Battery	No.	Caliber	Type Mount
Bankhead	8	12"	Mortar
Wilhelm	2	12"	Altered Gun Lift
Rawlins	2	10"	Barbette
Revere	2	10"	Barbette
Calwell	4	6"	Disappearing
Grattan	2	6"	Disappearing
Lee	2	5"	Balanced Pier Mount
Downes	2	3"	Pedestal Mount
Wansboro	2	3"	Pedestal Mount

Fort Flagler: photo of mule-drawn cab at dock. Photo used by permission of the Jefferson County Historical Society.

Housing at Fort Flagler, no date. From Post Card Album Accession #1995.327.2a-l. Used by permission of the Jefferson County Historical Society

Battery Thomas Wansboro, Fort Flagler. Photo by Author, July 2011

Fort Flagler ca. 1910-1915. Real Photo Post Card, Author's collection

Central Power Plant, Fort Flagler. Real Photo Post Card, Author's Collection

During World War I, the Army used Fort Flagler as a training center. At the beginning of the war there were 26 guns at Fort Flagler. During the war, 12 of the guns were removed and sent to the warfront in Europe. There they were converted to field artillery or railway artillery. After the war, the fort was used as a training site for the Washington National Guard and as a camp for the Army Reserve Officer Training Corps.

Buildings began to deteriorate with lack of maintenance, and in 1936, many were torn down. However, they were rebuilt during World War II and the Korean War when the Army used the fort for amphibious warfare training and for maneuvers. Some of the remaining gun emplacements were modified to accommodate anti-aircraft artillery. Construction of "temporary" barracks was undertaken, many of which are still at the present park.

In August 1941, over 300 men were assigned to the fort as a part of the 3rd Battalion, 14th Coast Artillery Regiment. Once again, Fort Flagler was an active base. The mission was training and routine garrison duties. Guns were renovated and restored during 1942 and 1943. By 1944, however, Batteries Downes, Wansboro, AA#2 and AMTB#5, were the only remaining active batteries at Fort Flagler and they were quickly reduced to Class C readiness.

Following the war, the business of mothballing military ships in local bays was discussed as an economic generator. Several ships went to Bremerton, but many others went to Kilisut Harbor between Indian Island and Marrowstone. From 1946 to 1948, Kilisut Harbor was the home for approximately 230 Army and/or Navy ships. They were tied side-by-side (or "nested") with each "nest" being allowed to move freely with wind and tide. Watchmen were hired to work 24 hour shifts to monitor the ships. Many lived onboard in the ships' quarters. The headquarters for these ships is just north of Nordland, in what is now Mystery Bay State Park.

Approximately 130 landing craft were beached on what is now the Fort Flagler campground. During the Korean War, the same area was used for target practice. When the fort was purchased as a state park, extensive clearing was required by demolition teams before it could be used as a public park.

In 1950, the Army moved the 56th Amphibious Tank and Tractor Battalion of approximately 600 men to Fort Flagler. During 1951 and 1952, troops of the 356th Engineer Batallion and SR Shore Battalion trained on Marrowstone Point. Shortly thereafter, there was a flurry of rumors that the fort was to be deactivated. In March 1953, the newspapers announced that the fort would be closed. The public clamored to keep it open. Congressional delegations were lobbied to keep it open, but by June 1953, Fort Flagler was essentially deserted of Army troops.

In 1954, the Department of Defense declared Fort Flagler to be excess to its needs and transferred the property to the General Services Administration for disposal. Fifty-four years of military jurisdiction had ended. It was put up for sale and purchased in various parcels between 1957 and 1962 by the Washington State Parks and Recreation Commission for use as a state park. In 1976, Fort Flagler was officially designated as an Historic Place.

A military museum and gift shop is operated by the Friends of Fort Flagler. This exceptional museum provides an outstanding overview of the history of Fort Flagler.

During summer months, volunteer camp hosts and Friends of Fort Flagler give tours of the gun emplacements and of the hospital. The restoration activities undertaken in the old hospital by the Friends of Fort Flagler received special recognition from the Jefferson County Historical Society.

Fort Flagler Parade Grounds and Barracks, 2011. Photo by Author

Gun at Battery Wansboro, Fort Flagler, 2011. Photo by Author

Fort Flagler State Park is one of the most popular parks on the Olympic Peninsula. Camping, hiking, fishing, and exploring the gun batteries provide recreational activities for the entire family. A boat launch and dock provide access to crabbing and fishing areas.

Marrowstone Point Lighthouse

Marrowstone Point Lighthouse keeper's home, ca. 2004. Photo by Author

The Marrowstone Point Light is the smallest lighthouse on Puget Sound. It was built in 1918 and marks the sandy, shallow shoal just off of Marrowstone Point on the north end of the island. Beginning in 1888, a post lantern was erected to mark the area. The main shipping channel is narrow at the tip of Marrowstone Point, and navigation was especially hazardous because the water is so shallow, fog is extremely common, and dangerous rocks are very close by. After many accidents and complaints from shipping companies, the Lighthouse Service responded with the 15 foot post lantern which displayed a red light. The post lantern was mounted on a scaffold structure, and had a large tank which encircled the top of the lens. This tank held fuel for eight days. The lighthouse keeper rowed out to the point every few days to polish the lens and replenish the fuel supply.

In most cases, post lanterns were a temporary structure. At Marrowstone Point, however, the Lighthouse Service didn't replace the post lantern for 30 years.

In spite of the post lantern signal, in October 1892, the SS *Premier* was sailing to Seattle from Port Townsend with 70 passengers on board. The ship collided with the freighter SS *Willamette* which was on its way to San Francisco loaded with 2,700 tons of coal. The vessels collided at full speed in the fog. The hulls became locked together and the ships could not be separated. Passengers from the *Premier* climbed on to the decks of the *Willamette*. Five people died and eighteen were badly injured in the process. With this disaster and with the increased traffic on the Sound, the Lighthouse Service realized that the light on Marowstone Point was even more critical. A fog bell was added in 1896, but mariners complained that it was inaudible. The Service also built a house for the light keeper.

The first light keeper was Osmond Hale Morgan. Born on Whidbey Island, he came to Marrowstone with his five children. Although the beach was isolated, it was well known for its good fishing, and accounts indicate that the keeper was well known for his fishing accomplishments.

In 1903, the SS *North Pacific,* a side-wheel steamship, lost her bearings in heavy fog and struck Craven Rock, just two miles south of the light. Survivors were brought ashore at the Fort Flagler wharf and Mr. Morgan provided hot beverages and food. An hour later the SS *Mainlander* ran ashore at Marrowstone Point. Passengers from the *North Pacific* loaded on the *Mainlander,* and when the tide came in the boat was refloated and passengers were on their way to Seattle.

In 1911, the Olympic Power Company strung transmission lines from their plant on the Elwha River to Marrowstone Island, thus providing electricity to both Fort Flagler and the Light Station.

Marrowstone Point Lighthouse, ca. 2004. Photo by Author

Several more ships lost their bearings in the fog. Many complained that the fog bell was inaudible and requested it be replaced with something more reliable. In 1918, the Lighthouse Service constructed a 20 foot high fog signal building on the most exposed part of the point. They equipped it with a Daboll three-trumpet fog signal.

Marrowstone Point Light, ca. 2005. Photo courtesy of the U.S. Coast Guard

Electrically powered air compressors activated the fog signal. The trumpets extended through the walls enabling a signal to be projected in three directions. Also in 1918, a new optic which could produce a 500-candlepower light was installed on a mast on the roof of the fog signal building.

The Coast Guard automated the light in 1962 but eventually it closed the Light Station. In 1974, the Department of the Interior's Fish and Wildlife Service acquired the Marrowstone Point Light Station to use as a fisheries center. Laboratory facilities were constructed in 1976. In the early 1990s, the U.S. Geological Survey, Biological Resources Division, inherited the station and invested approximately $40 million to remodel the facility. The light keeper's residence is used for office, library, and dorm space and is known as the Marrowstone Marine Field Station. The Station also houses a laboratory/office building, wet labs, tanks, and pumps.

The beacon still operates and is visible for nine miles. All of the light systems are monitored via computer from the Port Angeles Coast Guard Air Station. Maintenance of the light is the responsibility of the Aids to Navigation Branch of the Coast Guard located at Pier 36 in Seattle.

The facility can be easily seen from the beach, but the area is not open to the public. The beach area adjacent to the light is a popular site for fishing, picnics, and hiking on the beach.

Cape George Military Reservation

State highway maps still denote Cape George Military Reservation in an area just west of Port Townsend. Cape George is a promontory on the east side of Discovery Bay.

Only three miles from Fort Worden, positions for four 12-inch mortars and four 8-inch railway guns were constructed at Cape George when Fort Worden was in full operation. Connecting grades were built from the railway line which ran from Port Townsend to Port Angeles.

Fort Worden personnel manned the armaments, but the reservation's use was shortlived. The emplacement cuts for the firing position still remain, but the entire area is now private property. Today, the site is in Cape George Colony and not accessible to the public.

Naval Magazine Indian Island

Marrowstone and Indian Islands were once known as the Craven Peninsula. In 1841, Lieutenant Charles Wilkes of the U.S. Coast and Geodetic Survey Department visited the area and renamed many of George Vancouver's map annotations. Wilkes noted that the two islands appeared to be a peninsula. He changed the name of Marrowstone Point to Point Ringgold to honor Lieutenant Cadwalader Ringgold, a fellow officer who had been part of the United States Exploring Expedition in the Pacific. Wilkes subsequently named the island Craven's Peninsula in honor of his friend, Lieutenant Thomas Craven, who had been part of Wilkes' expedition in Antarctica.

Between Indian Island and the mainland was a narrow piece of land which Chimacum (also spelled Chimakum and Chemakum), Snohomish, and S'Klallam Indians had used as a canoe portage, and it was called by early settlers the Chimacum Canoe Portage. Natives used that narrow spit of ground as a seasonal fishing camp, but there is little evidence that they used either Indian or Marrowstone Islands as year-long settlements.

In 1889, Port Townsend residents requested that a deep channel passage be dug between the mainland and Indian Island. The Seattle Bridge and Dredging Company completed a navigable canal which truly separated the mainland from Indian Island. A small ferry operated for several years until the present bridge was completed in January 1951.

In 1939, the Navy purchased Indian Island. Port Townsend Bay had long been regarded as an important harbor because of its deep water, and its location at the entrance to Puget Sound made it strategically important. As a result, submarine nets were stretched from nearby Fort Flagler across Port

Townsend Bay and over to Indian Island to protect fleet anchorages in the case of war. One of the towers built to support the nets is still visible just off of Fort Flagler. The nets were anchored to piling towers at both ends. Admiralty Inlet is a very deep area, however, so nets were impractical in many places. Hydrophones were also placed on the bottom of the bay to listen for enemy ships.

In 1941, the new installation was commissioned as the U.S. Naval Net Depot and U.S. Naval Magazine, Indian Island. As a net depot, it had the responsibility for maintaining the nets. As a Naval Magazine, its mission was to store navy munitions and to assemble mines and submarine nets. Two large buildings on the west side of the island remain from this mission.

By 1945, the Naval Magazine and the Naval Net Depot were consolidated into one mission. In 1948, the name changed again to Indian Island Annex. By 1979, the activities at Indian Island were part of the Naval Undersea Warfare Engineering Station at Keyport.

Net Tower off Marrowstone Island. Photo by Glenn Davis, August 2011

Indian Island, Net Depot buildings. Photo by Glenn Davis, August 2011

The facility was placed in a reduced activity status in 1959. It was reactivated in 1979 when munitions storage and munitions handling facilities were discontinued at Bangor and the mission was moved to Indian Island.

After the Gulf War, NAVMAG Indian Island was selected as one of the West Coast ports to be upgraded to handle containerized ammunition. Several improvements were made, including an ordinance pier, a critical rail-to-truck transfer facility at Naval Base Kitsap and the largest crane in the Department of Defense at the ammunition pier in 2000. The crane "Big Blue" is capable of lifting 89,600 pounds. "Big Blue" can be seen from Port Townsend and has become a landmark in the Port Townsend area.

Indian Island remains as a wildlife reserve and NAVMAG is an exemplary steward of the environment. When trees needed to be removed to accommodate buildings and additional facilities, the Navy made the decision to log by horsepower. Horses cause less damage than machines to the forest floor. Navy environmentalists recognized that the NAVMAG Indian Island forest supports at least two eagles' nests, is the home for countless deer, and an occasional bear. As a result, protection of the environment was a necessity.

"Big Blue." Photo by Mark Wade

Logging by horses, NAVMAG Indian Island. U.S. Navy photo by Senior Chief Mass Communication Specialist Jerry McLain (Released)

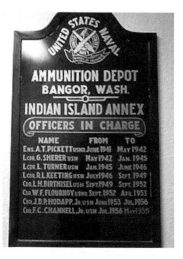

Officers in Charge 1941-1959, Indian Island Annex, Roster at Headquarters Building. Photo by Author

NAVMAG Mural painted by Paul Edwards, Headquarters Building, 2012. Photo by Author

NAVMAG Indian Island has also preserved tradition and has made a significant effort to preserve historically significant artifacts and military history.

When the commanding officer in 1942 asked a talented artist in his command to draw a mural, Paul Edwards agreed to the job. One wall shows Navy personnel working; the other shows Army personnel performing their duties. Interspersed are depictions of both soldiers and sailors on liberty.

Edwards eventually received a commission as an officer and served throughout the end of World War II. He then went on to become an animator for Walt Disney Productions.

NAVMAG Indian Island participates in several exercises each year. Transport of ammunition to and from the installation remains a focus as well as on-loading and offloading ammunition. Due to the need to maintain essential security measures, NAVMAG Indian Island is closed to the public.

Coast Guard in Jefferson County

Coast Guard history in Port Townsend goes back to the light at Point Wilson. The original light was put on Point Wilson in 1879. The current lighthouse was built in 1914. The keeper's quarters were occupied until 2000 by Coast Guard personnel.

Port Townsend, however, has a long history of maritime endeavors, and the agencies which would become predecessors to the Coast Guard were present during the early days as well. The U.S. Government moved the Puget Sound Customs Collection District to Port Townsend in 1854. Port Townsend was a hub for sailing ships and small steamships. Transportation of people and goods was a thriving industry for early Port Townsend. Every vessel that came from a foreign port and whose destination was Puget Sound was required to stop in Port Townsend.

Port Townsend was also home to the Marine Hospital and was headquarters for the U.S. Revenue Service along the Northwest coast. Immigration laws were supposed to be enforced by the U.S. Revenue Service, another predecessor to the Coast Guard. The Life Saving Service and the Revenue Service merged in 1915 to become the U.S. Coast Guard. Both the revenue cutters USRC *Ulysses Grant* and USRC *Thomas Corwin* were often in Port Townsend's port pursuing their missions.

When the Customs House moved into Seattle in 1913, the economic boom which was hoped for in Port Townsend was put to rest.

During World War II, Army, Navy, and Coast Guard units were all became involved in the defense of the Northwest coast. This mobilization was called Northwest Sea Frontier. The Coast Guard transferred to the command of the Navy on November 1, 1941, and was principally involved in what was known as the Coast Lookout System. The System had three objectives:

- prevent communication between persons on shore and the enemy;
- observe enemy vessels in coastal waters and provide information on those vessels to Naval or Army commands; and
- report encmy landings to Army or Navy commands and assist in preventing landings.

The Coastal Lookout System provided lookouts, lights, patrols, beach patrols, and aircraft warnings. On the west end of the county beach patrol outpost camps provided surveillance of the coast line. A light station on Destruction Island provided a lookout post for the coast. Similar activities took place at La Push and various other locations up and down the coast. Rangers from Olympic National Park moved supplies and maintained trails for the lookout stations. In return for their services, Coast Guard and Navy personnel were trained in fire-fighting to assist in the event of a forest fire.

The Coast Guard established a beach patrol station at Becker's Ocean Resort, now known as Kalaloch Lodge. The station included the main lodge, eighteen of the cabins, a store and a post office, and several outbuildings. The Coast Guard also constructed two barracks, dog kennels, and a laundry. The station existed for about a year and a half. Approximately 140 enlisted men and officers based there provided beach patrols and lookout services.

Dogs were an important adjunct to the patrolling mission, and were used up and down the beaches of the Pacific Coast. Patrols at Kalaloch were done during the hours of darkness and when visibility was decreased. Each patrolman was armed, had a portable radio and maintained hourly contact with his headquarters at Kalaloch station.

Wood frame coastal lookout towers were located at Hoh Head. Patrol and lookout activities were discontinued in late March 1944. Little remains of the Coast Guard stations. Kalaloch Lodge has seen many changes since World War II, and none of the original buildings is still standing.

In 1942 and 1943, the Coast Guard also assisted with the Aircraft Warning Service (AWS) operations. Several Coast Guard posts took on the responsibility for sighting and reporting enemy aircraft. Lookout posts in Jefferson County were located on Destruction Island and at Kalaloch. Much of the work was done by civilians. Information on each overhead aircraft, including altitude, type of plane and direction, was transmitted to AWS posts.

Spotting and investigating the landing of incendiary balloons was another task that fell to the Coast Guard along with the Navy, Army, and civilian spotters. These balloons were launched between November 1944 and July 1945 from Japan's Honshu Island. They measured approximately 35 feet in diameter and carried incendiary bombs. After they were launched the balloons would drift across the Pacific on prevailing air currents. A total of 25 balloons, or parts of balloons, landed in Washington.

The Coast Guard and Navy were instrumental in investigating a little-known incident of the landing of a Japanese incendiary balloon in Chimacum. On March 13, 1945, one of Japan's incendiary balloons, complete with ballasts and what remained of a bomb came to earth in a location near Chimacum. While many of these balloons were sighted by spotters, only this Chimacum balloon and one that landed near Gig Harbor fell on the Puget Sound area.

During the war, the Coast Guard also established boot camps at various places along the coast. One of the boot camps was in Port Townsend. A life-long Port Townsend resident commented that he marched down the street in the Port Townsend High School Band one day, and marched down the same street the next week wearing a Coast Guard uniform. These boot camps were discontinued after the war.

Coast Guard presence in Port Townsend was and continues to be seen in Coast Guard vessels on the waterfront. In 1966, the *Point Bennett* (WPB-82351) was assigned to the Port Townsend station. She was used for law enforcement and search and rescue operations, and was involved in several rescues including the grounded ferry *Hyak* near Anacortes. Her crew complement consisted of two officers and eight men. Decommissioned in February 1999, she was transferred to Trinidad and Tobago.

USCGC Osprey. *Photo courtesy of U.S. Coast Guard Digital Library*

The 13th Coast Guard District commissioned the U.S. Coast Guard Cutter *Osprey*, the first 87-foot cutter for the District, on June 19, 1999, at Union Wharf Pier in Port Townsend. The 87-foot cutter, built by Bollinger Shipyard in Lockport, Louisiana, was the first to arrive in the Northwest, replacing the 82-foot Point Class Patrol Boats. The *Osprey* is docked at the Port of Port Townsend Boat Haven near the Port Office.

Jefferson County International Airport

Prior to its utilization as an Army Air Force auxiliary field during World War II, the present site of the Jefferson County International Airport had another support role.

When Fort Townsend was the home base for soldiers protecting settlers from local Native Americans, the mess kitchen required vegetables to feed the troops. Many posts of the day had vegetable gardens on site. Troops were used to work in the gardens. Fort Townsend utilized a nearby area, which had a natural clearing and which would not require extensive logging and stump removal. The site is now the Jefferson County International Airport.

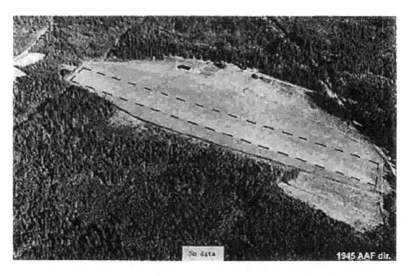

Jefferson County Airport, ca. 1945. Photo courtesy of National Archives

The general aviation airport was taken over by the Port of Port Townsend in 1959 and has a paved 3,000-foot east-west runway. Adjacent to the airport is the Port Townsend Aero Museum which houses an extensive collection of aircraft and provides restoration services. A youth mentorship program provides not only experience in aircraft restoration, but also hands-on experience in a wide variety of flight operations.

Memorial Sites

Memorial Field, Port Townsend

The athletic field in Port Townsend has an entrance which is flanked by two large cannons. The field, opened in 1946, was dedicated to servicemen from Jefferson County who died in battle.

Jefferson County Courthouse

On the walkway leading to the main entrance of the Jefferson County Courthouse is a bronze plaque listing the names of servicemen from Jefferson County who died in both World War I and World War II.

Point Hudson

Commander's House, built in 1934 for the Senior Surgeon, Public Health Department. Photo by Author

In the late 1890s, outbreaks of cholera and smallpox from ships arriving from all over the world prompted the federal government to provide more consistent, effective authority by imposing public health quarantine requirements for sailors and other travelers entering the United States.

Local authorities had

provided the first quarantine stations. However, as local authorities came to understand, there were financial and legal benefits to having the federal government involved in imposing quarantine on foreign citizens. Quarantine stations were gradually turned over to the federal government. By 1921, the quarantine system was fully nationalized and administration was transferred to the U.S. Public Health Service.

During the 1930s, the Works Progress Administration began the construction of several buildings which would serve as a quarantine station for visiting sailors and other foreign travelers entering Puget Sound. The quarantine station at Point Hudson opened in 1936. The Works Progress Administration constructed housing for both senior and junior officers, detention facilities, storage, and other buildings. The Commander's House, located at Point Hudson, was occupied by the senior surgeon for the Public Health Department.

The site also served as a vocational school for the National Youth Administration. When World War II broke out in Europe in 1939, the U.S. Coast Guard took over the buildings and operated them as a boot camp training facility. In 1941, the Navy took over command of the Coast Guard, and enlarged the harbor at what is now the Point Hudson Boat Haven. They also constructed a building to service minesweepers and patrol boats. A signal light at the station was used to illuminate passing ships for identification as friendly craft before allowing them to continue on to locations throughout Puget Sound.

The site served as a reception point for dignitaries visiting the area. In July 1943, Eleanor Roosevelt boarded a ship to travel to Port Angeles for a relative's christening. Stories indicate that she was entertained by the occupants of the Commander's House.

Following the war, the Point Hudson station was decommissioned in 1946 and placed in caretaker status and in 1947 it was designated as surplus property. It transferred six months later to the U.S. Army to be used as a training facility and a logistics base. When the Army moved out of these facilities and the facilities at Fort Worden, approximately one-third of Port Townsend's population went with it. In 1956, the Port of Port Townsend purchased the property; however, the costs of operation provide to be too expensive for the Port to operate. The facilities were leased to a harbormaster for approximately 40 years. It was sold again to the Point Hudson Company which developed the Point Hudson Resort and Marina. The properties are now once again on the property rolls of the Port of Port Townsend.

Port of Port Townsend Point Hudson Marina. Photo courtesy of Port of Port Townsend

The facilities provide a home to several maritime businesses and restaurants in Port Townsend. It is also home to the Wooden Boat Foundation headquarters and serves as the site for the Foundation's annual Wooden Boat Festival held each September. The Commander's House is available for rental as a guest house. The marina where patrol boats were once harbored is the home of one of the Olympic Peninsula's finest marinas.

Marvin G. Shields Memorial

Marvin G. Shields Memorial, Port Townsend, ca. 2012. Photo by Author

Marvin Glenn Shields, born in Port Townsend, was the first and only Navy Seabee and the first United States Navy sailor to receive the Medal of Honor for action in Vietnam.

Shields was with Seabee Team 1104 at Dong Xoai in South Vietnam. On June 10, 1965 the unit was attacked by a Viet Cong regiment. Despite being wounded, he continued to carry up ammunition to the firing line. Wounded again, he continued to fight and assisted a more severely wounded man to safety and then volunteered to help knock out a machine gun which had endangered the entire camp. He later died from his wounds.

Memorials to his life and service stand on Sims Way, Port Townsend, overlooking Port Townsend Bay. In downtown Port Townsend, American Legion Marvin G. Shields Post 26 also has a memorial outside of the building on Water Street. Inside, there are several tributes to his service.

Shields is buried at Gardiner, Washington.

Destruction Island Lighthouse

In 1775, Spanish explorer Juan Francisco de la Bodega y Quadra lost seven members of his crew after he sent them ashore for wood and water. They were massacred by local natives. In 1787, Charles Barkley, the captain of the British ship *Imperial Eagle* lost several members of his crew when he sent them ashore to explore the mouth of the river opposite the island. His crew was also massacred. Barkley named the river "Destruction." The name was eventually transferred to the island. The river was named the Hoh, its Indian name.

The island had been proposed as a site for a light many years prior to its actual construction in 1888, but funding issues delayed it.

The island has an elevation of about 80 feet above sea level. Construction crews transported the materials for the light station by boat to the island and then lifted them up via a derrick or hauled them up on their backs via a narrow trail.

Two houses and a barn were the first structures completed. The first keeper, Christian Zauner, arrived in 1889 while the tower and the fog signal were still being constructed. The tower, a 94-foot conical structure, was built from wood, and then completely enclosed in an iron skin to help protect it from the driving rains and high winds. A first-order Fresnel lens was assembled in the lantern room and became operational on New Years' Eve 1891. The fog signal was operational in November of that year.

Four keepers were usually assigned to the station at any one time. School classes were held for the keepers' children and a small herd of cattle and chickens helped sustain the little community.

The Coast Guard took over the responsibility for the light in 1939. Assigned keepers generally served an 18-month tour, with six weeks on the island followed by two and a half weeks of shore leave. The Coast Guard proposed that the station be abandoned in 1963, but mariners protested. It remained as a manned station until 1968.

The Fresnel lens was removed in 1995 and was replaced with an automatic beacon. Structures remaining on the island include two oil houses and the fog signal building. The keepers' houses were torn down many years ago. The fog signal building has been renovated to house maintenance crews if they are required to stay overnight during maintenance operations.

Destruction Island Lighthouse. U.S. Coast Guard photo

Destruction Island Lighthouse. NOAA photo

The Fresnel lens was taken to the Westport Maritime Museum, Westport, Washington, where it is on display. The presentation of the lens is exemplary. Housed in a 70-foot lens building, it is displayed so that a ramp allows viewing of the lens from various angles. The lens slowly rotates while its spotlights illuminate the room.

In 2008, the Destruction Island beacon was turned off for the final time. The Coast Guard indicated that it was no longer needed for navigation. The island is now a nature preserve, and is known as Station DESW1, for the National Weather Service.

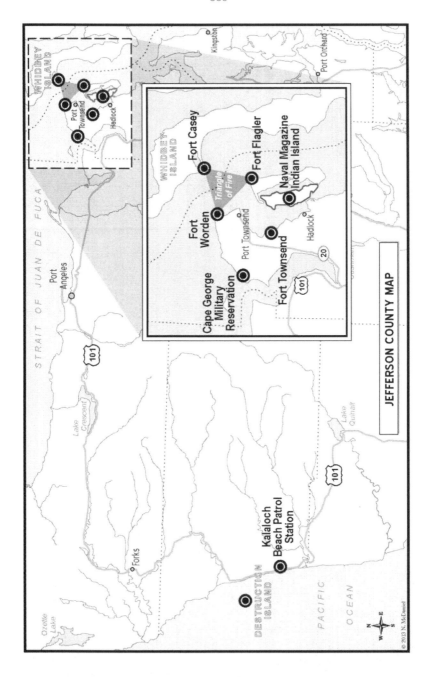

Chapter 12
Clallam County

Clallam County derives its name from the S'Klallam word, which means "strong people." Clallam County has the distinction of having the site of the oldest established military installation in the State of Washington.

Fort Núñez Gaona

The Spanish claims to Alaska and the Pacific Northwest date back to a 1493 papal bull and the rights contained in the 1494 Treaty of Tordesillas. These two acts gave Spain the exclusive rights to colonize the Western Hemisphere (excluding Brazil), including the west coast of North America.

By the late 1780s, Spain learned of British and Russian plans to explore, which suggested that Spanish claims might be encroached on by other countries. Manuel Quimper, sailing on the *Princesa Real,* landed near Neah Bay on July 24, 1790—two years before George Vancouver sailed into the area. He named the bay Bahio de Núñez Gaona after a Spanish admiral. Quimper took formal possession of the bay, which was already inhabited by the Makah peoples, in the name of Spanish King Carlos IV of Castile and Leon on August 1, 1790.

The bay was not ideal for large ships but the location was good for providing a base to protect Spain's potential new political, scientific, and commercial interests. As the British began to challenge Spain's interests in the area in the next few years, it would begin to play a role in the international arena as explorations turned into conquests. On May 29, 1792, Lieutenant Sálvador Fidalgo, under the orders of the

Viceroy of New Spain, officially established the Spanish settlement Fort Núñez Gaona.

Fidalgo's ship, the *San Carlos*, carried Spanish, Mexican, and Peruvian settlers. They started to clear the forest and brush across the creek from the Makah village. Approximately a week later, two more Spanish ships, the *Sutil* and the *Mexicana*, were welcomed to the land by Makah Chief Tetako.

The settlement consisted of storehouses, houses, a chapel, and a battery for cannons. There were also corrals for livestock. Garden areas consisted of vegetables and fruits. Trading of ceramic utensils and simple steel tools began with the Makah peoples. The new settlers also taught the Makah people about gardening.

Today, a fingerling potato type grown by the Makah tribe can be identified by phylogenetic analysis as originating in South America. In the late 1980s, the potato was catalogued and seed became available outside of the Makah nation. They are now often available in exclusive Pacific Northwest nurseries as seed potatoes.

The fort was occupied until late September 1792, when Fidalgo received orders to leave the Neah Bay area and move to Nootka, on Vancouver Island. Neah Bay's winters were not going to be conducive to harboring the ships, and some conflicts with neighboring Makahs reinforced the decision to leave the area, but it was not until 1819 that Spain gave up its claim to the area.

Diah Park, ca. 2008. Photo by Author

Today the site is marked by Diah Park, which pays tribute to the approximate 300 military veterans of Neah Bay, and to the legacy of the Spanish fort. The monument describes a shared past and the accomplishments of the Makah and Spanish cultures and memorializes the collaboration of the Spanish government, the State of Washington, and the Makah Tribal Council.

U.S. Coast Guard Station Neah Bay

The U.S. Coast Guard Station at Neah Bay is situated on the Northwestern-most tip of the Lower 48 States. As a result it holds the title as the most remote boat station in the contiguous States. It is surrounded by the Makah Indian Reservation. The Neah Bay Station is a detachment of the U.S. Coast Guard Sector Field Office in Port Angeles.

U.S. Coast Guard Station Neah Bay. Photo courtesy U.S. Coast Guard

One of the primary missions of the Neah Bay Station is that of heavy weather search and rescue. An advanced, state-of-the-art radio system allows the Station to monitor radio communications for vessels in distress. The area served by the Station consists of approximately 1,400 square nautical miles. The Station is also the primary contact for coordinating evacuation of injured or ill sailors requiring immediate medical attention.

The Station is located approximately one mile east of the Makah Marina in Neah Bay. The area has some of the roughest weather in the country. Lifeboat crews routinely undertake missions in 20-foot seas and 40-knot winds. Weather can change quickly in the area so fishing and tourist boaters are often the clients of the Neah Bay Station. The Station is also available to assist Canadian vessels if needed.

The Coast Guard Station has close ties to the Makah Tribe and often hosts aeromedical evacuation helicopters used to airlift injured or ill members to medical care facilities in Port Angeles or Seattle. The Neah Bay Station is known as the "Northwest Outpost" and also provides moorage facilities for Fish and Wildlife, National Ocean and Atmospheric Administration (NOAA), and National Marine Fisheries Service vessels. Approximately 35 active duty Coast Guard personnel are stationed at the Neah Bay Station.

United States Life Saving Service
Station #1: Station Waddah Island

The United States and the Makah Tribe signed a treaty in 1855. This treaty defined boundaries of lands ceded to the United States and tribal lands. With some liberal interpretation, it allowed some of the lands to be set aside for military use.

According to U.S. Coast Guard records, the original site of the United States Life Saving Station (USLSS) was somewhere on the Makah reserved lands, but was moved for undisclosed reasons. One remaining roster shows that C.L. Willoughby was the first keeper, appointed in October 1879. Charles Kloopman was subsequently appointed in 1882. Both had experience as seamen.

Waddah Island was part of the lands which were set aside. (It was also referred to as Baaddah Point.) Waddah Island had been occupied by three generations of native families. The sole resident in 1886 was a Makah man who was known as Young Doctor. Crippled, yet able to clear land, he asked the U.S. Government to pay $1,200 for the cleared land. The Government paid him $755.

Coast Guard history records vary. Some reports indicate that the station was moved to Waddah between 1905 and

1908. Newspaper and Coast guard records both agree, however, that by 1908, the station had been open for less than two years.

In early November 1908, the new power boat which had been assigned to the station was taken out on a trial run. The weather turned from light rain and winds into high winds and seas. The station keeper in 1908, George McAfee, described the stormy night and the eventual capsizing of the lifeboat. Station records show that the wind speed and gusts registered from 68 to 74 miles per hour. High seas, rocky reefs, and darkness resulted in the loss of two Surfmen, John Sundstrom and John Jacobsen. Their bodies were found at 4:00 p.m. the next day washed up on the rocks. Reports further indicate that a missionary to the Makahs, Miss Helen Clark, officiated at funeral services for the two men.

An official report of the USLSS indicated that the station was moved in 1910 after waves from a Pacific storm destroyed parts of the dock, its railing, and damaged a rescue boat belonging to the USLSS.

Camp Hayden and Striped Peak

Military planners recognized that in order to protect Puget Sound, Victoria British Columbia, and Canadian naval installations at Esquimalt from enemy ships, it would be necessary to monitor the entrance to the Strait of Juan de Fuca. Supplementing the fixed batteries at Fort Casey, Fort Flagler, and Fort Worden farther east, was an early temporary installation at Striped Peak Military Reservation, just west of Port Angeles. This was a Coastal Artillery Camp, established in 1941, at Tongue Point. Temporary guns were installed near Port Angeles and on Angeles Point. Within a few months, the temporary facilities were replaced by a more permanent structure. The permanent camp was named Camp Hayden in honor of Brigadier General John Hayden who had served as the commanding officer of the Puget Sound Harbor Defenses.

Camp Hayden had two fixed batteries, Battery 249 and Battery 131, supported by several fire control stations nearby.

Battery	No.	Caliber	Mount
Battery 249	2	6"	Shielded Barbette
Battery 131	2	16"	Casemated Barbette

Fire Control, observation, and spotting structures were also located at Tongue Point, Agate Rock, Gettysburg, Majestic, Twin, Pillar Point, Elwha East and Elwha West.

The 16-inch guns could fire a one ton projectile almost 28 miles. The 6-inch guns were rapid fire guns and could fire a 105-pound armor-piercing shell approximately 15 miles at the rate of 5 rounds per minute. Battery 131's plotting and switchboard room was located approximately 900 feet south of the battery itself. It was a self-contained unit with its own power plant and gas proof air locks on the doors. There were 11 fire control structures associated with it.

Camp Hayden Battery 131. Photo from FortWiki.com (Public domain)

Camp Hayden Battery 249. Photo from FortWiki.com, (Public domain)

The canopied bunkers were designed to take a direct hit. The turntable on which the gun and loading mechanism revolved was large enough and sturdy enough to turn a small locomotive. Three Worthington diesels supplied power that allowed soldiers operating the guns to revolve the turntables with a flick of the wrist. The diesels also fed the Camp Hayden power plant, which was buried under an embankment between the two guns. The plant included air conditioning and heating systems, which kept projectiles at consistent temperature and humidity.

Supporting Fort Worden was an auxiliary Harbor Entry/Harbor Defense Command Post located 900 feet up on Striped Peak which had SCR-682 radar #2. This facility helped manage ship traffic entering and exiting Puget Sound through the Strait of Juan de Fuca.

The Army built a road from the east into Camp Hayden Bay site and erected barracks along Salt Creek to house 150 soldiers. While on duty, the gun crews slept on cots in the tunnel linking the two batteries. Mess hall and kitchen facilities were also underground.

Camp Hayden, Battery 249 Gun Emplacement #1. Photo by Author, 2013

The guns were test fired once, prior to Camp Hayden's closure in 1948. No sooner had the guns been completed, they were considered nearly obsolete. When the installation was decommissioned, the guns were sold for scrap, 500 tons of steel which sold for approximately $30 per ton.

Today, the Camp Hayden site is part of Clallam County Parks' Salt Creek Recreation Area. Camping and picnic sites are a popular attraction for local residents and tourists alike. The site offers wonderful views of the Strait of Juan de Fuca and provides access to typical Olympic Peninsula natural areas. The gun emplacement sites are accessible to visitors.

Cape Flattery Lighthouse

Captain Cook visited the area around the Olympic Peninsula in 1778. Records indicate that the opening along the northwest tip of the peninsula "flattered" him into thinking that he had found a passage or at least a harbor. As a result, he named the area Cape Flattery. He noted in his records that he doubted that the Strait of Juan de Fuca ever existed.

Ten years later, Captain John Meares found the Strait and visited a small island just off of the cape. The Makah chief, Tatooche, had used the island as a summer camp for whaling and fishing. Meares named the island after the chief, and it was mapped as Tatoosh Island.

Almost 70 years later, in 1849-1850, William McArthur led an expedition which had the mission of locating potential sites for lighthouses along the coast of what would eventually become Washington State. He recommended that a light be put on Tatoosh Island and one at Dungeness Spit, west of Port Angeles.

Tatoosh Island, approximately 20 acres in size, is actually connected to Cape Flattery by underwater rock ledges. It is a windy, rainy place; rainfall averages 100 inches a year. A rocky island, it has cliffs approximately 100 feet high. Winds and tides make boating to the island difficult even under the best of conditions.

With the treaty of 1855, the government paid the Makah peoples $30,000 for the island. When the construction crew arrived, however, they were not warmly received. Smallpox had arrived with the white man, and having more "Bostons" around was not high on the priority list. The Makahs continued to use Tatoosh Island as their summer camp, and as a result, the construction crew also built a blockhouse on the island for their own protection. There were no incidents, but as construction progressed, a guard was always posted to assure some level of protection.

Completed in 1857, the lighthouse tower was in the center of the lightkeeper's house. The tower, 65 feet high, had a 10.5 foot high first-order Fresnel lens which had been built in Paris in 1854. It showed a fixed white light. A fog bell was also located near the house and tower. The keeper's house was a Cape Cod style sandstone with walls which were two feet thick. The kitchen, parlor, and the dining room were on the first floor, and sleeping rooms were located on the second floor.

The first lightkeeper, George Garrish, occupied the station with three assistants. After two months he and two others quit--too much work, too isolated, not enough pay for the job, and too much danger from the local natives. New assistants arrived within a few months. They, too, also lasted only a brief time.

Isaac Smith, the next lightkeeper, wrote to the Washington

Territory Indian Agent in 1858 that he was experiencing problems with the natives. They had broken into his house, into the light, and were threatening his life. The roof on the house was leaking, the chimney did not work well and smoke from the fires came right back into the house, and moss was growing on the walls inside of the house. Finally in 1875, the old house was repaired, but a new detached house was also constructed.

In 1872, a steam-driven fog horn replaced the bell, and the Department of Agriculture installed a weather station which would operate on the island until 1966. In 1887, a red panel was inserted into the Fresnel lens to cover the positions of Duncan and Duntze rocks which are located about a mile from the lighthouse. In those areas, only a red light was visible.

By 1885, relations with the Makahs had improved a bit, and a new keeper, Captain Henry Ayres, a Civil War veteran, arrived with his wife and daughter. Up until this time, families had been barred from being stationed there.

By 1887, the keeper no longer had to carry buckets of oil to the lamp, because a fuel storage tank had been installed which fed oil upwards using plungers which forced it through the tubes when needed. As a result, a keeper was required to stay at the top of the lighthouse through the night to make sure that oil was always available to the burning light.

A telegraph line was installed, at the time thought to be the longest in the world, which linked the island to Neah Bay. The telegraph is thought to have helped prevent shipwrecks because it could provide mariners heading out of the Strait of Juan de Fuca information on weather and conditions in the open water. Daily weather reports were relayed to Port Angeles and to Port Townsend from Neah Bay.

In 1886, the lighthouse at Tatoosh Island was designated as a fourth-class post office by the Postal Service. Mail arrived on the island by Makah canoes. Once near the island, the canoeist would throw packages to keepers hanging on the edge of the cliffs. A story about the supply system describes a Makah man by the name of Old Doctor who lost three dugout canoes in the surf while trying to deliver supplies. Supplies would arrive once or twice year. Because the cliff was so high and steep, supplies, people, and other goods had to be lifted up from the beach to the lighthouse via a derrick on the island. Other stories claim that cows and even a piano were delivered by this Makah supply system.

The Weather Bureau came back to the island in 1902 and

ran the station with full time weather observers on the island. A wireless radio station also began operating on the island in 1902 which could contact ships with weather and other information.

Cape Flattery Lighthouse, ca. 1930s. Photo courtesy U.S. Coast Guard

In 1904, Tatoosh became the junction point for the new undersea telegraph system which ran from Alaska to Seattle. By 1914, an oscillating light replaced the fixed beacon. The large first-order Fresnel lens was replaced with a more compact fourth-order lens in 1932. In the early 1930s, twelve families were living on Tatoosh Island. Fishing vessels, both commercial and sport, were becoming more popular and prevalent, and the light was becoming even more critical to the safety of the fleet.

In World War II, the Navy set up intercept stations to detect Japanese radio communications. Marines were stationed on the island to guard the new Naval station and the lighthouse. After the war, the Navy station closed, although LORAN (Long Range Navigation) was retained on the island and was used to assist mariners. The weather station was closed in 1966, and the buildings were removed. By 1977, it was no longer necessary to have full-time, year-round habitation; as technology came to the lighthouse mission, the facilities were automated and keepers were no longer required to live on the island. A solar-powered optic replaced the fourth-order Fresnel lens in 1996, so maintenance was also less frequent.

In 1999, any remaining structures were repaired and a fence was built around the keeper's house and a small cemetery which contained the graves of two of a keeper's children. In 2009, the Coast Guard began a clean-up project which removed old fuel tanks and generators, and the light was decommissioned.

Remaining lighthouse facilities are in the process of being turned over to the Makah Tribe, who will once again control the entire island.

U.S. Army Spruce Production Division Railroad

World War I aircraft production required a supply of high quality spruce. The new, and generally untried, airplane was being designed with increased speed, a large engine, and a greater payload. These airplanes' wings and fuselage were made from spruce. Propellers were also made from laminated spruce.

Sitka spruce was ideal because it was light, it had great strength, and did not splinter when it was struck by bullets because it has long tough fibers. The Pacific Northwest became the main supplier for aircraft produced not only in the United States, but in Great Britain and France, as well. By October 1917, the Allies were requesting a monthly production quota of 10,000,000 board feet. Northwest mills were not meeting the demand due in part to a labor strike. At the same time as mill owners were decreasing output and increasing product prices, unions were striking to obtain an eight-hour work day, better living conditions and union recognition.

As the United States found itself facing a major war effort, General Pershing appointed a former army captain, Brice Disque, to the Pacific Northwest to address labor issues which were occurring in the forest products industry. The Industrial Workers of the World (IWW) had been trying to organize sawmill operators, loggers, and truckers into their union. With a potential labor issue looming, the Army determined that without their intervention, the issues would not be resolved.

Captain Disque was assigned a special duty to put the labor problems in the Pacific Northwest to rest. Upon his advice to General Pershing, the U.S. Army Signal Corps became involved in resolving the labor-management question. He recommended that an army of soldier/loggers be put into the Northwest woods to start building railroads to haul the logs, to cut trees and to turn the trees into lumber. Without intervention, the Army determined that the regular supply of spruce and other timber products would be unreliable. As a result, Disque was given the job of reorganizing the industry.

The United States Army commissioned a unit in 1917 to supply spruce and other wood products. This unit, the Spruce Production Division, was part of the Signal Corps. Headquartered in Portland, Oregon, it had one of its main operations centers in Vancouver, Washington. It also had several camps around the Olympic Peninsula. Disque was promptly promoted to the rank of colonel and placed in charge of the Division.

Symbol of the Loyal Legion of Loggers and Lumbermen

Several soldier camps were scattered across the Pacific Northwest. Each camp had sleeping facilities, latrines, showers, and messing facilities. Workmen were recruited from experienced woodsmen in the Northwest. The Division could not take men who were considered to be in Class I draft status, but took men in Classes 2, 3, and 4 if they were in good enough health to be loggers or to help build railroads.

Civilian mill owners and lumbermen were skeptical of the Division and felt that they were, in reality, strikebreakers. Disque reminded them of the military requirements, of patriotism and the drastic actions that war demanded, and gradually overcame opposition to the Division. As a result, the early negotiations and steps to form a union turned into a new organization called the Loyal Legion of Loggers and Lumbermen (LLLL) or the "4 Ls." It met with opposition at first, but within six months, almost all the owners and nearly 100,000 wood workers joined the Legion.

On the Olympic Peninsula in the spring of 1918, the Spruce Production Division began construction of three separate railroads. Five miles of track were laid in the Quinault area and another five miles near Pysht. Thirty-six miles of Spruce Production Division Railroad No. 1 went from Port Angeles to the Hoko River area. Today, approximately 12 miles of that 36-mile stretch of railroad is within the boundary of the Olympic National Park.

Approximately 8,000 men (half of them soldiers) worked on that 36-miles stretch of railroad. The terrain is rugged, the soils are unstable, and heavily timbered areas combined with inclement weather made construction of this stretch a challenge. Around the north shore of Lake Crescent tunnels were bored through solid rock in two locations. Ballasting, cribbing, and extensive clearing made the construction a slow process.

Government spruce mill ca. 1918, Port Angeles. Real Photo Post Card, Author's collection.

The railroad cost the U.S. Government almost $30,000 per mile, making it the most expensive railroad per mile constructed by the government. It was also one of the fastest construction projects. Fourteen months after construction began, the project was nearly complete. As the final rail was laid, the armistice also ended World War I. Despite all the engineering, labor, and outlay of funds, the Spruce Production Division Railroad No. 1 never hauled a single log for wartime effort.

The mill at Port Angeles, which operated until 1997, was also constructed as a government mill. It was completed too late -- only 70% was finished by Armistice Day (November 11, 1918) -- to contribute any lumber for the war effort. It cost approximately $750,000 to build. Another Spruce Products Division mill was planned to be built at Lake Pleasant near Forks, Washington, but was never completed.

The railroad grade can still be seen when looking across Lake Crescent from Highway 101. Tunnels can still be explored by hikers.

The Army Air Corps in Port Angeles

The 40th Pursuit Squadron was activated at Selfridge Field, Michigan, on December 22, 1939 as part of the 31st Pursuit Group along with the 39th and 41st Squadrons. The squadron was at Baer Field, Fort Wayne, Indiana, when Pearl Harbor was bombed on December 7, 1941.

Deployed in response to Pearl Harbor, the unit's ground echelon headed to Port Angeles on December 10. The pilots and crews took the P-39s via the southern route to avoid the winter weather enroute to the Pacific Northwest.

The 31st Group was recalled to Selfridge Field and took half of the 40th to become the 308th Squadron. The remaining 40th cadre of 14 officers and 76 enlisted men along with 39th and 41st cadres remained in Port Angeles until mid-January 1941, and then shipped from San Francisco aboard the USAT *Ancon* (a United States Army Transport ship) on January 31, 1942 for Australia.

The unit was a decorated squadron with several missions over Papua, New Guinea in 1943–1944, and other locations. The unit received the Presidential Unit Citation for its efforts in the Papua Campaign which took place from November 1942 through January 1943.

Slip Point Lighthouse

Slip Point Lighthouse in 1916. Photo courtesy U.S. Coast Guard

The original fog signal station at the Slip Point site was constructed in the 1890s on Slip Point; Slip Point forms the eastern side of Clallam Bay. The face of the point is marked by a landslide which was often used as a reference for mariners. The location is about one–third of the way along the Strait of Juan de Fuca and was built so mariners could avoid the rocks on the south side of the strait. Local labor from the Clallam Bay area built the first facility. A fog signal building and the keeper's residence were built. A light, however, was not built due to a lack of funding. A lens lantern was mounted on the side of the fog-signal building and was lit for the first time in 1905 by the keeper, Hans Score.

In 1906, a square tower was built and equipped with a

fourth-order Fresnel lens. The newly upgraded light could now be seen from the Canadian side of the Strait. The keeper's house was not located adjacent to the light and the keeper had to walk on an elevated catwalk to access the fog signal and the light. During storms, the catwalk was often threatened by high seas pounding against the beach.

Original Slip Point Lighthouse in 1905. Photo courtesy U.S. Coast Guard.

1951 Slip Point Tower and Catwalk. Photo courtesy U.S. Coast Guard

During the 1950s the tower was torn down and the light was replaced by an automated light on a white tower. The light was fully automated in 1977. In the 1990s, that light was also deactivated.

While the light is gone, the lightkeeper's house still stands and has recently been used by both the Clallam County Sheriff and the Coast Guard for housing personnel in Clallam Bay.

In 2000, 26 acres was ceded to Clallam County for inclusion in Clallam Bay Spit County Park. The remnants of the catwalk and the tower were removed. Cement footings which supported the catwalk can still be seen.

The residence and the steel tower are located in Clallam Bay Spit County Park off of Highway 112.

Lookout Stations
Aircraft Warning Service (AWS)

After the attack on Pearl Harbor on December 7, 1941, many military strategists considered the Olympic Peninsula to be one of the most threatened and vulnerable places in the United States. Many felt that the Peninsula could be the first to feel an attack from an enemy coming from the west.

All of the military branches and the Coast Guard became involved in what was to become extremely accelerated on-alert status at Forts Casey, Worden and Flagler. Camp Hayden (Striped Peak) was intended to provide an additional layer of protection. Anti-aircraft guns were placed on Ediz Hook at the entrance to the Port Angeles Harbor and at various locations on Puget Sound. Within days after the attack, army troops were scattered along the Washington coast from Canada to the Columbia. The strongest sites were established in Clallam County west of Port Angeles.

By the spring of 1943, a joint agreement between the Army and the Navy articulated the roles of each service in coastal defense. The Army was to be responsible for conducting military operations in defense of the territory. The Navy's role was to gain and maintain control of the sea areas and to protect sea lanes. The Navy was further directed to establish communications and an intelligence system for sea defense and an information system which would utilize coast guard stations, lighthouses, and ships.

The Coast Guard was transferred to the command of the Navy on November 1, 1941. Coastal lookout systems were to become the main role of the Coast Guard. The mission was to prevent communications between persons on the shore and the enemy; to observe actions of enemy vessels on the water; transmit information to the Army and Naval commands; and to assist in preventing any enemy actions. Lookouts and lights, patrols, life-saving boats, and aircraft warning were missions performed by the Coastal Lookout System.

By late April 1942, coastal lookout stations and lifeboat stations dotted the shoreline. The 13th Naval District, which at that time comprised both Washington and Oregon, was divided into three sectors. One of the sector headquarters was at Port Angeles. The other two were at Astoria and Coos Bay, Oregon.

The Port Angeles sector extended from Cape Flattery south to Cape Elizabeth, approximately 65 miles along the coast. Some of the greatest physical obstacles existed in this area. Virgin forests with undergrowth which was almost impenetrable, rocky beaches, vertical cliffs, and uncertain weather made the area difficult to guard.

In addition to the beach patrol and lookout activities of the Coast Guard in 1942 and 1943, other Coast Guard posts on the Olympic Peninsula coastline provided the Aircraft Warning Service operation. Several Coast Guard posts took responsibility for watching the skies and sending reports to the Port Angeles center. Aircraft Warning Service posts were located at Tatoosh Island, Ozette, Cape Alava, Quillayute River, Kalaloch, Destruction Island, and Whale River.

Many other small observation posts were established along the coastal areas and were manned by trained civilians. These dedicated volunteers provided services twenty-four hours a day and had the responsibility to report all planes seen or heard. When an aircraft was spotted, "flash" messages were sent from the AWS posts by telephone and provided information to the Port Angeles center on altitude, types and numbers of aircraft, and the flight direction.

The Army also had AWS posts in remote and isolated areas. Many times these posts were on U.S. Forest Service and National Park Service lands and rangers were instrumental in helping to provide supplies and equipment. Often supplies had to be packed in by horseback or by manpower. Park Service personnel were instrumental in laying and maintaining telephone lines to the sites. Many of the Forest Service fire lookouts were utilized as observation posts.

During the winter of 1942-1943, thirteen AWS observation posts were located within the Olympic National Park. These sites included Dodger Point, Hurricane Ridge, Deer Park, and Enchanted Valley. New structures were built at Pyramid Peak, Warkum Point, Indian Pass, and Geodetic Hill. By late 1943, ultra-high frequency radio service was utilized to communicate between many of the stations.

AWS stations were also located along the Strait of Juan de Fuca. One of the stations at Dungeness, built in 1941, was constructed from donated materials on the Cook farm. Located adjacent to the farmhouse, the tower was 35 feet high and had a view of the Strait. It had three stories, each with a single room which could be accessed by an exterior doorway. Windows were located on each level. The largest window was on the top floor and was surrounded by a balcony.

Jean Cook, the chief observer, recruited a team numbering nearly 300 observers to maintain a 24-hour watch. If an aircraft was sighted a report was made to the Port Angeles filter center, which compiled the observer reports for the Army.

The Cook tower was moved from Dungeness to the property of Harriet Fish in Agnew in 1992. It was placed on the National Register of Historic Places in 1993.

Pyramid Peak AWS Station. Photo courtesy U.S. Forest Service

The perceived threats, which engendered lookouts, patrols, and volunteer services were greatly diminished by the close of 1943. Most of the quickly-constructed structures were just as quickly abandoned, and the structures soon disappeared. AWS structures which remain on their original sites include cabins at Dodger Point and Pyramid Peak.

The lookout at Dodger Point, west of Hurricane Ridge overlooking the Elwha Valley, was originally built in 1933 as a fire lookout. It was named for Dodger Bender, who performed telephone maintenance and construction work for the Forest Service. It is accessible, but it is a challenging 13.5- mile hike starting from the Whiskey Bend trailhead.

The Pyramid Peak site was refurbished in 2008 and provides a look into the past at what conditions were like for the watcher. A 3.5-mile trail departs from the north side of Lake Crescent, and gains 2,400 feet elevation to the cabin. The cabin is an excellent place to view the Olympics and the Strait of Juan de Fuca.

Ozette Lake Coast Guard Station

Barracks at Lake Ozette, ca. 1943. Photo courtesy of Olympic National Park

On September 1, 1942, Coast Guard men departed Seattle for Ozette Lake, northwest of Forks. By the following morning, the men had established two tent camps on the beach three miles west of Ozette Lake. At the end of two weeks, five beach camps and trails had been constructed between Lake Ozette and the beach.

The men on patrol covered approximately twelve miles of the coast each day, cooked meals over campfires and slept on the ground. Each patrol stayed on the beach anywhere from two to twelve days.

At the peak of these patrols, several beach patrols and three lookout towers were being used. The outposts were located at the mouth of the Ozette River, Cape Alava, Sand Point, Wind Trail, Yellow Banks, Township Trail, Allen Trail, Lone Tree Rock, and Cape Johnson. The three lookout towers were located at Cape Alava, Eagle Point, and at the mouth of Starbuck Creek.

Materials to build the towers and the camps were shipped in by raft from Neah Bay or were packed in from Lake Ozette. Telephone lines and radios were used for communication between the outposts, various patrol stations, and the main station at Lake Ozette. Dogs were used on the patrols and sentry dogs were kept at the camps from the spring of 1943 until the stations were closed. By June 1943, nearly 40 dogs were at the Ozette Lake Coast Guard Station.

Station buildings were built at the beach patrol station at the north end of the lake. By the end of 1942, personnel had completed several buildings including barracks, a storeroom, and an armory. By summer of 1943, two barracks, a galley and a mess hall, a cook's quarters, officers' quarters, a study, library, dog kennels, and other assorted buildings had been completed.

By later that summer, however, the danger of enemy attacks had declined and the patrols were deemed to not be necessary. By March 1944, the beach patrol activities at Ozette were discontinued.

Little remains of the site. The former mess hall and kitchen were remodeled and turned into a residence for the park ranger in the area. The trail system which had been built between the lake and the beach is still in use by hikers and campers in the area.

La Push and Kalaloch Beach Patrol Stations

La Push Beach Patrol Station, located on the mouth of the Quillayute River, and Kalaloch Beach Patrol Station were headquarters for beach patrol outposts which had been established between Cape Johnson and Cape Elizabeth on the coast. The LaPush Station, commissioned on October 15,

1942, was the headquarters station for outposts established at Toleak Point, Mosquito Creek, Mora, and Third Beach. The structures at Toleak Point were remodeled trapper's cabins. The camp at Mosquito Creek was a frame and tent.

As at the Lake Ozette station, dogs were used extensively to help patrol along the beach. Continuous day and night patrols were established along the area. As part of the system, La Push Beach Patrol also had a lookout tower on James Island and a light station on Destruction Island. Because James Island obstructs a full view of the horizon from the village, a lookout tower next to the Lifeboat Station house was complemented by a second lookout structure on the island.

A shipwreck in 1943 among the treacherous rocks of Teahwhit Head. Crew members of the Russian freighter rescued by members of the U.S. Coast Guard from the knife-edge cliff above the wreck. Photo courtesy U.S. Coast Guard

The boredom of the patrols was interrupted on April 1, 1943, when the Russian steamship *Lamut*, which was on its way to Vladivstok, was caught in a severe storm. *Lamut* ran into the rocks just off Teahwit Head. The ship was lodged between a cliff and a small island. It was just after 11 p.m. and the ship was listing dangerously. An oil drum broke free and struck a young, pregnant woman in the head. She was killed and knocked overboard into the cold, turbulent water.

A distress signal was sent out and subsequently heard at the Coast Guard station. Rescue boats were deployed to search for the shipwreck. Survivors were found clinging to the sloping deck. A sea rescue was not possible due to dangerous waves, so a land rescue was undertaken.

Coast Guard personnel cut their way through the brush to the beach and found their way to the cliffs above the ship. They had gone out on a search mission, not a rescue mission. Having no rescue gear, they tied their shoelaces together, forming a line which was dropped over the cliff to the deck of the ship. The Russian crew attached a heavier line and this was pulled up to the cliff top. A life line was lowered to the ship and one by one the survivors were lifted off of the ship and taken to waiting ambulances and trucks.

One woman was killed when a lifeboat overturned in the high surf. The remaining 51 people on the ship were rescued despite the heavy seas, the terrain, and the weather.

An interesting sidelight on this story is that after the rescue, many of the American rescue crew wrote personal letters to Premier Stalin explaining the extraordinarily difficult conditions in the area, and asking that the captain of the *Lamut* not be punished because of the loss of the ship. Capital punishment was the common fate at that time for Russian captains who lost their ships.

The beach patrol units were discontinued in late March 1944 and the units were decommissioned. Little remains of the site. Portions of the trails near Mora leading to the beach are part of the original trails.

Quillayute Naval Auxiliary Field

World War II activities in the "West End" of the Olympic Peninsula included the construction of a Naval Auxiliary Air Station built on Quillayute Prairie, as part of the fortifications along the Pacific Coast and the Strait of Juan de Fuca to help guard against a possible attack by Japan.

West Enders were warned that in the event of an attack, the sole highway (Highway 101) would be used exclusively as military transport. Like all communities along the coast, West Enders were advised to use only the dim headlight setting for automobile travel after dark.

Aerial view of NAS Quillayute, August 1945. U.S. Navy photo.

Construction had started on the field in the late 1930s and by 1944, the field was a base for approximately 2,500 sailors. The small town of Forks was the closest and basically the only area for recreation for sailors at the nearby Quillayute Naval Auxiliary field. Its remote location and proximity to the Pacific made Quillayute a focal point for the protection of the Pacific Coast. The field provided maintenance, assembly, and class "C" repair facilities for naval aircraft units. Various aircraft made landings and were temporarily based at the field. Records indicate that VC-82, a composite squadron made up of fighters and torpedo bombers, arrived at Quillayute on June 12, 1945 and departed for reassignment to Pasco, Washington on August 5-6, 1945.

One of the eight "lighter than air" aircraft (blimps) assigned to Tillamook Naval Air Station in Oregon was usually assigned to Quillayute during the summer. Quillayute also provided an emergency landing base for blimps stationed at Tillamook.

Although blimps were not permanently based at Quillayute,

they often landed there for temporary stays. In one case on January 4, 1944, the K-39 made an emergency landing at Quillayute. While ground crews attempted to secure the ship, winds came up and caused the ship to roll over. Both propellers were bent which resulted in both engines being cut.

As the wind continued to blow, heavy gusts tore the lines loose from the ground party and the line from the winch. The airship became airborne and then crashed and was a total loss.

When the war was over, the Navy departed Quillayute and the airfield was closed. The airport was turned over to the Washington Department of Transportation (DOT), and subsequently deeded to the City of Forks in 1999.

Buildings from the World War II era still exist, although many are in disrepair. The tower facility was destroyed by fire in 2007. An adjacent hangar, which housed several aircraft, did not sustain serious damage. The runways are being used by general aviation and some charter services today. The National Oceanic and Atmospheric Administration maintains a weather station at the airport which provides critical forecast information for all of Western Washington.

USN photograph of K-87 taken at Quillayute, Sept 1944. Photo from www.warwingsart.com/LTA/zp-33.html

Crash of K-39 at Quillayute NAS, January 1944. Photographer unknown, U.S. Navy photo

Firefighters douse hot spots inside the former control tower at Quillayute Airport west of Forks. Lonnie Archibald, for Peninsula Daily News, *November 11, 2007*

Ediz Hook Lighthouse

In 1862, mariners looked for a driftwood fire burning at the top of a tripod on the end of Ediz Hook to mark the end of the spit which protects Port Angeles harbor. Shipping into Port Angeles harbor was becoming a vital industry. Shipping into Port Townsend was also a booming business.

The U.S. Customs House was located in Port Townsend. Ships entering Puget Sound from all over the world were obliged to stop there. Victor Smith arrived in the area in August 1862, having been appointed as Customs Inspector.

Smith wrote letters to Salmon P. Chase, President Lincoln's Secretary of the Treasury, imploring him to change the Customs House location from Port Townsend to Port Angeles. His letters do not deny the fact that he owned property in Port Angeles, and was hopeful to develop this property. Congress subsequently passed the act which removed the Customs House from Port Townsend and sent it to Port Angeles. Smith returned to Port Townsend to collect the papers, money and government property. When he was refused he had the Revenue Cutter *Shubrick* train its guns on the Customs House and demanded its records. Under those circumstances the papers and property were released. He kept the Customs function aboard the ship until he could personally build a structure in Port Angeles and then rent it to the government. With the blessing of Washington D.C., he moved the Port of Entry to Port Angeles, a city with a population of ten people.

Questions over shortages of funds and mismanagement of the Port of Entry functions continued. Smith's reputation as a difficult individual was widely known. Most notably, President Lincoln had written a letter to Salmon P. Chase, Secretary of the Treasury indicating that, "My mind is made up to remove Victor Smith as collector of the customs in the Puget Sound district. Yet in doing this I do not decide that the charges against him are true. I only decide that the degree of dissatisfaction with him is too great from him to be retained. But I believe he is your personal acquaintance and friend, and if you desire it I will try to find some other place for him."

Smith remained in place. As a result of the town's new mission, he was subsequently successful in getting the approval for a formal lighthouse on Ediz Hook. The bonfire was extinguished in 1865 when the lighthouse was established. Some described the new structure as something akin to a country schoolhouse. In fact, it was a two story house with a small tower on one end. A fixed, fifth-order Fresnel lens showed its first light on April 2, 1865. A fog bell was added in 1885.

In his role as Customs Inspector, Smith was also in charge of appointing lightkeepers. He subsequently appointed his sister Mary as assistant and his father George K. Smith as the chief light keeper. Three years later Victor died in a shipwreck off of California.

Even at his death there were questions about his affairs. Stories regarding his loss at sea also included stories that the safe aboard the wrecked steamship *Brother Jonathan* was found with its doors open and the cash missing. His father continued to serve as lightkeeper until 1870, followed by his sister who served until 1874.

By the end of the 1800s, the dwelling/lighthouse was in need of some serious repairs. Mariners had complained that the fog bell was not loud enough, so an octagonal tower was constructed near the old structure in 1908. The lantern and lens were removed and placed in the new tower. The old tower was removed from the lightkeepers' house.

1865 Ediz Point Lighthouse. Photo courtesy of the U.S. Coast Guard

The new light tower remained in use only until 1946 when it was replaced by a beacon at the Port Angeles Coast Guard Air Station.

The lightkeeper's house was floated across the Port Angeles harbor and moved up the hill to become a private residence in Port Angeles. It is still in use as such at Fourth and Albert Street.

Ediz Hook Lighthouse, 1908. Photo courtesy U.S. Coast Guard.

U.S. Coast Guard Air Station Port Angeles

Coast Guard history in Port Angeles reaches back to 1862 with the presence of the revenue cutter *Shubrick*. She was the first revenue cutter to be homeported on the Olympic Peninsula. In 1863, the Ediz Hook spit was designated as a lighthouse reservation and the light became functional in 1865. Ediz Hook would be the eventual home of the Coast Guard in Port Angeles.

The Coast Guard Air Station on Ediz Hook was commissioned in 1935 and became the first permanent Coast Guard air station on the Pacific Coast. Its first aircraft, a Douglas RD-4 amphibian aircraft, arrived in June of 1935.

During World War II, the station took on a training mission to provide aerial gunner training and also to train local defense forces. The site also served as a training site for Navy pilots learning to do carrier landings when a short runway was added to the hook. Its wartime mission was even more diversified when it served as the host for a Naval Intelligence unit and also as the Headquarters for the Air Sea Rescue System for the Northwest Sea Frontier Area. By the summer of 1942, aircrews stationed in Port Angeles were busy investigating reports of enemy submarines off the coast and in the Strait of Juan de Fuca. Other aircraft served in the role of escorts for convoys and for towing practice targets. The roles expanded by 1943 when the Air Station was given the responsibility for all Coast Guard anti-submarine activity and rescue activities all of the way to the California border.

U.S. Coast Guard Station Port Angeles. Photo courtesy U.S. Coast Guard

By September 1944 the unit became Coast Guard Group Port Angeles. When the war ended, the station was serving as home base for 29 aircraft. Patrol boats were also assigned to the unit.

Helicopters stated to arrive in 1946. The first helicopter assigned was the Sikorsky HO35-16, followed in 1951 by the Sikorsky HO43. The last fixed wing aircraft, a Grumman HU-16E, was retired in 1973, and the station has since been the home only for helicopters. The HH-52A was assigned in 1965 to be replaced by the American Eurocopter HH-65A Dolphin in 1988. Today, Coast Guard Group and Air Station responds to more than 400 search and rescue missions each year.

In July 2010, Group/Air Station Port Angeles was reorganized to become Air Station Sector Field Office Port Angeles, providing support to Station Neah Bay, Station Port Angeles, Station Quillayute River, and several Coast Guard cutters stationed around the area. Air Station Sector Field Office Port Angeles is responsible for conducting Search and Rescue, Law Enforcement, Homeland Security, and Resource Protection activities that include the Strait of Juan de Fuca, and the northwestern coast of Washington around the Olympic Peninsula to the mouth of Puget Sound.

Motor Lifeboat Station Quillayute River

Memorial at Quillayute River. U.S. Coast Guard photo

Approximately 30 Coast Guard personnel are currently stationed at the Lifeboat Station in LaPush. The primary mission of the base is search and rescue in addition to law enforcement. The current primary boats are the 47-foot lifeboats.

In February 1997, a sailboat off the coast near LaPush radioed that it was in distress and in danger of crashing into the rocks just off of the beach. The craft had lost its mast, and was in danger of sinking. Coast Guard personnel in two boats quickly deployed to answer the call. Two boats went out and only one came back. The U.S. Coast Guard Motor Lifeboat 44363 did not return.

High winds and rough seas capsized the Coast Guard lifeboat, killing three of the four personnel on board. The two people on the sailboat *Gale Runner* were hoisted to safety by a Coast Guard helicopter.

Following the accident, the Coast Guard took the opportunity to refine training procedures, to emphasize risk assessment and team coordination, and to upgrade the rescue vessels themselves with updated safety features and communication capabilities.

A memorial at the station depicts a lifeboat battling the seas. The memorial is located on the Quillayute Reservation in LaPush. A nearby resort is available for overnight accommodations.

New Dungeness Lighthouse

Captain George Vancouver named the spit jutting out into the Strait of Juan de Fuca New Dungeness Spit after Dungeness Point in southeast England. The spit, six miles long, is one of the largest natural spits in the world. Captain Vancouver was somewhat prophetic in assigning the name. The English Dungeness Point had had a light since around 1600. It took over a half century to get a light on the New Dungeness Spit, but on December 14, 1857, the light shone for the first time. It was the second lighthouse to be established in Washington Territory.

The first lighthouse at New Dungeness was a one and a half story duplex built in a Cape Cod style. It had a 92-foot tower rising out of the roof. Painted in a unique style, the original tower was white on the bottom half, black on the top half, and it had a red lantern room.

New Dungeness Lighthouse, ca. 1868. Photo courtesy U.S. Coast Guard.

The spit had seen its share of shipwrecks and it was also the site of several Native American battles. It had often been the location for raids on the S'Klallam peoples by Tsimshian natives who paddled war canoes from Canada. These raids continued after the light was in place. Tsimshian, Haida, and other natives would often use the site to camp on their way to pick hops in south Puget Sound.

A band of Tsimshian warriors were camped there one night, when S'Klallam warriors decided that they were tired of the Tsimshian intrusions. A recent raid had resulted in the kidnapping of one of Lame Jack's wives and his son. The S'Klallams attacked. The story continues that all eighteen Tsimshian were killed with the exception of one pregnant woman, Nusee-chus. She was wounded but made her way to the lighthouse where the lightkeeper and his wife took her in and treated her.

Lame Jack, however, did not have total success. When he was trying to escape with a chest of gold coins and other souvenirs, one of his fellow S'Klallams killed him, and left him for dead with the Tsimshians.

The S'Klallams followed the trail of blood from the Tsimshian woman to the lighthouse. The lightkeeper, William Blake and his wife, Mary Ann, when confronted by the S'Klallams refused to turn her over to them. They later took her to Dungeness to the home of Benjamin Rainey, whose wife was also Tsimshian. When she recovered, she was sent to Victoria only to discover that her husband had died two weeks earlier there of smallpox.

She was then sent home to Fort Simpson. The United

New Dungeness Light Station, 1898. Photo courtesy U.S. Coast Guard

States Bureau of Indian Affairs sent money and gifts with her to help appease the warring situation between the Tsimshians and the S'Klallams. Then U.S. Commissioner James G Swan later reported "the Indians were all satisfied."

Two assigned light keepers manned the New Dungeness station until 1895 when two more were added to the roster.

Additional living quarters were added in 1905. As the years went by, the tower developed some cracks and in 1927, it was shortened by 30 feet. With these structural changes the original lantern was too large. As a result, it was replaced by the fourth-order lens from the Admiralty Head light. At this time, the tower was repainted completely white.

In 1976, the Fresnel light was turned off and replaced with a modern optic. The Fresnel lens can still be seen at the Coast Guard Museum in Seattle. The New Dungeness light was the last Coast Guard manned lighthouse on the West Coast.

Today, volunteers from the New Dungeness Chapter of the U.S. Lighthouse Society have acquired the station from the Coast Guard by a lease. Volunteers are invited to come and man the station for a week at a time, greet visitors, and do basic maintenance around the station. To spend a week there, visitors must be members of the New Dungeness Lighthouse Society. It is a popular opportunity, and the waiting list to visit as a volunteer "keeper" is approximately two years.

Located in the Dungeness Wildlife Refuge, the site provides a wonderful opportunity to observe over 250 species of birds, and a host of other animals. To get to the lighthouse, follow Kitchen-Dick Road from Highway 101 to the Dungeness Recreation Area. From there it is approximately a five-mile hike to the lighthouse.

New Dungeness Lighthouse 1944. Photo courtesy U.S. Coast Guard

758th Radar Squadron

Cape Flattery Military Reservation
Makah Air Force Station

In 1942, the U.S. Army established Cape Flattery Military Reservation on 4,024 acres leased from the Makah Tribe of Indians, as a coastal defense installation to protect the entrance to Puget Sound. The Military Reservation originally consisted of several non-contiguous sites which were acquired to house two 6-inch and two 16-inch coastal gun batteries, approximately 25 fire control stations, a magazine and numerous radar sites.

Building sites were cleared, roads were built, but the project was terminated in October 1943 before the batteries could be built. Few buildings were completed. The lease from the Makah Tribe was terminated in 1945 and, with the exception of 10 acres at Bahokus Peak, the property was transferred back to the Tribe.

Prompted by the Korean War in 1950, Makah Air Force Station was one of twenty-eight stations built as part of the Air Defense Command radar network. The 758th Aircraft Control and Warning (AC&W) Squadron was activated at Bohokus Peak in November 1950. The 758th started operating the AN/FPS-3 long-range search radar and an AN/CPS-4 height-finder radar. In its early years, the station functioned as a Ground-Control Intercept (GCI) station. As a GCI station, the primary role was to guide interceptor aircraft toward unidentified intruders when they were picked up the radar.

In 1960, Makah AFS joined the SAGE system (Semi-Automatic Ground Environment), and fed data to McChord AFB. After joining the SAGE system the squadron was re-designated as the 758th Radar Squadron (SAGE). By 1963, the squadron operated an AN/FPS-7A search radar and AN/FPS-90 and AN/FPS-26A height finder radars. In the 1970s the AN/FPS-7A was upgraded to an AN/FPS-16.

There was base housing available for seven officers and 38 enlisted at the site. Housing shortages at the site often resulted in personnel's families living in Port Angeles, 75 miles away.

The unit became part of the Tactical Air Command (TAC) in 1979 when the Aerospace Defense Command was inactivated. In the early 1980s, technology and upgrades resulted in the installation of an AN/FPS-91A search set and an AN/TPS-43E.

In June 1988, the 758th Radar Squadron was inactivated and the Air Force closed most of its facilities. The radar site was turned over to the FAA. A detachment from McChord continued to maintain the radars until the late 1990s. The FAA now maintains the radar at the site as part of the Joint Surveillance System (JSS).

The station facilities and the housing areas were turned over to the Makah Tribe. Some facilities are currently being used by the tribe.

Cover of the Makah AFS Welcome Brochure, 1974. U.S. Air Force photo

Makah Air Force Station ca. 1974. U.S. Air Force photo

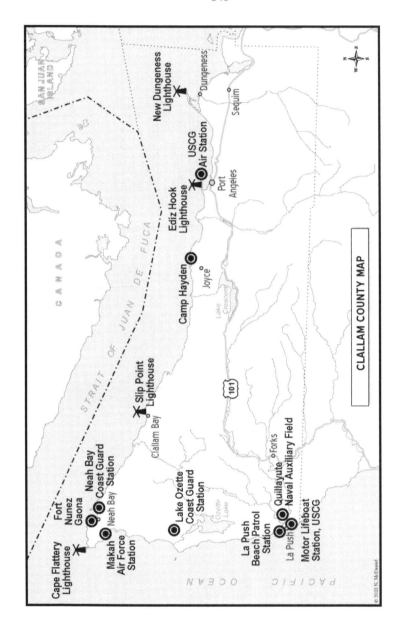

Notes

Whatcom County

- Oakley, Janet, "Captain George Pickett begins construction of Fort Bellingham on August 26, 1856," *HistoryLink*, www.historylink.org, Essay 7098.

- *Northwest Ethnohistory Collection, Center for Northwest Studies. Inspector General Mansfield's Report of the Inspection of the Fort Bellingham in December 1858.* Western Washington University, Bellingham.

- Port Angeles: Supported Units Station Bellingham. http://www.uscg.mil/d13/stabellingham

- Historic Light Information and Photography, Washington: http://www.uscg.mil/history/weblighthouses.lhwa.asp

- Blaine AFS, 757th Radar Squadron http://home.comcast.net/~blaine757/757thart.htm

Skagit County

- Burrows Island, WA http://www.lighthousefriends.com/light.asp?ID=107

- Port of Skagit, Air Port History http://www.portofskagit.com/skagit-regional-airport/airport-history/

- Fortwiki.com/Fort_Whitman

Snohomish County

- Mukilteo Light Station http://www.lighthousefriends.com/light.asp?ID=32

- *Mukilteo Multimodal Project, Draft Environmental Impact Statement.* Cultural Resources Discipline Report, Washington State Department of Transportation, U.S. Department of Transportation, Federal Transit Administration; Washington State Ferries, January 2012.

- Paine Field History, http://www.painefield.com/history/history_corner.html

- Naval Station Everett, Wikipedia.org/wiki/Naval_Station_Everett

- CNIC Naval Station Everett.
  http://www.cnic.navy.mil/everett/index.htmCity of Arlington, WA Airport History.
- http://www.arlingtonwa.gov/index.aspx?page=101
- Flying Heritage Collection.
  http://www.flyingheritage.com/TemplateHome.aspx?contentId=1
- Lesson Eleven: Overview of American Indian Policies, Treaties, and Reservations in the Northwest, Center for the Study of the Pacific Northwest, Washington
  http://www.washington.edu/uwired/outreach/cspn/Website/Classroom

Island County

- Military History of Whidbey Island
  http://www.whidbeycamanoislands.com/arts_history/military
- Gregory, V. J. *Keepers at the Gate*. Port Townsend: Port Townsend Publishing Co. 1976
- Admiralty Head Lighthouse   www.admiraltyhead.wsu.edu

San Juan County

- The Pig War
  http://whidbeycamanoislands.com/arts_history/military
- A Short History of Patos Island and its Lighthouse.
  www.patoslightkeepers.org/history/html
- Turn Point, WA.
  www.lighthousefriends.com/light.asp?/ID=104
- Lime Kiln WA,
  www.lighthousefriends.com/light.asp?/ID=105
- Lime Kiln and Cattle Point Lighthouse San Juan Island HistoryLink.org Essay: 7704
  www.historylink.org/index.cfm?DisplayPage=output.cfm@File_II=7704

King County

- Wilma, David. "Fort Lawton is Established on February 9, 1900," HistoryLink.org Essay 1757,
  http://www.historylink.org/essays/output.cfm?file_id=1757

- Aki Point WA.
  www.lighthousefriends.com/light.asp?ID=112
- West Point, WA.
  www.lighthousefriends.com/light.asp?ID=33
- Andrews, Mildred Tanner, *Woman's Place: A Guide to Seattle and King County History.* Seattle: Gemil Press, 1994, 307-308.
- "Dead Seattle Ex-Service Women to be Honored," *Seattle Times,* February 22 and February 26, 1922.
- Bill Lightfoot, *Beneath the Surface: Submarines Built in Seattle and Vancouver 1909-1918.* Vancouver, BC: Cordillera Books, 2005
- Morgan, Mark "Nike Sites in Washington State and Travis AFB," http://ed-helen.org/MMTravis.html
- Saxe, William E. "Arming the Soviets," *Columbia, the Magazine of Northwest History,* Summer 2006, Volume 20, No.2
- Warren, James R. "World War II Home Front on Puget Sound— A Snapshot History" HistoryLink Essay, File #1664, http://www.historylink.org/essays/output.cfm?file_id=1664
- Wilma, David, "WAACs Women's Auxiliary Corps, First in the Northwest, Arrive at Fort Lawton in April 1943," HistoryLink.org Essay 2920, http://www.historylink.org/essays/output.cfm?file_id=2920

Pierce County

- Wayne Shoemaker, "Working in a World War II Prisoner of War Camp," *Banner,* Fort Lewis Military Museum Association Newsletter, Vol 7, No. 1 Winter 1993
- Huddleston, Joe D, "Fort Lewis: A History" Fort Lewis, WA: Headquarters, I Corps and Fort Lewis, 1986
- Denfeld, Duane Colt, PhD "Fort Lewis, Part 2, 1927-2008," HistoryLink.org Essay 8493. http://www.historylink.org/index.cfm?DisplayPage=output.cfm&file_id=8493
- *The Official History of the Washington National Guard,* Vol 5. Camp of the Adjutant General

- Archambault, Alan H, *Images of Fort Lewis*. San Francisco: Arcadia Publishing, 2002.
- Lakewood Veterans Memorial, Dedicated on Memorial Day, May 26, 2003, The Historical Marker Database, http://www.hmdb.org/marker.asp?marker=41552
- History of Fort Steilacoom, http://www.historicfortsteilacoom.com/history.php
- Browns Point, WA http://www.lighthousefriends.com/light.asp?ID=121
- Fort Nisqually Living History Museum http://www.metroparkstacoma.org/page.php?id=862

Thurston County

- Blankenship, Georgiana Mitchell, *Early History of Thurston County, Washington: Together With Biographies and Reminiscences of Those Identified with Pioneer Days*. Nabu Press, 2010, page 128—131.

Mason County

- Sanderson Field, Wikipedia.org/wiki/Sanderson_Field

Kitsap County

- Graff, Cory, Puget Sound Navy Museum, *Images of America, the Navy in Puget Sound*. Arcadia Books, 2010.
- Morgan, Mark "Nike Sites in Washington State and Travis AFB," http:L//ed-thelen.org/MMTravis.html
- Poole, Lisa and Dianne Robinson "Torpedo Town U.S.A., A History of the Naval Undersea Warfare Engineering Station 1914—1989," www.hnsa.org/doc/torpedotown
- Naval Undersea Warfare Center Division Keyport, Test and Training Environments Department. *The History of the Naval Torpedo Tracking Ranges at Keyport,"* Report No. 2254. Keyport, Washington. August 1998.
- Department of the Navy, Bureau of Yards and Docks. *Building the Navy's Base's in World War II: History of the Bureau of Yards and Docks and the Civil Engineer Corps (1940-1946)*, Chapter XIII, The Ammunition Depots.

- *Naval Undersea Museum, Keyport, Washington.* Published for the Naval Undersea Museum Foundation by Historical Publishing Network.
- Wilma, David. "Haida Raiders Kill Gustave Englebrecht, First U.S. Navy Battle Death in the Pacific at Port Gamble on November 21, 1856", HistoryLink.org. http://www.historylink.org/index.cfm?DisplayPage=output.cfm&File_Id=5500
- "Kitsap County: Home Sweet Home to the U.S. Navy" *Kitsap Sun,* March 25, 2005. http://www.kitsapsun.com/bsun/ah_km_all-about/article/0.2666.BSUN_21200_3649006,00.html

Jefferson County

- Cowell, Theodore, Ray, "History of Fort Townsend," *Washington Historical Quarterly,* Vol 16. No 4
- Stevens, Lawrence, G. *Fort Townsend and Its Soldiers, 1856 to 1895.* Jefferson County Historical Society, 2006
- Gregory, V. J. *Keepers at the Gate.* Port Townsend: Port Townsend Publishing Co. 1976
- Derr, Rex "Fort Flagler State Park Commemorates Restored Historic Gun with Weekend of Activities." A press release from Washington State Parks and Recreation Commission, April 27, 2005
- Gregory, V.J. et. al, *With Pride in Heritage, History of Jefferson County.* Professional Publishing Printing, Inc. Portland, Oregon, 1966
- McClary, Daryl C. "Marrowstone Light Station," HistoryLink.org, Essay 5702, www.historylink.org/index.cfm?DisplayPage+output.cfm&File_Id=5702
- McShane, Dan, "Reading the Landscape, Observations of Washington State Landscapes, Geology, Geography, Ecology, History and Land Use," http://washingtonlandscape.blogspot.com/2010/08/indian-island-jefferson-county.html
- Camfield, Thomas, *Port Townsend, An Illustrated History of Shanghaiing, Shipwrecks, Soiled Doves and Sundry Souls.* Port Townsend: Ah Tom Publishing, Inc., 2000
- "Ear to the Sound: Bunker Remnant of Military Presence at Fort Worden." *Peninsula Daily News,* May 25, 2009, page C-1

- Fort Flagler: Over 100 Years of History . . .from Exemplary Coast Defense to Beautiful State Park, a Friends of Fort Flagler publication, 2nd edition, August 2006.
- O'Connor, Kenan, Petty Officer 3rd Class "World War II Navy Vet Returns to Indian Island to See His Artwork." ptleader.com, July 3, 2012.

Clallam County

- Oldham, Kit, "Clallam County—Thumbnail History," File #7576 http://www.historylinkl.org/essays/output.cfm?file_id=7576
- Cape Flattery Lighthouse www.uscg.mil/history/LHWA.asp
- Hanable, William S. "Cape Flattery Light on Tatoosh Island Begins Operating on December 28, 1857," HistoryLink.org Essay 5703, http://www.historylink.org/essays/output.cfm?file_id=5703
- "Fort Hayden", http://www.clallam.net/CountyParks/html/parks_fthayden.htm
- Evans, Gail H.E. & T. Allan Comp (Project Supervisor) "Mobilized for War: World War II Military Involvement." Chapter VI in *Olympic National Park Historic Resource Study*, Seattle: National Park Service, Department of the Interior, Pacific Northwest Region, 1983
- "Spruce Production Division, Railroad No. 1," www.craigmagnuson.com/spdrr01.htm
- Gerald W. Williams "The Spruce Production Division," *Forest History Today*, Spring 1999.
- Chidlow, Nora L. "The Inauguration of the Coast Guard's Only Air-Land Rescue Unit at CGAS Port Angeles: The Rescue of the Crew of a Navy Bomber," www.uscg.mil/history/articles/ChidlowNavy1945.pdf
- Noble, Dennis L. "The Coast Guard in the Pacific Northwest," http://www.uscg.mil/hq/g-cp/history/h_PacNW.html
- Evans, Gail H.E. & T. Allan Comp (Project Supervisor) "Skid Roads and Slice Boxes: Commercial Development and Industrial Development," Chapter 3 in *Olympic National Park Historic Resource Study*, Seattle: National Park Service, Department of the Interior, Pacific Northwest Region, 1983.
- Williams, Gerald "The Spruce Production Division." Paper presented with Gail E. H. Evans at the Washington State Military History Conference held at Camp Murray, WA, March 30, 1984.

- McClary, Daryl C. "Dungeness Massacre Occurs on September 21, 1868." HistoryLink.org Essay 5743 http://www.historylink.org/index.cfm?DisplayPage=output.cfm&file_id=5743

- Nicolay, John and John Hay. *Complete Works of Lincoln, Volume VIII,* New York: Francis C. Tandy. page 270, 1905.

Index

A

A-1	6
A-20	175
A-26	175
Acquisition Radar	93
Admiralty Head Light	46, 60-61, 72-75
Admiralty Inlet	61, 70, 259
Air Force Fuels Lab	26
Air Mail Service	28
Aircraft Warning Service	291, 318
Air Defense Control Site (P-1)	176
Air Force Northwest	173
Air Defense Command	10, 175-176, 337, 337
Air Defense Radar Veterans	12
Air Sea Rescue System	331
Airship Squadron ZP-33	207
Alki Point Lighthouse	91
Alaska Airlines	30
Alden Point	45
Alexander Blockhouse	75-77
Allen, John B	81
Allen, Paul	36
American Camp	40, 42, 52
American Express	245
American Lake	145
AN/FPS-3	337
AN/CPS-4	337
AN/FPS-6	10
AN/FPS-6A	10
AN/FPS-20	10
AN/FPS-24	11
AN/FPS-26A	11
Anders, Maj Gen William	5
Anderson, Albert	92
Andrew Chambers Donation Claim	197
"An Officer and a Gentleman"	266
Appleby, Stephen	145
Applied Physics Lab	228
Arlington School of Aeronautical Engineering	35
Arlington Airport	32-35
Army Air Corps	27
Army Corps of Engineers	62, 68, 85
Army Amphibious Brigade	267
Army Quartermaster Corps	99, 100
Army ROTC	178
Army Service Forces Training Ctr	150
Army Transportation Corps	86, 117
Army Transportation Svc	100
"The Arsenal"	182
Artillery Hill	264
AT-6	175
A-26	175
Auburn	137
Ault, Commander William	59
Ault Field	57, 59, 209
Ayres, Captain Henry	310

B

B-17	109-110, 173-175
B-18	175
B-23	175
B-24	173
B-25	29
B-26	29
B-29	109
Babcock, General	254
Bachelder, James	164
Bahio de Nunez Gaona	
Bainbridge Memorial Field	247
Bainbridge Island	213
Bainbridge Island Japanese American Memorial	247
Bangor	234
Bangor Naval Ammunition Depot	235

Barkley, Charles	298	Battle Point	215
Barrage Balloon	125	Baynes, Rear Admiral	
Base Support Unit		Robert	41
Seattle	98	Beans Point	213
Bataan Park	247	*Bear*	101
Battery 131	305-306	Becker's Ocean Resort	291
Battery 248	67	Belle Vue Farm	40
Battery 249	305-307	Bellingham Bay	2
Battery B, 3rd Coastal		Bellingham Int. Airpt	5
Artillery	275	"Big Blue"	286
Battery C, 14th		Birch Bay AFS	10-12
Coast Artillery	21	Black River Blockhouse	114
Battery Ash	263	Blaine	9
Battery Bankhead	274-275	Blaine AFS	10-12
Battery Benson	264, 267	Blankenship,	
Battery Brannan	263	Georgiana Mitchell	195, 197
Battery Calwell	275	Blue Star Memorial Hwy	248
Battery Downes	275	Boeing Co.	31, 108
Battery Grattan	275	Bonney Lake	189
Battery Harrison	20-21	*Boston*	138
Battery Kingsbury	62-63	Bothell / Kenmore Site	
Battery Kinzie	264	(S-03)	96
Battery Lee	274-175	Bowman Bay	78
Battery Mitchell	241	Brannon's Prairie	137
Battery Moore	62-63	Bremer, William	217
Battery Nash	214	Bremerton	611
Battery Powell	263	Bremerton Historic	
Battery Putnam	264	Ships Association	239
Battery Quarles	263	Bremerton Memorial	
Battery Randol	263	Stadium	248
Battery Rawlins	274-275	Bremerton Shipyards	27
Battery Revere	274-275	British Camp	40
Battery Schenck	62-63	*Brontes*	111
Battery S-13 / S-14	94	Brooks, Edward	24
Battery S-32 / S-33	94	Browns Point Lighthouse	167
Battery Seymour	62-63	Buchanan, President	41, 71
Battery Stoddard	264	Buena Vista Cemetery	247
Battery Thornburgh	62-62	Buffalo Soldiers	82
Battery Thomas		Bureau of Docks and	
Wansboro	275, 277	Yards	218
Battery Trevor	62-63	Bureau of Land Mgmt	46
Battery Tolles	264	Bureau of Lighthouses	79
Battery Turman	62-63	Burrows Island	15
Battery Valleau	62-63	Bush Point Lighthouse	79
Battery Van Horn	62-63	Bush Prairie	196
Battery Vicars	263	Bush Prairie	
Battery Vinton	214	Airfield Site	203
Battery Walker	264	Bush, President George W	87
Battery Warner	214		
Battery Wilhelm	274-275		
Battery Worth	62-63		
Battle of Connell's		**C**	
Prairie	189		
Battle of the Coral Sea	59		
Battle of Gettysburg	2, 42	C-17	178
Battle of Seattle	110-113	C-54 Skymaster	176

Cable Controlled		Clark, D.W.	9
Underwater Vehicle	231	Clark Hall	139
Camp Bonneville	151	Clark, Helen	305
Camp Fred Steele	43	Clinton	23
Camp Harmony	151	Clover Park School	
Camp Hayden	305	Dist	156
Camp Lewis	83, 103,	Clover Valley	57
146, 148, 172		Coast Artillery	62, 68,
Camp Montgomery	191	82, 256, 260	
Camp Muckleshoot Prairie	114	Coast Guard Station	
Camp Murray	180-185	Port Angeles	74
Camp Nisqually		Commandant, 13th	
Camp Pickett	42	Naval District	57
Camp Reynolds	43	Company D	2
Camp San Juan	43, 255	Connell's Prairie	189
Camp Steilacoom	182	Continental Air Command	177
Canadian National Dock	129	Cook Blockhouse	76
Canal de Haro	48	Cook, Jean	320
Cape Alava	320, 322	Cottman, Rear Admiral	226
Cape Disappointment	90	Coastal Lookout System	290
Cape Flattery Lighthouse	308-312	Coast Artillery Corps	98, 213,
Cape Flattery Military		261, 269	
Reservation	336	Coast Guard	
Cape George Military		Investigative Svc	6
Reservation	283-284	Coast Guard – Jefferson	
Casey, Brig Gen T.L.	62	County	289
Casey, Lt Col Silas	43, 163,	Coast Guard Museum	
246		Northwest	101-102
Casey's Camp	43	Coast Guard Station	
Cattle Point Lighthouse	51-54	Port Angeles	16
Centralia (Skookumchuck)	196	Commission on Training	
Central Whidbey Island		Camp Activities	147
Historic District	73	Composite Squadron	
Chambers Prairie	196	Sixty-Six	207
Chehalis Tribe	196	Congressional Record	15
Chenoweth, Francis	192	*Constellation*	250
Chief Naval Operations	34, 57	Coquilton	111
Chimacum	291	Cougar Mountain /	
Chimacum Canoe		Issaquah (S-20)	96
Portage	284	Coupeville	59, 65,
Chimacum (Chemakum)		73	
Tribe	244, 284	Court martial	87
Chinook Indian Jargon	91	Craven, Lt Thomas	284
Chiswell, Alfred	270	Craven's Peninsula	284
Christiansen, Peter	24, 48	Crescent Harbor	57
City of Seattle	88	Crockett Blockhouse	75-77
Civil Air Patrol	209	Crown Aviation	30
Civil Control Stations	161	Curtiss-Wright Flt	
Civil War Memorial,		Systems	30
Retsil	248	Curtiss JN-4D Jenny	36
Civil War Memorial		Curtiss P-40C	
Masonic Cemetery		Tomahawk	36
Olympia	198-199	Cutlar, Lyman	4, 40
Clallam Bay Spit			
County Park	318		
Clallam County	301-340		

D

Dabob Bay Range	229-230
Daughters of the American Revolution	197
Davis Blockhouse	75-77
Davis, Charles	71
Davis, Jefferson	2
Davis, 1Lt Robert	2, 4
Davis, Sam	4
Decatur	111-113, 195
Deception Pass	78
Deer Park	320
Defense Logistics Agency	26
Delridge Playground	124
Dennis Shoal	15
Department of Columbia	256
Department of Oregon	40
Destruction Island	291
Des Moines Memorial Drive	134
Destruction Island Lighthouse	298, 319, 323
Deterrent Park	239
Detlie, John Stewart	109
Diah Park	302
Discovery Island	48
Discovery Park	89
Disque, Brice	312
Distant Early Warning Line (DEW Line)	177
Dodger Point	320
Doffelmeyer's Point	196
Double Bluff	61, 259
Douglas, James	41
Drag racing	35
DuPont	169
Durgan, Edward	8, 45, 48
Durgan, Estelle	8
Dutch Elm disease	135
Duwamish Tribe	111

E

86th Air Base Squadron	29
EA-6B Prowler	59
EA-18G Growler	59
Eagle Point	322
Earl Faulkner Post, American Legion	28
Eastwind	102
Eastwood, Corporal Thad	20
Eaton, Nathan	195
Eaton's Rangers	191
Ebey Blockhouse	75-77
Ebey, Col. Isaac N.	67, 76, 247
Ebey, Emily	76
Ebey's Landing Natl Historic Reserve	65
Edwards, Paul	288-289
Ediz Hook	318, 328
Eisenhower, Dwight	152
Eisenhower, Mamie	152
Elliott, Charles	91
Enchanted Valley	320
Endicott Board	20, 213, 256
Endicott Period	241
Endicott, William	20, 256
Englebrecht, Gustave	246
Enterprise	48
Ethan Allen class	239
Evans, Henry	71
Evans, Joseph	71
Evergreen Rotary Park	247
Exact	91
Experimental Aircraft Assoc. (EAA)	35
Externsteine	102

F

1st Battalion, 1st Infantry	85
1st Bomb Wing	175
1st Cavalry	83
1st Combined Air Div.	37
14th Coast Artillery	265
14th Infantry Regiment	83
40th Pursuit Squadron	315
41st Infantry Division	153
44th Infantry Regiment	85
49th Parallel	39
56th Amphibious Tank & Tractor Battalion	279
57th Fighter Group	29
505th Aircraft Control and Warning Group	175
529th Air Defense Gp	29
4753rd Air Base Sqdn	29
F-Boats	120
F-4F Wildcat	59, 207

F-6F Hellcat	59
F-82F	175
F-84	29
F-86	29
F-89 Scorpion	6
F-102	29
F-106	29
Farmer family	79
Federal Aviation Admin	88
Federation of Improvement Club Committee	185
Fellows, Deborah Copenhaver	201
FEMA Region X Hdqtrs	97
Fidalgo, Lt Salvador	302
Fircrest Naval Hospital	138
Fircrest School	140
Firlands Sanitarium	140
First Regiment Armory Association	181
Fish, Harriet	320
Flagler, Brig Gen Daniel Webster	273
Fleet Ballistic Missile	235
Fletcher Class	122
Flying Heritage Collection	31, 35-37
Fonda, George	90
Forbes Point	57
Forrest Sherman Class	250
Forsythe, 2 Lt J.W.	2
Fort Alden (Alder)	114
Fort Bellingham	2-5, 254-55
Fort Casey	60-66, 82, 149, 261, 265
Fort Chambers	197
Fort Dent	114
Fort Duwamish	114
Fort Eaton	198
Fort Ebey	65, 67-69
Fort Flagler	60, 62, 67, 82, 261, 265, 273-280
Fort Hays	189
Fort Henderson	114
Fort Henness	196
Fort Hicks	190
Fort Lander	114
Fort Lawton	81-89, 94, 125, 151
Fort Lewis	85, 145-160
Fort Lewis Logistics Ctr	158
Fort Lewis Motor Base	156
Fort Lewis Museum	148, 159
Fort Lewis Ordnance Base	156
Fort Lewis Quartermaster Motor Base	156
Fort Henness	196
Fort Maloney	189-190
Fort McAllister	190
Fort Nisqually	169
Fort Nunez Gaona	301
Fort Nugent	78
Fort Slaughter	114
Fort Ward	213-216, 241
Fort Ward State Park	216
Fortson Park	131
Fort Steilacoom	2, 112, 190, 255
Fort Thomas	114
Fort Tilton	114
Fort Townsend	253, 293
Fort White	189
Fort Whitman	20
Fort Worden	60, 62, 67, 82, 258, 261
Fort Worden Military Cemetery	268
Forty-one for Freedom	2239
Foulweather Bluff	60-61, 259
Franklin class	239
Friends of Fort Flagler	279
Froula Playground	124
Full Fuselage Trainer	109
Future of Flight Aviation Ctr	31

G

Gale Runner	333
"Galloping Gertie"	185
Garrish, George	309
Gearing class	122
General Svc. Administration	35, 117
Geodetic Hill	320
Gerber, Marvin	90
Gleaves Class	122
Glendale (Burien) Post American Legion	135
Glidden, Helen	45
Goat Island	21
Goodrich Aviation Tech Svcs	30

Grand Mound Prairie	196	Historic Flight	
Grand Army of the		Foundation	31
Republic Cemetery	124	Historic Fort Steilacoom	
Grant, William	130	Association	165
Gray Airfield	149, 153	HMS *Bounty*	102
Gray, Capt. Lawrence C	149	HMS *Discovery*	89
Great White Fleet	121	Holding & Reconsignment	115
Greenling	233	Honeywell	30
Green River	137	Hooverville	99
Greene, Maj. Gen Henry	147	Hornby, Captain Geoffrey	41
Greene Park	148	Hudson's Bay Co 1,4, 39-40, 51,	
Gregory, Captain Luther	103	180	
Griffin Bay	52	Hurley-Mason	146
Ground Control Intercept	10, 337	Hurricane Ridge	320
Grumman HU-16E	331		
Gun Point	78		

H

I

H-13 Sioux	6	*Imperial Eagle*	298
Haida Tribe	71	Incendiary balloons	291
Hadlock	275	Indian Island	57, 279
Hal's Corner	247	Indian Island Annex	285
Halleck, General	254	Indian Pass	320
Haller, Captain G.O.	253	Industrial Workers	
Hamann, Jack	87	Of the World	312
Hamlin Park	138	Infantry Divisions at Ft	
Handley, Thomas	4	Lewis (2nd, 3d, 32nd, 33rd, 40th,	
Hanson, Hans Martin	91	41st, 44th, 96th)	150-152
Harbor Defense Command	65, 263,	165	
266, 275		Insane Asylum of	
Harbor Entrance		Washington Territory	
Control Post	266, 270	Integrated Border	
Harbor Island	122	Enforcement Team	7
Harbor Tug BITT	6	Integrated Support	
Harney, Brig. Gen	40, 253	Command Seattle	98, 100
Haro Strait	40	Interceptor Squadrons	175
Haskett, Maj. General		International Geo-	
George	184	Physical Year	177
Hastings, Loren	272	Isla de Patos	45
Hastings, Maria	272	Island County	57-80
Hayden, Brig. Gen John	305	Island Co. Historical	
Hays, Major Gilmore	189	Society	73, 76
Healy, Capt Mike	101	Island of Ducks	45
Healy	102	Italian POWs	86, 117
Hensel, Henry Paul	217	Italian Service Unit	157
Henry R. Johnson		IX Army Corps	150
World War I Memorial	248		
Heritage Flight Museum	5-6		
Heather	167	# J	
Henness, Benjamin and			
Lucretia	196		
Hicks, Capt. Urban	189	Jacobsen, John	305
Highland Park	124		

Jackson, Senator Henry M.	237
Jakle, George	52
James, Frances	245
James Island	323
James Madison class	239
Jaworski, Lt Col Leon	87
JBLM Units	155, 179
Jefferson County	253-300
Jefferson Co. Courthouse	294
Jefferson Co. Intl. Airport	293-294
Jefferson Co. Historical Society	254, 260, 276, 279
Jefferson Davis	195
Jefferson Park Golf Course	103, 124
JM-1	208
Johnston, Maj. Gen William	148
Joint Base Lewis-McChord	155
Joint Surveillance System	337
Joy, Admiral Charles Turner	249

K

K-9 Corps	73
K-39 (lighter than air)	326
Kaiser Wilhelm I	42
Kalakala	221
Kalaloch Beach Patrol	322
Kalaloch Lodge	291, 319
Keepers of the Patos Light	46
Kellogg, Dr. John C	62, 70
Kelley, Maj. Samuel C.	68
Kent	94
Kent / Midway (S-43)	97
Keyes, Captain Erasmus Darwin	163
Keyport	225-231
Keyport Torpedo Station	225
Keystone Harbor	57
Keystone Spit	65
Kilisut Harbor	279
King County	103
King County Airport	127
King County Memorials	137
Kingston	240
Kitsap	113
Kitsap County	213-252
Kitsap Co. Fairgrounds	248
Kitsap Co. Veterans Memorial	248
Klickitat Tribe	111
Kloopman, Charles	304
Kogan, Simon	200
Korean Conflict	27
Korean War Memorial	201

L

L-13	6
Ladies of the Roundtable	76
Lake Tribe	111
Lake Ozette	57, 319
Lake Union	89
Lake Washington	89
Lake Washington Ship Canal	89
Lake Youngs	94
Lake Youngs / Renton (S32 / 33)	97
Lamut	323-324
Lander, Judge Edward	192
LsPush Beach Patrol	322
Larson AFB	176
Laurel Grove Cemetery	71
Laurelhurst Playground	124
Lawson Reef	152
Lawton, Maj. Gen Henry	8
Legend Flyers	31
Lend-Lease	36, 115
Lend-Lease Depot Auburn	115-118
Leschi	111, 163-4, 189, 191
Lewis, Capt Meriwether	146
Lewis Hall	139
Lewis, Victor Alonzo	199
Liberty Bay Park	248
Liberty Gate	147
Lieck, Carl	16, 24
Lighter than Air	207
Lightfoot, Bill	121
Lighthouse Board	8, 24, 48, 79, 167
Lighthouse Digest	9
Lighthouse Service	16, 24, 25, 52, 91-92
Lindsey, Marie	53

Lime Kiln Lighthouse	49-51
Littlefield, David	272
Loback, Wesley	34
Lomax, Private Clyde	86
Lone Tree Point	18
Long Range Radar	11
Lookout Stations	318
LOPAR	96
LORAN	311
Loyal Legion of Loggers and Lumbermen	313
Lummi (Tribe)	1

M

M-47 Tank	184
MacArthur, General Arthur	182
MacDonald, Archibald	170
Madigan Army Medical Center	155
Madigan, Col. Frank	150
Maggs, John	245
Magnuson, Senator Warren	130
Magnuson Park	107
Makah Air Force Station	336-339
Makah Tribe	301, 309, 338
Malakoff	246
Maloney, Maurice	189
Manchester Annex	243
Manchester Navy Fuel Depot	243
Manchester Naval Supply Depot	242
Manchester State Park	242
Manchester Veterans Memorial	248
Mansfield, I.G. George	3
March Field	28
Marine Hospital, Port Townsend	290
Marrowstone Island	61, 79
Marrowstone Point Lighthouse	281-283
Mark 8 / 9-1 torpedoes	227
MARS	10
Marvin G. Shields Memorial	297
Mason County	207-211
Mason County Airport	207
Mason, Governor	163, 195
Massachusetts	246
McAfee, George	305
McAllister, James	190
McArthur, William	309
McCann, Richard	3-4
McChord AFB	11, 26, 94, 149, 172-179
McChord AFB Units	177-178
McChord Air Museum	180
McChord Field	185, 203
McChord, Col William C	149-172
McCloskey, Captain Manus	262
Meares, Capt. John	309
Medicine Creek Treaty	162
Memorial Armory, Kitsap	248
Memorial Field, Port Townsend	294
Merrill Ring Logging	27
Meuse-Argonne	148
Mexicana	302
Middle Point Military Reservation	240-242
Miles, Joseph	163
Miller Woodlawn Cemetery	248
Milroy, Maj Gen Robert	198
Military Air Transportation Service	100
Militia Act	182
Militia Law	181
Mirckenmeir, Mr.	32
Missile Tracking Radar	93
Monday Civic Club of Tacoma	192
Monitor	259
Montgomery, John	191
Moran Brothers Co.	121
Moran, Robert	121
Morgan, Osmond Hale	282
Morning Mist	4
Morrow, Edward R.	186
Morrow, Lacey	186
Moses, Abram	163
Moses Lake AFB	176
Motor Lifeboat Station Quillayute River	332
Mount Rainier Ordnance Depot	153, 156
Mount St. Helens	178
Muckleshoot Tribe	113
Muhlenberg, Maj. Henry	104
Mukilteo	23, 25
Mukilteo Defense Fuel Support Point	26

Mukilteo Explosive Loading Terminal	25-26
Mukilteo Tank Farm	25-26
Mukilteo Lighthouse	16, 23-25
Murray Creek	181
Museum of Flight	108-109
Museum of Flight Restoration Ctr	31, 109
Mystery Bay State Park	279

N

National Air and Space Administration	109
National Historic Lighthouse Preservation Act	18, 90, 245
National Oceanic Atmospheric Administration	26, 243, 326
National Postal Museum	28
National Youth Administration	295
Naval Magazine Indian Island	284
Naval Receiving Facility	132
Naval Air Station Astoria	209
Naval Air Station Seattle	208
Naval Air Auxiliary Station Shelton	207
Naval Air Stn Whidbey	34, 59-60
Naval Base Kitsap	236, 286
Naval Intermediate Maintenance Facility	224
Naval Ordnance Depot	230
Naval Radio School	216
Naval Radio Station Bainbridge Island	215
Naval Reserve Armory	129
Naval Station Everett	31-32
Naval Station Seattle	107
Naval Submarine Base Bangor	234-239
Naval Supply Center	243
Naval Supply Depot	133
Naval Support Complex	31
Naval Training Ctr, U. of Washington	138
Naval Undersea Museum	232-234
Naval Undersea Warfare Engineering Station, Keyport	225, 231, 285
Navy Fire Fighting School	243
Navy Yard Puget Sound	219
New Dungeness Light-House Society	335
New Dungeness Light Station	24, 52, 73, 333-336
Nessels, Lawrence	71
Net Control and Plotting Center	215
Nike Ajax batteries	94
Nike Hercules Missiles	94
Nike Missile	88-89, 93-97
9th Infantry Division	152
91st Division	147
Ninth Infantry Reg.	2, 40
Nisqually Tribe	111, 163
Nixon, President	88
Nooksack (Tribe)	1
NORAD	29
North Beach	78
Northwest Businessmen's Preparedness League	145
Northwest Schooner Society	18
Northwest Sea Frontier	290. 331

O

115th Cavalry Regiment	153
126th Coast Artillery	262
146th Field Artillery	136
O-1	6
Oak Harbor	57, 78
O'Brien	94
O'Brien, Rossell	181
Ohio-class	235
Olalla	240
Old Doctor	310
Old Navy Dump	243
"Old Reliables"	152
Olivotto, Guglielmo	87-88
Olmsted, John	83
Olympia Airport	203
Olympic Flight Museum	204

Olympic National Park	320	Pierce County	145-193
Olympic Power Company	282	"Pig War"	39-43, 48, 51
On American Soil	87		
Oozelfinch	98	Pigeon Point	65
Operation Sea Dragon	250	Pioneer Company, Washington Territorial Volunteers	189
Orcas Island	45		
Orcas Island Fire Dept.	46		
Ordnance Investigative Laboratory (OIL)	257	*Point Bennett*	272, 292
Oregon Treaty	39	Point Brown	167
Overseas Replacement Station	151	Point Defiance	169
		Point Hudson	294-296
Owhi	111	Point Elliott Treaty	24, 162
Ozette Lake Coast Guard Station	321	Point No Point Treaty	1, 162
		Point No Point Light Station	167, 244-254
P		Point Ringgold	285
		Point Wilson	61, 70, 72, 258
P-38	29	Point Wilson Lighthouse	270-273
P-39	29	Polaris Missile	231, 235
P-40	29, 132, 173	Polaris Missile Facility Atlantic	235
P-51	6	Polaris Missile Facility, Pacific	235
Pacific Coast Torpedo Station	225	*Polar Star*	102
Pacific Steamship Co	99-100	*Polar Sea*	102
Paine, 2Lt Topliff Olin	27	Polikarpov U-2/PO2	36
		Pope and Talbot	27
Paine Air Field	10, 26-31	Port Angeles Coast Guard Station	283
Palouse Tribe	111	Port Angeles Spruce Mill	314
Parks, Capt. Richard	145	Port of Blaine	9
Path of Freedom Memorial	248	Port Discovery	259
Patkanim	111-112	Port of Embarkation	86
Patos Island Light	45-47	Port of Everett	26
Patos Island State Park	46	Port of Seattle	133
Patrol Sqdn VP 46	59	Port of Shelton	209
PBY	59	Port Hadlock	62
PBY Memorial Foundation	59	Port Gamble	62, 246
Pearl Harbor	57	Port Orchard Bay	81
Pearson, Daniel	71	Port Townsend	2, 57, 61-62, 70, 71, 82, 253, 258
Peary, Admiral Robert E	101		
Penn Cove	57	Port Townsend Aero Museum	293
Phantom Lake	94		
Phelps, Lt. T.S.	111	*Port Townsend Daily Leader*	82
Pickering, Governor	181		
Pickett, Captain George	2, 40-42	Post of San Juan	43
Pickett's Charge	2	Possession Sound	23
Pickett House	4	Poulsbo	240
Pickett, Jason Tilton	4-5	POW Camp	86
Pier 36	98-101	*Princesa Real*	301
Pier 70	98	Prisoners of War	153, 159
Pier 91	98, 132	Priteca, B. Marcus	130

Puget Sound Coast Artillery Museum	269
Puget Sound Mounted Volunteers	195
Puget Sound Navy Museum	224-225, 247
Puget Sound Naval Shipyard	72, 81, 185, 216-224, 226, 260
Puget Sound Naval Shipyard Hospital	139
Puget Sound Naval Stn	61-62
Puyallup Assembly Ctr	161
PT-19	6
Puyallup Tribe	111
PV-1 Ventura	59

Q

Quadra, Juan Francisco De la Bodega	298
Queen Charlotte Islands	1
Quiemuth	163
Quillayute Naval Auxiliary Field	324-327
Quillayute River	319
Quimper, Manuel	301

R

Red Barn	108
Red Bluff Lighthouse	70-72
Redmond	94
Redmond (S13 / 14)	97
Red Shield Inn	148
Relocation Centers	161
Renton (S33C)	97
Reservation Bay	78
Reservation Head	78
Revenue Cutter Service	101
Rich Passage	213
Rickover, Admiral Hyman	237
Ringgold, Lt Cadwalader	284
Robert, 2Lt Henry M.	41
Robert's Rules of Order	41
Roberts, Mr & Mrs	3
Roberts, Maria	3, 4
Robertson, Capt. William	71
Robertson, Mary	71

Robins Dry Dock and Repair Co.	121
Robinson Point Lighthouse	140-142
Roosevelt	101
Roosevelt, Franklin D	226
Rose Point	24
Rosario Strait	15-16, 40

S

2nd Balloon Company	265
2nd Bomb Wing	175
62nd Medical Group	151
62nd Troop Carrier Wing	176-177
66th Field Artillery Brigade	136
71st Coast Artillery Corps	64
757th AC&W	10-13
758th AC&W	337
1705th Air Transport Group	176
SA-10A	175
SA-16 Albatross	175
S-03 Bothell/Kenmore	94
S-20 Cougar Mtn / Issaquah	94
S-43 Kent / Midway	94
S-61 Vashon Island	94
S-62 Olalla	94
S-81 Poulsbo	94
S-82 Winslow / Bain- Bridge Island	94
S-92 Kingston	94
Sakis Tiigang	4
Salt Creek	307
Samish (Tribe)	1
San Carlos	302
San Juan Channel	48
San Juan County	39-55
Sand Point Naval Air Stn	102-108
Saratoga Sound	21
San Juan Islands	2, 39, 40
San Juan Island Natl. Historic Park	43
Sanderson Field	209
Sanderson, Maj Gen Lawson	209
Sautter, L & Cie	25
Saxe, William	118
SBD Dauntless	59

Scott, General Winfield	41	S'Klallam Tribes	244, 284, 301
Seaman, DD 791	122		
Sears Building, Seattle	124, 126	Skookumchuck (Centralia)	196
Seaplane base	57	Smith, Isaac	310
Sea Ranger	110	Skokomish Tribe	244
Seattle Air Defense Wing	131	Slaughter, Lt. William	114, 137
Seattle Army Depot	100	Slip Point Lighthouse	316
Seattle Armory	135	Smith Island	52, 71
Seattle Blockhouse	111	Smith, Victor	328
Seattle Center House	135	Smokey Point	31
Seattle Chamber of Commerce	81	Snohomish County	23-55
		Snohomish Tribe	75, 111, 284
Seattle City Hall Park	131		
Seattle City Light	129	Snoqualmie Tribe	111
Seattle City Parks	83	Soroptomist Park	247
Seattle Construction & Dry Dock Co.	121	Spanish American War	8, 71
		Spanish American War Memorial, Retsil	248
Seattle Ex-Service Women's Club	134	Spatz, General Andrew	109
Seattle Garden Club	134	Spokane Tribe	111
Seattle General Strike	85	Spruce Production Division	313-315
Seattle Memorial Stadium	138		
Seattle Museum of History & Industry	131	Squamish Tribe	113
		SS *Governor*	272
Seattle Naval Hospital	139-140	SS *Mainlander*	282
Seattle Nike Missile Defense System	267	SS *Majestic*	263
		SS *North Pacific*	282
Seattle Pacific University	65	SS *Premier*	281
Seattle Parks & Rec Dept	91	SS *West Hartland*	272
Seattle Post #1, American Legion	135	SS *Willamette*	281
		Starbuck Center	124
Seattle-Tacoma Airport	127	Station DESW1	299
Seattle Tacoma Ship-Building	122-123	Station S	215-216
		Statue of the Lone Sailor	247
Seattle World's Fair	117, 136		
Selective Service Act	150	Steamship Terminal Office Bldg	100
Semiahmoo Harbor Light	8-9	Stevens, Gov. Isaac	78, 111, 191
Semiahmoo (Tribe)	1		
Semi-Automatic Ground Environment (SAGE)	11, 177, 337	Stillaguamish Tribe	75
		Stinson, Henry L.	156
		St. Paul's Episcopal Church	270
Sequim	24		
Shelton	235	Strategic Air Command	177
Sherman, Gen. William T.	255	Strategic Homeporting	31
Shilshole Bay	81	Strategic Weapons Facility Pacific (SWFPAC)	235
Shoemaker, Wayne	159		
Shubrick	328, 330		
Sikorsky HO35-16	331	Striped Peak	305
"Silent Service"	228	Stryker Brigades	152
Simard, Cyril Thomas	59	Stryker, Robert	152
Skagit County	15-38	Stryker, PFC Stuart	152
Skagit County Airport	19	Stuart Island	48
Skagit Tribe	75	Submarines	119-121
Skagit Wildlife Area	21	Submarine nets	285
Skinner & Eddy Corp	99	*Sumner* Class	122

Sundstrom, John	305
Sunnydale School	135
Sunnyside Cemetery	76
Sunnyside Farm	76
Sutil	302
Swinomish (Tribe)	4, 18

T

3-D Tracking Range	228
3rd Infantry Division	149, 153
12th Co. Army Infantry	28
12th Bombardment Wing	173
13th Coast Guard District	92
13th Naval District	319
25th Air Division	175
25th Infantry Regiment	82
25th NORAD Region	29, 176
248th Coast Artillery	68
325th Fighter Group	175
326th Fighter Gp	29
Tacoma Narrows Bridge	185-188
Tacoma News Tribune	149
Tacoma Rotary Club	149
Tactical Air Command	176, 337
Tala Point	259
Target Tracking Radar	93
Tarquina	71
Tatoosh Island	309, 319
TBF Avenger	207
T-6 Texan	6
Tethered Remotely Operated Vehicle	231
"The Harbor Bell"	271
The Light on the Island	45
"The Point"	117
Third Judicial Dist.	4
Thousand Trails Campgrounds	18
Thurston County	195-206
Ticonderoga	250
Tillamook Naval Air Station	325
Todd Dry Dock & Construction Co.	123
Todd and Kaiser Shipbuilding	122
Tolmie, Dr. William F.	170
Tomb of the Unknown Soldier	247
Torpedo Station Puget Sound	225
Totten, General	259
Traffic Triangle	248
Treaty of Point Elliott	1
Treaty of Tordesillas	301
Triangle of Fire	60, 273
Trident Missile	235
Trieste II	234
Tsimshian Tribe	334
Tuck, Mrs. Maria	4
Turn Point Light	45, 47-49
Turn Point Lighthouse Preservation Society	49
Tumwater	196

U

University of Puget Sound	168
University of Washington	28, 49, 228
USAF Aerospace Defense Command	28
U.S. Army Signal Corps	313
U.S. Army Training Ctr	151
U.S. Army Spruce Production Div. Railroad	312
U.S.C.G. Station Bellingham	6
U.S.C.G Station Neah Bay	303
U.S. C.G. Station Port Angeles	320
USCGC *Osprey*	292-293
USCGC *Sea Lion*	7
USCGC *Terrapin*	7
U.S. Forest Service	33
U.S. Geological Survey	283
U.S.L.S.S Waddah Island	304
U.S. Naval Auxiliary Air Stn Arlington	33
U.S. Naval Magazine, Indian Island	285
U.S. Naval Net Depot	285
U.S. Naval Ordnance Depot Puget Sound	225
U.S. Naval School Communications-Technicians	216

U.S. Revenue Service	290
USRC *Thomas Corwin*	290
USRC *Ulysses Grant*	290
USS *Abraham Lincoln*	32
USS *Alabama*	236
USS *Alaska*	236
USS *Bremerton*	248
USS *California*	221
USS *Callaghan*	31
USS *Card*	123
USS *Carl Vinson*	223
USS *Chandler*	32
USS *Coontz*	222-3
USS *Coral Sea*	222
USS *David R. Ray*	32
USS *Durant*	102
USS *Eagle*	129
USS *Elder*	*268*
USS *Essex*	222
USS *Fife*	32
USS *Florida*	236
USS *Ford*	31
USS *Franklin D. Roosevelt*	222
USS *Georgia*	236
USS *Hancock*	222
USS *Henry M. Jackson*	236, 238
USS *Ingraham*	31
USS *John C. Stennis*	225
USS *Kearsarge*	222
USS *King*	222-3
USS *Lexington*	222
USS *Louisville*	249
USS *Maine*	62
USS *Maryland*	221
USS *Massachusetts*	41
USS *Michigan*	236
USS *Missouri*	222
USS *Momsen*	32
USS *Nebraska*	121
USS *Nevada*	221, 236
USS *Nimitz*	223
USS *Ohio*	236
USS *Paul F. Foster*	31
USS *Robert E. Lee*	236
USS *Rodney M Davis*	32
USS *Sacramento*	222
USS *Saratoga* Memorial	247
USS *Shangri-La*	222
USS *Shoup*	32
USS *Stonewall Jackson*	235
USS *Tennessee*	221
USS *Turner Joy*	247, 249
USS *West Virginia*	221
USS *Woodrow Wilson*	239
USS *Yorktown*	222
Utility Squadron 13	207

V

Vancouver Barracks	151, 165, 257
Vancouver, Capt. George	24, 89, 301
Vancouver Island	39-40
Vandergraft X-Ray	257
Vashon Island (S-61)	97
Vashon Island Equestrian Park	97
VB-139	34
VC-3	34
VC-4	34
VC-55	34
VC-66	207
VC-77	34
VC-78	34
VC-87	34
VC-90	34
Veterans Memorial Park Retsil	248
VF-38	34
VF-49	34
VJ-13	207
VT-38	34
Vietnam Veterans Memorial Mason County	210-211
Vietnam Veterans Memorial Olympia	202
Volunteer Park	124

W

Waddah Island Station	304
Wakefield, Lt. Newton	59
Walla Walla Tribe	111
Ward, Col. George H	214
Warkum Point	320
Warrior Rock Lighthouse	90
Wartime Civil Control Administration	161
Washington class	239
Washington National Guard	181-183, 264

Washington St. Advisory Council On Historic Preservation	25
Washington State Emergency Mgmt. Division	183
Washington St. Ferry	23
Washington St. Game Dept	21
Washington State Military Dept	183
Washington St. Parks	18, 65, 258, 269
Washington State Patrol	204
Washington State Toll Bridge Authority	185
Washington St. University Lighthouse Docents	74
Washington Territory	15, 40,
Washington Territorial Militia	181
Washington Territorial Volunteers	18, 189, 190, 196
Washington Veterans Home Cemetery	248
WAVES	215
Webb, Roland H	121
West Beach	78
West Coast High Frequency Direction Net	215
Western Defense Sector	177
Western Washington Fairgrounds	162
West Point Lighthouse	89-91
Whale River	319
Whatcom Creek	2
Whatcom County	1-14, 40
Whatcom Museum of History & Art	4
Whidbey Island	2, 57, 61, 82
Whidbey Island Naval Air Station	19
White, Capt. Joseph A	189
White River	137
White River Massacre	137
Whitman, Dr. Marcus	162
Wilkes, Charles	244, 284
Willard Flying School	30
William H. Todd Corp.	121
Willoughby, C.L.	304
Wiltse, Dick	270
Wind Trail	322
Winslow	240
Wittich, Lt Willis	255
Woodland Park	125
Worden, Rear Admiral John L.	259
Works Progress Administration	27, 32, 99, 129, 172-173, 219, 295
World War I Memorial, Olympia	199
World War II Memorial, Kitsap Co Courthouse	248
World War II Memorial Olympia	200
Wounded Knee	2
Women Ordnance Workers (WOWS)	157
Wyckoff, Lt Ambrose	217

Y

Yakima Tribe	111
Yakima Indian War	76, 78
Yates, John	271
Yelm Prairie	196
Yellow Banks	322
Yeoman "F"	138
Young Doctor	304

Z

Zauner, Christian	298
Zelatched Point	229
Zimmerman, Kurt	160
ZP-33	207

JEFFERSON COUNTY LIBRARY
620 Cedar Avenue
Port Hadlock, WA 98339
(360) 385-6544   www.jclibrary.info

About the Author

Retired from the U.S. Air Force as a Medical Service Corps officer, Nancy McDaniel grew to appreciate the contributions of United States military personnel. A native of the Olympic Peninsula, she became familiar with the old forts at an early age and became curious about the personal stories of people who served there and the historical significance of these installations.

She graduated from the University of Puget Sound, Tacoma, Washington with a Bachelor of Arts in business management, and subsequently earned a Master of Science in Healthcare Administration from Trinity University, San Antonio, Texas. She retired from the Air Force at the rank of Colonel in 1997.

She also authored *"The Snohomish Tribe of Indians—Our Heritage, Our People,"* published in 2004.

She resides in Chimacum, Washington with husband Colonel (Ret) Glenn L. Davis, numerous horses, cats and a dog.

Nancy McDaniel, photo by husband Glenn L. Davis